Learn
Kubernetes Security

Securely orchestrate, scale, and manage your microservices in Kubernetes deployments

Kaizhe Huang

Pranjal Jumde

BIRMINGHAM—MUMBAI

Learn Kubernetes Security

Commissioning Editor: Vijin Boricha
Acquisition Editor: Meeta Rajani
Senior Editor: Arun Nadar
Content Development Editor: Romy Dias
Technical Editor: Sarvesh Jayant
Copy Editor: Safis Editing
Project Coordinator: Neil Dmello
Proofreader: Safis Editing
Indexer: Rekha Nair
Production Designer: Aparna Bhagat

First published: July 2020

Production reference: 2270820

Published by Packt Publishing Ltd.
Livery Place
35 Livery Street
Birmingham
B3 2PB, UK.

ISBN 978-1-83921-650-3

www.packt.com

For my lovely wife, Melody, who encouraged me to step out of my comfort zone and take on challenges.

– Kaizhe Huang

To my family and all the avid readers.

– Pranjal Jumde

Packt.com

Subscribe to our online digital library for full access to over 7,000 books and videos, as well as industry leading tools to help you plan your personal development and advance your career. For more information, please visit our website.

Why subscribe?

- Spend less time learning and more time coding with practical eBooks and Videos from over 4,000 industry professionals

- Improve your learning with Skill Plans built especially for you

- Get a free eBook or video every month

- Fully searchable for easy access to vital information

- Copy and paste, print, and bookmark content

Did you know that Packt offers eBook versions of every book published, with PDF and ePub files available? You can upgrade to the eBook version at packt.com and as a print book customer, you are entitled to a discount on the eBook copy. Get in touch with us at customercare@packtpub.com for more details.

At www.packt.com, you can also read a collection of free technical articles, sign up for a range of free newsletters, and receive exclusive discounts and offers on Packt books and eBooks.

Foreword

If you aren't using Kubernetes yet, you will be soon.

Kubernetes is not only the de facto platform to run modern, service-based applications. With cloud vendors quickly embracing it, it's also becoming the Operating System of the cloud. The reason for this success is that Kubernetes is powerful, versatile, and designed with modern software lifecycles in mind. On the other hand, Kubernetes is also a complicated beast. Gone are the days when running software meant managing processes on a single server. Now you have to deal with containers running in clusters that can reach thousands of machines in size, accessed by many developers organized in teams with different responsibilities.

Security has traditionally been an important area of focus when running software applications, either large or small. However, the dramatic increase in complexity and the additional degrees of freedom make Kubernetes security even more critical and harder!

Without doubt, security is one of the most important aspects of running Kubernetes applications in production. A correct Kubernetes security methodology involves, among other things, protecting the pipeline through image scanning, ensuring that the principle of least privilege is respected, defending pods at runtime, and segmenting the network. All of this while gathering enough information to understand when a threat is happening and what the blast radius was after it happened.

This is a lot to handle and requires a substantial amount of learning. One of the things that I love most about Open Source is that all you need to educate yourself is available for you in a number of forums: docs, tutorials, slack channels, conferences. Kubernetes, from this point of view, is no exception. Its huge community has produced a lot of content and you can definitely use it to become an expert. Alternatively, by studying this book, you can become a Kubernetes security expert by taking advantage of the wisdom of two seasoned operators, who live and breathe Kubernetes security and have done so for years.

The book will guide you gently, starting from a high-level introduction to the concepts at the base of Kubernetes before diving into the more advanced and nuanced aspects of securing a production cluster. It will do it in a way that is digestible even if you are not an expert, but at the same time will provide useful information even if you already have experience in the field. While reading it, I particularly appreciated the section questions at the end of each chapter, where you can test what you learned. I also loved the links section showing where you can go to get additional details.

Having founded Sysdig, one of the leading companies in Kubernetes security, I consider myself pretty knowledgeable on the subject. At the same time, the authors of this book are people I go to when things go beyond my skill level or when I want to learn something new. You won't be disappointed if you do the same.

Happy reading.

Loris Degioanni

Founder and CTO at Sysdig

Contributors

About the authors

Kaizhe Huang is a security researcher at Sysdig, where he researches how to defend Kubernetes and containers from attacks ranging from web attacks to kernel attacks. Kaizhe is one of the maintainers of Falco, an incubation-level CNCF project, and the original author of multiple open source projects, such as kube-psp-advisor. Before joining Sysdig, as an employee at Stackrox, Kaizhe helped build a detection data pipeline, conducted security research, and innovated detection based on machine learning. Previously, as a senior security engineer at Oracle, he helped build security products: Database Vault, Database Privilege Analyzer, and Database Assessment Tool. Kaizhe holds an MS degree in information security from Carnegie Mellon University.

I want to thank my lovely wife, Melody, and my family members – without your support and prayers, I wouldn't have been able to finish the book. Thanks to my manager, Omer, for giving me the opportunity and freedom to explore and innovate. Thanks to my Sysdig coworkers; you always inspire me. Thank you, Pranjal – without your commitment, I wouldn't have been able to do this. Thanks to everyone on my publishing team. Thanks to my dog, Emma, who helped me relax during writing.

Pranjal Jumde is a senior security engineer at Brave Inc. In the security industry, he has worked on different aspects of security, such as browser security, OS/kernel security, DevSecOps, web application security, reverse engineering malware, security automation, and the development of security/privacy features. Before joining Brave, as an employee at Stackrox, Pranjal helped in the development of detection and enforcement features for the runtime detection platform. He has also worked at Apple and Adobe, where he worked on the development of features to harden various platforms. Pranjal holds an MS degree in information security from Carnegie Mellon University. He has also presented his research at different conferences, such as ACM CCS and BSides SF/Delhi.

I would like to thank my co-author, Kaizhe, for all his trust in me. Without your support and commitment, completing this book wouldn't have been possible. Family is the strongest support that anyone can have – without the support of mine, this book would not have been possible. A special thanks to my wife, Swetha, for her patience, encouragement, and support. A special thanks to the editorial team for all their help.

About the reviewer

Madhu Akula is a cloud-native security researcher with extensive experience in cloud, container, Kubernetes, and automation security. He frequently speaks and trains at security conferences around the world, including DEFCON, BlackHat, USENIX, GitHub, OWASP Appsec, AllDayDevOps, DevSecCon, Nullcon, and c0c0n conferences. His research has identified vulnerabilities in more than 200 companies and products, including Google, Microsoft, AT&T, Wordpress, Ntop, and Adobe. He is a co-author of Security Automation with Ansible 2, a book that is listed as a technical resource by Red Hat. Madhu is an active member of international security, DevOps, and cloud native communities and holds industry certifications such as OSCP and CKA.

Packt is searching for authors like you

If you're interested in becoming an author for Packt, please visit authors. packtpub.com and apply today. We have worked with thousands of developers and tech professionals, just like you, to help them share their insight with the global tech community. You can make a general application, apply for a specific hot topic that we are recruiting an author for, or submit your own idea.

Table of Contents

3

Threat Modeling

4

Applying the Principle of Least Privilege in Kubernetes

5

Configuring Kubernetes Security Boundaries

Section 2: Securing Kubernetes Deployments and Clusters

6

Securing Cluster Components

7

Authentication, Authorization, and Admission Control

8
Securing Kubernetes Pods

9
Image Scanning in DevOps Pipelines

10

Real-Time Monitoring and Resource Management of a Kubernetes Cluster

11

Defense in Depth

Section 3:
Learning from Mistakes and Pitfalls

12
Analyzing and Detecting Crypto-Mining Attacks

13
Learning from Kubernetes CVEs

Assessments

Other Books You May Enjoy

Index

Preface

The growing complexity and scalability of real-world applications has led to a transition from monolithic architecture to microservices architecture. Kubernetes has become the de facto orchestration platform for deploying microservices. As a developer-friendly platform, Kubernetes enables different configurations to suit different use cases, making it the primary choice among most DevOps engineers. The openness and highly configurable nature of Kubernetes increases its complexity. Increased complexity leads to misconfigurations and security issues, which if exploited, can cause a significant economic impact on an organization. If you are planning to use Kubernetes in your environment, this book is for you.

In this book, you'll learn about how to secure your Kubernetes cluster. We briefly introduce Kubernetes in the first two chapters (we expect you to have a basic understanding of Kubernetes before you begin). We then discuss the default configurations of different Kubernetes components and objects. Default configurations in Kubernetes are often insecure. We discuss different ways to configure your cluster correctly to ensure that it is secure. We dive deep to explore different built-in security mechanisms, such as admission controllers, security contexts, and network policies, that are provided by Kubernetes to help secure your cluster. We also discuss some open source tools that complement the existing toolkits in Kubernetes to improve the security of your cluster. Finally, we look at some real-world examples of attacks and vulnerabilities in Kubernetes clusters and discuss how to harden your cluster to prevent such attacks.

With this book, we hope you will be able to deploy complex applications in your Kubernetes clusters securely. Kubernetes is evolving quickly. With the examples that we provide, we hope you will learn how to reason about the right configurations for your environment.

The Secure DevOps Platform. Scale-up Kubernetes. Scale-down risk.

Learn more at https://sysdig.com/

Who this book is for

This book is for DevOps/DevSecOps professionals who have started adopting Kubernetes as their main deployment/orchestration platform and have a basic understanding of Kubernetes. The book is also for developers who'd like to learn how to secure and harden a Kubernetes cluster.

What this book covers

Chapter 1, Kubernetes Architecture, introduces the basics of Kubernetes components and Kubernetes objects.

Chapter 2, Kubernetes Networking, introduces Kubernetes' networking model and dives deep into the communication among microservices.

Chapter 3, Threat Modeling, discusses important assets, threat actors in Kubernetes, and how to conduct threat modeling for applications deployed in Kubernetes.

Chapter 4, Applying the Principle of Least Privilege in Kubernetes, discusses the security control mechanisms in Kubernetes that help in implementing the principle of least privilege in two areas: the least privilege of Kubernetes subjects and the least privilege of Kubernetes workloads.

Chapter 5, Configuring Kubernetes Security Boundaries, discusses the security domains and security boundaries in Kubernetes clusters. Also, it introduces security control mechanisms to strengthen security boundaries.

Chapter 6, Securing Cluster Components, discusses the sensitive configurations in Kubernetes components, such as `kube-apiserver`, `kubelet`, and so on. It introduces the use of `kube-bench` to help identify misconfigurations in Kubernetes clusters.

Chapter 7, Authentication, Authorization, and Admission Control, discusses the authentication and authorization mechanisms in Kubernetes. It also introduces popular admission controllers in Kubernetes.

Chapter 8, Securing Kubernetes Pods, discusses hardening images with CIS Docker Benchmark. It introduces Kubernetes security contexts, Pod Security Policies, and `kube-psp-advisor`, which helps to generate Pod security policies.

Chapter 9, Image Scanning in DevOps Pipelines, introduces the basic concepts of container images and vulnerabilities. It also introduces the image scanning tool Anchore Engine and how it can be integrated into DevOps pipelines.

Chapter 10, Real-Time Monitoring and Resource Management of a Kubernetes Cluster, introduces built-in mechanisms such as resource request/limits and LimitRanger. It also introduces built-in tools like Kubernetes Dashboard and metrics server, and third-party monitoring tools, such as Prometheus and a data visualization tool called Grafana.

Chapter 11, Defense in Depth, discusses various topics related to defense in depth: Kubernetes auditing, high availability in Kubernetes, secret management, anomaly detection, and forensics.

Chapter 12, Analyzing and Detecting Crypto-Mining Attacks, introduces the basic concepts of cryptocurrency and crypto mining attacks. It then discusses a few ways to detect crypto mining attacks with open source tools such as Prometheus and Falco.

Chapter 13, Learning from Kubernetes CVEs, discusses four well-known Kubernetes CVEs and some corresponding mitigation strategies. It also introduces the open source tool `kube-hunter`, which helps identify known vulnerabilities in Kubernetes.

To get the most out of this book

Before starting this book, we expect you to have a basic understanding of Kubernetes. While reading this book, we expect you to look at Kubernetes with a security mindset. This book has a lot of examples of hardening and securing Kubernetes workload configurations and components. In addition to trying out the examples, you should also reason about how these examples map to different use cases. We discuss how to use different open source tools in this book. We hope you spend more time understanding the features provided by each tool. Diving deep into different features provided by the tools will help you understand how to configure each tool for different environments:

Software covered in the book	OS requirements
Kubernetes 1.14.3	Linux or macOS
Anchore 0.6.1	Linux or macOS
Prometheus 2.17.0	Linux or macOS
Sysdig Inspect 0.5.0	Linux or macOS
Kube-hunter 0.3.1	Linux or macOS
Minikube v1.10.1	Linux or macOS
Falco 0.20.0	Linux or macOS
Grafana 7.0.1	Linux or macOS
Kube-bench 0.3.0	Linux or macOS
kube-psp-advisor 1.8.0	Linux or macOS

If you are using the digital version of this book, we advise you to type the code yourself or access the code via the GitHub repository (link available in the next section). Doing so will help you avoid any potential errors related to the copying/pasting of code.

Download the example code files

You can download the example code files for this book from your account at www.packt.com. If you purchased this book elsewhere, you can visit www.packtpub.com/support and register to have the files emailed directly to you.

You can download the code files by following these steps:

1. Log in or register at www.packt.com.
2. Select the **Support** tab.
3. Click on **Code Downloads**.
4. Enter the name of the book in the **Search** box and follow the onscreen instructions.

Once the file is downloaded, please make sure that you unzip or extract the folder using the latest version of:

*   WinRAR/7-Zip for Windows
*   Zipeg/iZip/UnRarX for Mac
*   7-Zip/PeaZip for Linux

The code bundle for the book is also hosted on GitHub at https://github.com/PacktPublishing/Learn-Kubernetes-Security. In case there's an update to the code, it will be updated on the existing GitHub repository.

We also have other code bundles from our rich catalog of books and videos available at https://github.com/PacktPublishing/. Check them out!

Code in Action

Code in Action videos for this book can be viewed at https://bit.ly/2YZKCJX.

Download the color images

We also provide a PDF file that has color images of the screenshots/diagrams used in this book. You can download it here: http://www.packtpub.com/sites/default/files/downloads/9781839216503_ColorImages.pdf.

Conventions used

There are a number of text conventions used throughout this book.

`Code in text`: Indicates code words in text, database table names, folder names, filenames, file extensions, pathnames, dummy URLs, user input, and Twitter handles. Here is an example: "This attribute is also available in `PodSecurityContext`, which takes effect at the pod level."

A block of code is set as follows:

```
{
  "filename": "/tmp/minerd2",
  "gid": 0,
  "linkdest": null,
}
```

When we wish to draw your attention to a particular part of a code block, the relevant lines or items are set in bold:

```
{
  "scans": {
    "Fortinet": {
      "detected": true,
    }
  }
}
```

Any command-line input or output is written as follows:

```
$ kubectl get pods -n insecure-nginx
```

Bold: Indicates a new term, an important word, or words that you see onscreen. For example, words in menus or dialog boxes appear in the text like this. Here is an example: "The screenshot shows the CPU usage of the **insecure-nginx** pod monitored by Prometheus and Grafana."

> **Tips or important notes**
> Appear like this.

Get in touch

Feedback from our readers is always welcome.

General feedback: If you have questions about any aspect of this book, mention the book title in the subject of your message and email us at customercare@packtpub.com.

Errata: Although we have taken every care to ensure the accuracy of our content, mistakes do happen. If you have found a mistake in this book, we would be grateful if you would report this to us. Please visit www.packtpub.com/support/errata, selecting your book, clicking on the **Errata Submission Form** link, and entering the details.

Piracy: If you come across any illegal copies of our works in any form on the internet, we would be grateful if you would provide us with the location address or website name. Please contact us at copyright@packt.com with a link to the material.

If you are interested in becoming an author: If there is a topic that you have expertise in and you are interested in either writing or contributing to a book, please visit authors.packtpub.com.

Reviews

Please leave a review. Once you have read and used this book, why not leave a review on the site that you purchased it from? Potential readers can then see and use your unbiased opinion to make purchase decisions, we at Packt can understand what you think about our products, and our authors can see your feedback on their book. Thank you!

For more information about Packt, please visit packt.com.

Section 1: Introduction to Kubernetes

In this section, you will grasp the fundamental concepts of Kubernetes' architecture, network models, threat models, and the core security principles that should be applied to a Kubernetes cluster.

The following chapters are included in this section:

- *Chapter 1, Kubernetes Architecture*
- *Chapter 2, Kubernetes Networking*
- *Chapter 3, Threat Modeling*
- *Chapter 4, Applying the Principle of Least Privilege in Kubernetes*
- *Chapter 5, Configuring Kubernetes Security Boundaries*

1
Kubernetes Architecture

Traditional applications, such as web applications, are known to follow a modular architecture, splitting code into an application layer, business logic, a storage layer, and a communication layer. Despite the modular architecture, the components are packaged and deployed as a monolith. A monolith application, despite being easy to develop, test, and deploy, is hard to maintain and scale. This led to the growth of microservices architecture. Development of container runtimes like Docker and **Linux Containers** (**LXC**) has eased deployment and maintenance of applications as microservices.

Microservices architecture splits application deployment into small and interconnected entities. The increasing popularity of microservices architecture has led to the growth of orchestration platforms such as Apache Swarm, Mesos, and Kubernetes. Container orchestration platforms help manage containers in large and dynamic environments.

Kubernetes is an open source orchestration platform for containerized applications that support automated deployment, scaling, and management. It was originally developed by Google in 2014 and it is now maintained by the **Cloud Native Computing Foundation** (**CNCF**). Kubernetes is the first CNCF-graduated project that graduated in 2018. Established global organizations, such as Uber, Bloomberg, Blackrock, BlaBlaCar, The New York Times, Lyft, eBay, Buffer, Ancestry, GolfNow, Goldman Sachs, and many others, use Kubernetes in production at a massive scale (`https://kubernetes.io/case-studies/`). Large cloud providers, such as **Elastic Kubernetes Service** (Amazon), **Azure Kubernetes Service** (Microsoft), **Google Kubernetes Engine** (Google), and **Alibaba Cloud Kubernetes** (Alibaba), offer their own managed Kubernetes services.

In a microservices model, application developers ensure that the applications work correctly in containerized environments. They write a Docker file to bundle their applications. DevOps and infrastructure engineers interact with the Kubernetes cluster directly. They ensure that the application bundles provided by developers run smoothly within the cluster. They monitor the nodes, pods, and other Kubernetes components to ensure the cluster is healthy. However, security requires the joint effort of both parties and the security team. To learn how to secure a Kubernetes cluster, we will first have to understand what Kubernetes is and how it works.

In this chapter, we will cover the following topics:

- The rise of Docker and the trend of microservices
- Kubernetes components
- Kubernetes objects
- Kubernetes variations
- Kubernetes and cloud providers

The rise of Docker and the trend of microservices

Before we start looking into Kubernetes, it's important to understand the growth of microservices and containerization. With the evolution of a monolithic application, developers face inevitable problems as the applications evolve:

- **Scaling**: A monolith application is difficult to scale. It's been proven that the proper way to solve a scalability problem is via a distributed method.

- **Operational cost**: The operation cost increases with the complexity of a monolith application. Updates and maintenance require careful analysis and enough testing before deployment. This is the opposite of scalability; you can't scale down a monolithic application easily as the minimum resource requirement is high.

- **Longer release cycle**: The maintenance and development barrier is significantly high for monolith applications. For developers, when there is a bug, it takes a lot of time to identify the root cause in a complex and ever-growing code base. The testing time increases significantly. Regression, integration, and unit tests take significantly longer to pass with a complex code base. When the customer's requests come in, it takes months or even a year for a single feature to ship. This makes the release cycle long and impacts the company's business significantly.

This creates a huge incentive to break down monolithic applications into microservices. The benefits are obvious:

- With a well-defined interface, developers only need to focus on the functionality of the services they own.

- The code logic is simplified, which makes the application easier to maintain and easier to debug. Furthermore, the release cycle of microservices has shortened tremendously compared to monolithic applications, so customers do not have to wait for too long for a new feature.

When a monolithic application breaks down into many microservices, it increases the deployment and management complexity on the DevOps side. The complexity is obvious; microservices are usually written in different programming languages that require different runtimes or interpreters, with different package dependencies, different configurations, and so on, not to mention the interdependence among microservices. This is exactly the right time for Docker to come into the picture.

Let's look at the evolution of Docker. Process isolation has been a part of Linux for a long time in the form of **Control Groups** (**cgroups**) and **namespaces**. With the cgroup setting, each process has limited resources (CPU, memory, and so on) to use. With a dedicated process namespace, the processes within a namespace do not have any knowledge of other processes running in the same node but in different process namespaces. With a dedicated network namespace, processes cannot communicate with other processes without a proper network configuration, even though they're running on the same node.

Docker eases process management for infrastructure and DevOps engineers. In 2013, Docker as a company released the Docker open source project. Instead of managing namespaces and cgroups, DevOps engineers manage containers through Docker engine. Docker containers leverage these isolation mechanisms in Linux to run and manage microservices. Each container has a dedicated cgroup and namespaces.

The interdependency complexity remains. Orchestration platforms are ones that try to solve this problem. Docker also offered Docker Swarm mode (later renamed Docker **Enterprise Edition**, or Docker **EE**) to support clustering containers, around the same time as Kubernetes.

Kubernetes adoption status

According to a container usage report conducted in 2019 by Sysdig (`https://sysdig.com/blog/sysdig-2019-container-usage-report`), a container security and orchestration vendor says that Kubernetes takes a whopping 77% share of orchestrators in use. The market share is close to 90% if OpenShift (a variation of Kubernetes from Red Hat) is included:

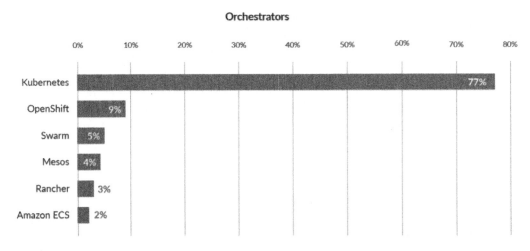

Figure 1.1 – The market share of orchestration platforms

Although Docker Swarm was released around the same time as Kubernetes, Kubernetes has now become the de facto choice of platform for container orchestration. This is because of Kubernetes' ability to work well in production environments. It is easy to use, supports a multitude of developer configurations, and can handle high-scale environments.

Kubernetes clusters

A Kubernetes cluster is composed of multiple machines (or **Virtual Machines (VMs)**) or nodes. There are two types of nodes: master nodes and worker nodes. The main control plane, such as `kube-apiserver`, runs on the master nodes. The agent running on each worker node is called `kubelet`, working as a minion on behalf of `kube-apiserver`, and runs on the worker nodes. A typical workflow in Kubernetes starts with a user (for example, DevOps), who communicates with `kube-apiserver` in the master node, and `kube-apiserver` delegates the deployment job to the worker nodes. In the next section, we will introduce `kube-apiserver` and `kubelet` in more detail:

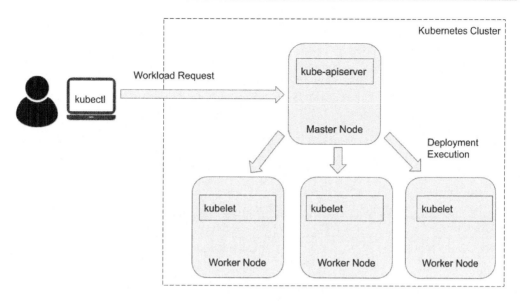

Figure 1.2 – Kubernetes deployment

The previous diagram shows how a user sends a deployment request to the master node (`kube-apiserver`) and `kube-apiserver` delegates the deployment execution to `kubelet` in some of the worker nodes.

Kubernetes components

Kubernetes follows a client-server architecture. In Kubernetes, multiple master nodes control multiple worker nodes. Each master and worker has a set of components that are required for the cluster to work correctly. A master node generally has `kube-apiserver`, `etcd` storage, `kube-controller-manager`, `cloud-controller-manager`, and `kube-scheduler`. The worker nodes have `kubelet`, `kube-proxy`, a **Container Runtime Interface (CRI)** component, a **Container Storage Interface (CRI)** component, and so on. We will go through each of them in detail now:

- `kube-apiserver`: The Kubernetes API server (`kube-apiserver`) is a control-plane component that validates and configures data for objects such as pods, services, and controllers. It interacts with objects using REST requests.

- `etcd`: `etcd` is a high-availability key-value store used to store data such as configuration, state, and metadata. The watch functionality of `etcd` provides Kubernetes with the ability to listen for updates to configuration and make changes accordingly.

- `kube-scheduler`: `kube-scheduler` is a default scheduler for Kubernetes. It watches for newly created pods and assigns pods to the nodes. The scheduler first filters a set of nodes on which the pod can run. Filtering includes creating a list of possible nodes based on available resources and policies set by the user. Once this list is created, the scheduler ranks the nodes to find the most optimal node for the pod.

- `kube-controller-manager`: The Kubernetes controller manager is a combination of the core controllers that watch for state updates and make changes to the cluster accordingly. Controllers that currently ship with Kubernetes include the following:

Controllers	Description
Replication controller	This maintains the correct number of pods on the system for every replication controller object.
Node controller	This monitors changes to the nodes.
Endpoints controller	This populates the endpoint object, which is responsible for joining the service object and pod object. We will cover services and pods in more detail in the next section.
Service accounts and tokens controller	This creates default accounts and API tokens for new namespaces.

- `cloud-controller-manager`: The cloud container manager was introduced in v1.6; it runs controllers to interact with the underlying cloud providers. This is an attempt to decouple the cloud vendor code from the Kubernetes code.

- `kubelet`: `kubelet` runs on every node. It registers the node with the API server. `kubelet` monitors pods created using Podspecs and ensures that the pods and containers are healthy.

- `kube-proxy`: `kube-proxy` is a networking proxy that runs on each node. It manages the networking rules on each node and forwards or filters traffic based on these rules.

- `kube-dns`: DNS is a built-in service launched at cluster startup. With v1.12, CoreDNS became the recommended DNS server, replacing `kube-dns`. CoreDNS uses a single container (versus the three used for `kube-dns`). It uses multithreaded caching and has in-built negative caching, thus being superior to `kube-dns` in terms of memory and performance.

In this section, we looked at the core components of Kubernetes. These components will be present in all Kubernetes clusters. Kubernetes also has some configurable interfaces that allow clusters to be modified to suit the organizational needs.

The Kubernetes interfaces

Kubernetes aims to be flexible and modular, so cluster administrators can modify the networking, storage, and container runtime capabilities to suit the organization's requirements. Currently, Kubernetes provides three different interfaces that can be used by cluster administrators to use different capabilities within the cluster.

The container networking interface

Kubernetes has a default networking provider, `kubenet`, which is limited in capability. `kubenet` only supports 50 nodes per cluster, which obviously cannot meet any requirements of large-scale deployment. Meanwhile, Kubernetes leverages a **Container Networking Interface (CNI)** as a common interface between the network providers and Kubernetes' networking components to support network communication in a cluster with a large scale. Currently, the supported providers include Calico, Flannel, `kube-router` and so on.

The container storage interface

Kubernetes introduced the container storage interface in v1.13. Before 1.13, new volume plugins were part of the core Kubernetes code. The container storage interface provides an interface for exposing arbitrary blocks and file storage to Kubernetes. Cloud providers can expose advanced filesystems to Kubernetes by using CSI plugins. Plugins such as MapR and Snapshot are popular among cluster administrators.

The container runtime interface

At the lowest level of Kubernetes, container runtimes ensure containers start, work, and stop. The most popular container runtime is Docker. The container runtime interface gives cluster administrators the ability to use other container runtimes, such as `frakti`, `rktlet`, and `cri-o`.

Kubernetes objects

The storage and compute resources of the system are classified into different objects that reflect the current state of the cluster. Objects are defined using a `.yaml` spec and the Kubernetes API is used to create and manage the objects. We are going to cover some common Kubernetes objects in detail.

Pods

A pod is a basic building block of a Kubernetes cluster. It's a group of one or more containers that are expected to co-exist on a single host. Containers within a pod can reference each other using localhost or **inter-process communications (IPCs)**.

Deployments

Kubernetes deployments help scale pods up or down based on labels and selectors. The YAML spec for a deployment consists of `replicas`, which is the number of instances of pods that are required, and `template`, which is identical to a pod specification.

Services

A Kubernetes service is an abstraction of an application. A service enables network access for pods. Services and deployments work in conjunction to ease the management and communication between different pods of an application.

Replica sets

Replica sets ensure a given number pods are running in a system at any given time. It is better to use deployments over replica sets. Deployments encapsulate replica sets and pods. Additionally, deployments provide the ability to carry out rolling updates.

Volumes

Container storage is ephemeral. If the container crashes or reboots, it starts from its original state when it starts. Kubernetes volumes help solve this problem. A container can use volumes to store a state. A Kubernetes volume has a lifetime of a pod; as soon as the pod perishes, the volume is cleaned up as well. Some of the supported volumes include `awsElasticBlockStore`, `azureDisk`, `flocker`, `nfs`, and `gitRepo`.

Namespaces

Namespaces help a physical cluster to be divided into multiple virtual clusters. Multiple objects can be isolated within different namespaces. Default Kubernetes ships with three namespaces: `default`, `kube-system`, and `kube-public`.

Service accounts

Pods that need to interact with `kube-apiserver` use service accounts to identify themselves. By default, Kubernetes is provisioned with a list of default service accounts: `kube-proxy`, `kube-dns`, `node-controller`, and so on. Additional service accounts can be created to enforce custom access control.

Network policies

A network policy defines a set of rules of how a group of pods is allowed to communicate with each other and other network endpoints. Any incoming and outgoing network connections are gated by the network policy. By default, a pod is able to communicate with all pods.

Pod security policies

The pod security policy is a cluster-level resource that defines a set of conditions that must be fulfilled for a pod to run on the system. Pod security policies define the security-sensitive configuration for a pod. These policies must be accessible to the requesting user or the service account of the target pod to work.

Kubernetes variations

In the Kubernetes ecosystem, Kubernetes is the flagship among all variations. However, there are some other ships that play very important roles. Next, we will introduce some Kubernetes-like platforms, which serve different purposes in the ecosystem.

Minikube

Minikube is the single-node cluster version of Kubernetes that can be run on Linux, macOS, and Windows platforms. Minikube supports standard Kubernetes features, such as `LoadBalancer`, services, `PersistentVolume`, `Ingress`, container runtimes, and developer-friendly features such as add-ons and GPU support.

Minikube is a great starting place to get hands-on experience with Kubernetes. It's also a good place to run tests locally, especially cluster dependency or working on proof of concepts.

K3s

K3s is a lightweight Kubernetes platform. Its total size is less than 40 MB. It is great for Edge, **Internet of Things (IoT)**, and **ARM**, previously **Advanced RISC Machine**, originally **Acorn RISC Machine**, a family of **reduced instruction set computing (RISC)** architectures for computer processors, configured for various environments. It is supposed to be fully compliant with Kubernetes. One significant difference from Kubernetes is that it uses `sqlite` as a default storage mechanism, while Kubernetes uses `etcd` as its default storage server.

OpenShift

OpenShift version 3 adopted Docker as its container technology and Kubernetes as its container orchestration technology. In version 4, OpenShift switched to CRI-O as the default container runtime. It appears as though OpenShift should be the same as Kubernetes; however, there are quite a few differences.

OpenShift versus Kubernetes

The connections between Linux and Red Hat Linux might first appear to be the same as the connections between OpenShift and Kubernetes. Now, let's look at some of their major differences.

Naming

Objects named in Kubernetes might have different names in OpenShift, although sometimes their functionality is alike. For example, a namespace in Kubernetes is called a project in OpenShift, and project creation comes with default objects. Ingress in Kubernetes is called routes in OpenShift. Routes were actually introduced earlier than Ingress objects. Underneath, routes in OpenShift are implemented by HAProxy, while there are many ingress controller options in Kubernetes. Deployment in Kubernetes is called `deploymentConfig`. However, the implementation underneath is quite different.

Security

Kubernetes is open and less secure by default. OpenShift is relatively closed and offers a handful of good security mechanisms to secure a cluster. For example, when creating an OpenShift cluster, DevOps can enable the internal image registry, which is not exposed to the external one. At the same time, the internal image registry serves as the trusted registry where the image will be pulled and deployed. There is another thing that OpenShift projects do better than `kubernetes` namespaces—when creating a project in OpenShift, you can modify the project template and add extra objects, such as `NetworkPolicy` and default quotas, to the project that are compliant with your company's policy. It also helps hardening, by default.

Cost

OpenShift is a product offered by Red Hat, although there is a community version project called OpenShift Origin. When people talk about OpenShift, they usually mean the paid option of the OpenShift product with support from Red Hat. Kubernetes is a completely free open source project.

Kubernetes and cloud providers

A lot of people believe that Kubernetes is the future of infrastructure, and there are some people who believe that everything will end up on the cloud. However, this doesn't mean you have to run Kubernetes on the cloud, but it does work really well with the cloud.

Kubernetes as a service

Containerization makes applications more portable so that locking down with a specific cloud provider becomes unlikely. Although there are some great open source tools, such as `kubeadm` and `kops`, that can help DevOps create Kubernetes clusters, Kubernetes as a service offered by a cloud provider still sounds attractive. As the original creator of Kubernetes, Google has offered Kubernetes as a service since 2014. It is called **Google Kubernetes Engine (GKE)**. In 2017, Microsoft offered its own Kubernetes service, called **Azure Kubernetes Service (AKS)**. AWS offered **Elastic Kubernetes Service (EKS)** in 2018.

Kubedex (`https://kubedex.com/google-gke-vs-microsoft-aks-vs-amazon-eks/`) have carried out a great comparison of the cloud Kubernetes services. Some of the differences between the three are listed in the following table:

Parameters	Google GKE	Amazon EKS	Microsoft AKS
Year started (GA)	2014	2018	2017
Kubernetes GA Versions	1.14/1.15	1.14	1.13 and 1.14
Regions Supported	Worldwide	North America, Ireland, London, Frankfurt, Singapore, Sydney, Tokyo, Seoul, and Paris	Almost worldwide
Cluster Create Time	3 minutes	20 minutes	15 minutes
Price	Free	20 cents per hour per master	Free

Parameters	Google GKE	Amazon EKS	Microsoft AKS
Kubernetes Marketplace	Yes	No	No
Integrations	GCP Ecosystem	AWS Ecosystem	Azure Ecosystem
Managed Worker Nodes	Yes	No	Yes
Application Layer Secret Encryption	Yes	No	No
Network Policy Support	Yes (Calico)	Yes (Calico)	Yes (kube-router and Calico)
Monitoring Integration	Yes (Stackdriver)	Yes (Container Insights)	Yes
Sandbox support (for example, gVisor)?	Yes (beta)	No	No
Binary Authorization Support	Yes (beta)	No	No
Ingress managed SSL Certificate	Yes	No	No
Release Channels	Yes (stable, regular, and rapid)	No	No
Compliance	PCI DSS, ISO, SOC, HIPAA	HIPAA, PCI, PCI DSS, ISO	PCI DSS, ISO, SOC, HIPAA
Maximum nodes per cluster	5000	500+	100
Cross region load balancing	Yes	No	No

Some highlights worth emphasizing from the preceding list are as follows:

- **Scalability**: GKE supports up to 5,000 nodes per cluster, while AKS and EKS only support a few hundred nodes or less.

- **Advanced security options**: GKE supports Istio service meshes, Sandbox, Binary Authorization, and ingress-managed **secure sockets layer** (**SSL**), while AKS and EKS cannot.

If the plan is to deploy and manage microservices in a Kubernetes cluster provisioned by cloud providers, you need to consider the scalability capability as well as security options available with the cloud provider. There are certain limitations if you use a cluster managed by a cloud provider:

- Some of the cluster configuration and hardenings are done by the cloud provider by default and may not be subject to change.

- You lose the flexibility of managing the Kubernetes cluster. For example, if you want to enable Kubernetes' audit policy and export audit logs to `splunk`, you might want to make some configuration changes to the `kube-apiserver` manifest.

- There is limited access to the master node where `kube-apiserver` is running. The limitation totally makes sense if you are focused on deploying and managing microservices. In some cases, you need to enable some admission controllers, then you will have to make changes to the `kube-apiserver` manifest as well. These operations require access to the master node.

If you want to have a Kubernetes cluster with access to the cluster node, an open source tool—`kops`—can help you.

Kops

Kubernetes Operations (**kops**), helps in creating, destroying, upgrading, and maintaining production-grade, highly available Kubernetes clusters from the command line. It officially supports AWS and supports GCE and OpenStack in the beta version. The major difference from provisioning a Kubernetes cluster on a cloud Kubernetes service is that the provisioning starts from the VM layer. This means that with `kops` you can control what OS image you want to use and set up your own admin SSH key to access both the master nodes and the worker nodes. An example of creating a Kubernetes cluster in AWS is as follows:

```
# Create a cluster in AWS that has HA masters. This cluster
# will be setup with an internal networking in a private VPC.
# A bastion instance will be setup to provide instance
access.
export NODE_SIZE=${NODE_SIZE:-m4.large}
export MASTER_SIZE=${MASTER_SIZE:-m4.large}
export ZONES=${ZONES:-'us-east-1d,us-east-1b,us-east-1c'}
export KOPS_STATE_STORE='s3://my-state-store'
kops create cluster k8s-clusters.example.com \
--node-count 3 \
```

```
--zones $ZONES \
--node-size $NODE_SIZE \
--master-size $MASTER_SIZE \
--master-zones $ZONES \
--networking weave \
--topology private \
--bastion='true' \
--yes
```

With the preceding `kops` command, a three-worker-nodes Kubernetes cluster is created. The user can choose the size of the master node and the CNI plugin.

Why worry about Kubernetes' security?

Kubernetes was in general availability in 2018 and is still evolving very fast. There are features that are still under development and are not in a GA state (either alpha or beta). This is an indication that Kubernetes itself is far from mature, at least from a security standpoint. But this is not the main reason that we need to be concerned with Kubernetes security.

Bruce Schneier summed this up best in 1999 when he said *'Complexity is the worst enemy of security'* in an essay titled *A Plea for Simplicity*, correctly predicting the cybersecurity problems we encounter today (`https://www.schneier.com/essays/archives/1999/11/a_plea_for_simplicit.html`). In order to address all the major orchestration requirements of stability, scalability, flexibility, and security, Kubernetes has been designed in a complex but cohesive way. This complexity no doubt brings with it some security concerns.

Configurability is one of the top benefits of the Kubernetes platform for developers. Developers and cloud providers are free to configure their clusters to suit their needs. This trait of Kubernetes is one of the major reasons for increasing security concerns among enterprises. The ever-growing Kubernetes code and components of a Kubernetes cluster make it challenging for DevOps to understand the correct configuration. The default configurations are usually not secure (the openness does bring advantages to DevOps to try out new features).

With the increase in the usage of Kubernetes, it has been in the news for various security breaches and flaws:

- Researchers at Palo Alto Networks found 40,000 Docker and Kubernetes containers exposed to the internet. This was the result of misconfigured deployments.

- Attackers used Tesla's unsecured administrative console to run a crypto-mining rig.

- A privilege escalation vulnerability was found in a Kubernetes version, which allowed a specially crafted request to establish a connection through the API server to the backend and send an arbitrary request.

- The use of a Kubernetes metadata beta feature in a production environment led to an **Server-Side Request Forgery** (**SSRF**) attack on the popular e-commerce platform Shopify. The vulnerability exposed the Kubernetes metadata, which revealed Google service account tokens and the `kube-env` details, which allowed the attacker to compromise the cluster.

A recent survey by The New Stack (`https://thenewstack.io/top-challenges-kubernetes-users-face-deployment/`) shows that security is the primary concern of enterprises running Kubernetes:

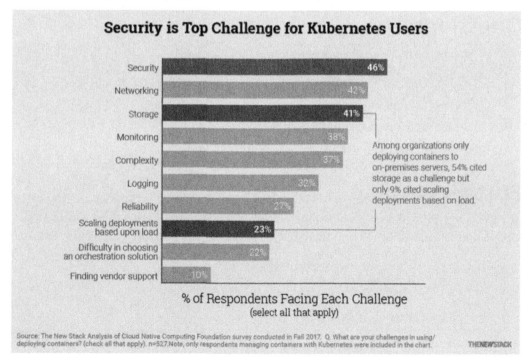

Figure 1.3 – Top concerns for Kubernetes users

Kubernetes is not secure by default. We will explain more about this in later chapters. Security becoming one of the primary concerns of users totally makes sense. It is a problem that needs to be addressed properly just like other infrastructure or platform.

Summary

The trend of microservices and the rise of Docker has enabled Kubernetes to become the de facto platform for DevOps to deploy, scale, and manage containerized applications. Kubernetes abstracts storage and computing resources as Kubernetes objects, which are managed by components such as `kube-apiserver`, `kubelet`, `etcd`, and so on.

Kubernetes can be created in a private data center or on the cloud or hybrid. This allows DevOps to work with multiple cloud providers and not get locked down to any one of them. Although Kubernetes is in GA as of 2018, it is still young and evolving very fast. As Kubernetes gets more and more attention, the attacks targeted at Kubernetes also become more notable.

In the next chapter, we are going to cover the Kubernetes network model and understand how microservices communicate with each other in Kubernetes.

Questions

1. What are the major problems of monolith architecture?
2. What are Kubernetes' master components?
3. What is deployment?
4. What are some variations of Kubernetes?
5. Why do we care about Kubernetes' security?

Further reading

The following links contain more detailed information about Kubernetes, `kops`, and the OpenShift platform. You will find them useful when starting to build a Kubernetes cluster:

- `https://kubernetes.io/docs/concepts/`
- `https://kubernetes.io/docs/tutorials/`
- `https://github.com/kubernetes/kops`
- `https://docs.openshift.com/container-platform/4.2`
- `https://cloud.google.com/kubernetes-engine/docs/concepts/kubernetes-engine-overview`

2
Kubernetes Networking

When thousands of microservices are running in a Kubernetes cluster, you may be curious about how these microservices communicate with each other as well as with the internet. In this chapter, we will unveil all the communication paths in a Kubernetes cluster. We want you to not only know how the communication happens but to also look into the technical details with a security mindset: a regular communication channel can always be abused as part of the kill chain.

In this chapter, we will cover the following topics:

- Overview of the Kubernetes network model
- Communicating inside a pod
- Communicating between pods
- Introducing the Kubernetes service
- Introducing the CNI and CNI plugins

Overview of the Kubernetes network model

Applications running on a Kubernetes cluster are supposed to be accessible either internally from the cluster or externally, from outside the cluster. The implication from the network's perspective is there may be a **Uniform Resource Identifier** (**URI**) or **Internet Protocol** (**IP**) address associated with the application. Multiple applications can run on the same Kubernetes worker node, but how can they expose themselves without conflicting with each other? Let's take a look at this problem together, and then dive into the Kubernetes network model.

Port-sharing problems

Traditionally, if there are two different applications running on the same machine where the machine IP is public and the two applications are publicly accessible, then the two applications cannot listen on the same port in the machine. If they both try to listen on the same port in the same machine, one application will not launch as the port is in use. A simple illustration of this is provided in the following diagram:

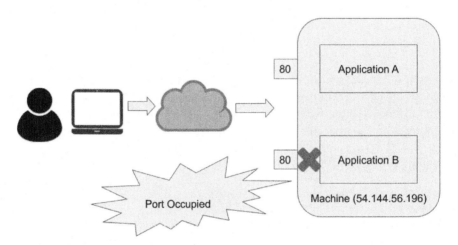

Figure 2.1 – Port-sharing conflict on node (applications)

In order to address the port-sharing confliction issue, the two applications need to use different ports. Obviously, the limitation here is that the two applications have to share the same IP address. What if they have their own IP address while still sitting on the same machine? This is the pure Docker approach. This helps if the application does not need to expose itself externally, as illustrated in the following diagram:

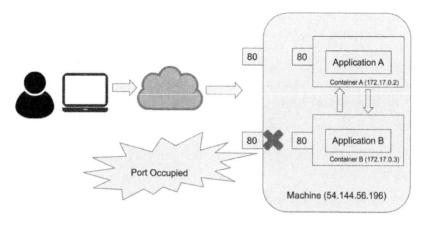

Figure 2.2 – Port-sharing conflict on node (containers)

In the preceding diagram, both applications have their own IP address so that they can both listen on port **80**. They can communicate with each other as they are in the same subnet (for example, a Docker bridge). However, if both applications need to expose themselves externally through binding the container port to the host port, they can't bind on the same port **80**. At least one of the port bindings will fail. As shown in the preceding diagram, container **B** can't bind to host port **80** as the host port **80** is occupied by container **A**. The port-sharing confliction issue still exists.

Dynamic port configuration brings a lot of complexity to the system regarding port allocation and application discovery; however, Kubernetes does not take this approach. Let's discuss the Kubernetes approach for solving this issue.

Kubernetes network model

In a Kubernetes cluster, every pod gets its own IP address. This means applications can communicate with each other at a pod level. The beauty of this design is that it offers a clean, backward-compatible model where pods act like **Virtual Machines (VMs)** or physical hosts from the perspective of port allocation, naming, service discovery, load balancing, application configuration, and migration. Containers inside the same pod share the same IP address. It's very unlikely that similar applications that use the same default port (Apache and nginx) will run inside the same pod. In reality, applications bundled inside the same container usually have a dependency or serve different purposes, and it is up to the application developers to bundle them together. A simple example would be that, in the same pod, there is a **HyperText Transfer Protocol (HTTP)** server or an nginx container to serve static files, and the main web application to serve dynamic content.

Kubernetes leverages CNI plugins to implement the IP address allocation, management, and pod communication. However, all the plugins need to follow the two fundamental requirements listed here:

1. Pods on a node can communicate with all pods in all nodes without using **Network Address Translation** (**NAT**).

2. Agents such as `kubelet` can communicate with pods in the same node.

These two preceding requirements enforce the simplicity of migrating applications inside the VM to a pod.

The IP address assigned to each pod is a private IP address or a cluster IP address that is not publicly accessible. Then, how, can an application become publicly accessible without conflicting with other applications in the cluster? The Kubernetes service is the one that surfaces the internal application to the public. We will dive deeper into the Kubernetes service concept in later sections. For now, it will be useful to summarize the content of this chapter with a diagram, as follows:

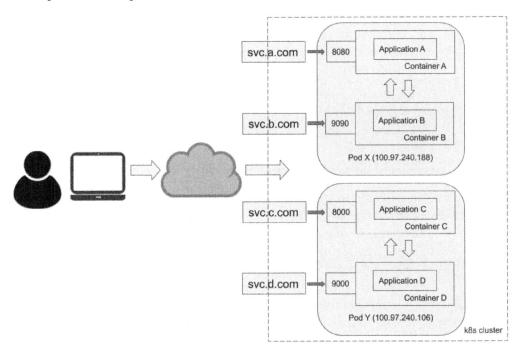

Figure 2.3 – Service exposed to the internet

In the previous diagram, there is a **k8s cluster** where there are four applications running in two pods: **Application A** and **Application B** are running in **Pod X**, and they share the same pod IP address—**100.97.240.188**—while they are listening on port **8080** and **9090** respectively. Similarly, **Application C** and **Application D** are running in **Pod Y** and listening on port **8000** and **9000** respectively. All these four applications are accessible from the public via the following public-facing Kubernetes services: **svc.a.com**, **svc.b.com**, **svc.c.com**, and **svc.d.com**. The pods (**X** and **Y** in this diagram) can be deployed in one single worker node or replicated across 1,000 nodes. However, it makes no difference from a user's or a service's perspective. Although the deployment in the diagram is quite unusual, there is still a need to deploy more than one container inside the same pod. It's time to take a look into the containers' communication inside the same pod.

Communicating inside a pod

Containers inside the same pod share the same pod IP address. Usually, it is up to application developers to bundle the container images together and to resolve any possible resource usage conflicts such as port listening. In this section, we will dive into the technical details of how the communication happens among the containers inside the pod and will also highlight the communications that take place beyond the network level.

Linux namespaces and the pause container

Linux namespaces are a feature of the Linux kernel to partition resources for isolation purposes. With namespaces assigned, a set of processes sees one set of resources, while another set of processes sees another set of resources. Namespaces are a major fundamental aspect of modern container technology. It is important for readers to understand this concept in order to know Kubernetes in depth. So, we set forth all the Linux namespaces with explanations. Since Linux kernel version 4.7, there are seven kinds of namespaces, listed as follows:

- **cgroup**: Isolate cgroup and root directory. cgroup namespaces virtualize the view of a process's cgroups. Each cgroup namespace has its own set of cgroup root directories.

- **IPC**: Isolate System V **Interprocess Communication (IPC)** objects or **Portable Operating System Interface (POSIX)** message queues.

- **Network**: Isolate network devices, protocol stacks, ports, IP routing tables, firewall rules, and more.

- **Mount**: Isolate mount points. Thus, the processes in each of the mount namespace instances will see distinct single-directory hierarchies.

- **PID**: Isolate **process IDs (PIDs)**. Processes in different PID namespaces can have the same PID.

- **User**: Isolate user IDs and group IDs, the root directory, keys, and capabilities. A process can have a different user and group ID inside and outside a user namespace.

- **Unix Time Sharing (UTS)**: Isolate the two system identifiers: the hostname and **Network Information Service (NIS)** domain name.

Though each of these namespaces is powerful and serves an isolation purpose on different resources, not all of them are adopted for containers inside the same pod. Containers inside the same pod share at least the same IPC namespace and network namespace; as a result, K8s needs to resolve potential conflicts in port usage. There will be a loopback interface created, as well as the virtual network interface, with an IP address assigned to the pod. A more detailed diagram will look like this:

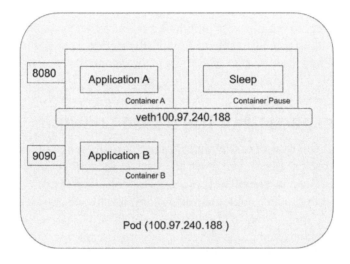

Figure 2.4 – Containers inside a pod

In this diagram, there is one **Pause** container running inside the pod alongside containers **A** and **B**. If you **Secure Shell (SSH)** into a Kubernetes cluster node and run the docker ps command inside the node, you will see at least one container that was started with the pause command. The pause command suspends the current process until a signal is received. Basically, these containers do nothing but sleep. Despite the lack of activity, the **Pause** container plays a critical role in the pod. It serves as a placeholder to hold the network namespace for all other containers in the same pod. Meanwhile, the **Pause** container acquires an IP address for the virtual network interface that will be used by all other containers to communicate with each other and the outside world.

Beyond network communication

We decide to go beyond network communication a little bit among the containers in the same pod. The reason for doing so is that the communication path could sometimes become part of the kill chain. Thus, it is very important to know the possible ways to communicate among entities. You will see more coverage of this in *Chapter 3, Threat Modeling*.

Inside a pod, all containers share the same IPC namespace so that containers can communicate via the IPC object or a POSIX message queue. Besides the IPC channel, containers inside the same pod can also communicate via a shared mounted volume. The mounted volume could be a temporary memory, host filesystem, or cloud storage. If the volume is mounted by containers in the Pod, then containers can read and write the same files in the volume. Last but not least, in beta, since the 1.12 Kubernetes release, the shareProcessNamespace feature finally graduates to stable in 1.17. To allow containers within a pod to share a common PID namespace, users can simply set the shareProcessNamespace option in the Podspec. The result of this is that **Application A** in **Container A** is now able to see **Application B** in **Container B**. Since they're both in the same PID namespace, they can communicate using signals such as SIGTERM, SIGKILL, and so on. This communication can be seen in the following diagram:

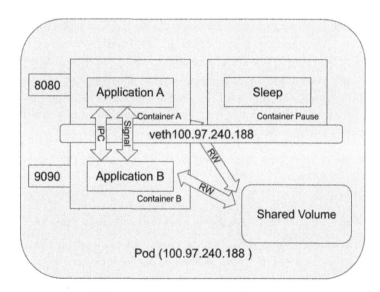

Figure 2.5 – Possible communication between containers inside a pod

As the previous diagram shows, containers inside the same pod can communicate to each other via a network, an IPC channel, a shared volume, and through signals.

Communicating between pods

Kubernetes pods are dynamic beings and ephemeral. When a set of pods is created from a deployment or a DaemonSet, each pod gets its own IP address; however, when patching happens or a pod dies and restarts, pods may have a new IP address assigned. This leads to two fundamental communication problems, given a set of pods (frontend) needs to communicate to another set of pods (backend), detailed as follows:

- Given that the IP addresses may change, what are the valid IP addresses of the target pods?
- Knowing the valid IP addresses, which pod should we communicate to?

Now, let's jump into the Kubernetes service as it is the solution for these two problems.

The Kubernetes service

The Kubernetes service is an abstraction of a grouping of sets of pods with a definition of how to access the pods. The set of pods targeted by a service is usually determined by a selector based on pod labels. The Kubernetes service also gets an IP address assigned, but it is virtual. The reason to call it a virtual IP address is that, from a node's perspective, there is neither a namespace nor a network interface bound to a service as there is with a pod. Also, unlike pods, the service is more stable, and its IP address is less likely to be changed frequently. Sounds like we should be able to solve the two problems mentioned earlier. First, define a service for the target sets of pods with a proper selector configured; secondly, let some magic associated with the service decide which target pod is to receive the request. So, when we look at pod-to-pod communication again, we're in fact talking about pod-to-service (then to-pod) communication.

So, what's the magic behind the service? Now, we'll introduce the great network magician: the kube-proxy component.

kube-proxy

You may guess what kube-proxy does by its name. Generally, what a proxy (not a reverse proxy) does is, it passes the traffic between the client and the servers over two connections: inbound from the client and outbound to the server. So, what kube-proxy does to solve the two problems mentioned earlier is that it forwards all the traffic whose destination is the target service (the virtual IP) to the pods grouped by the service (the actual IP); meanwhile, kube-proxy watches the Kubernetes control plane for the addition or removal of the service and endpoint objects (pods). In order to do this simple task well, kube-proxy has evolved a few times.

User space proxy mode

The `kube-proxy` component in the user space proxy mode acts like a real proxy. First, `kube-proxy` will listen on a random port on the node as a proxy port for a particular service. Any inbound connection to the proxy port will be forwarded to the service's backend pods. When `kube-proxy` needs to decide which backend pod to send requests to, it takes the `SessionAffinity` setting of the service into account. Secondly, `kube-proxy` will install **iptables rules** to forward any traffic whose destination is the target service (virtual IP) to the proxy port, which proxies the backend port. The following diagram from the Kubernetes documentation illustrates this well:

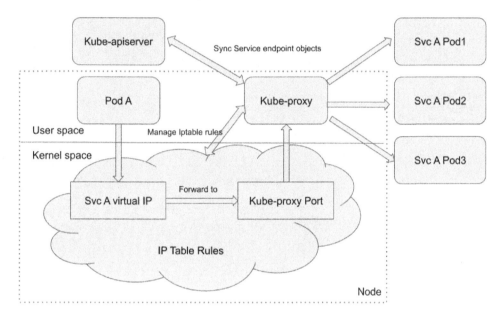

Figure 2.6 – kube-proxy user space proxy mode

By default, `kube-proxy` in user space mode uses a round-robin algorithm to choose which backend pod to forward the requests to. The downside of this mode is obvious. The traffic forwarding is done in the user space. This means that packets are marshaled into the user space and then marshaled back to the kernel space on every trip through the proxy. The solution is not ideal from a performance perspective.

iptables proxy mode

The kube-proxy component in the iptables proxy mode offloads the forwarding traffic job to netfilter using iptables rules. kube-proxy in the iptables proxy mode is only responsible for maintaining and updating the iptables rules. Any traffic targeted to the service IP will be forwarded to the backend pods by netfilter, based on the iptables rules managed by kube-proxy. The following diagram from the Kubernetes documentation illustrates this:

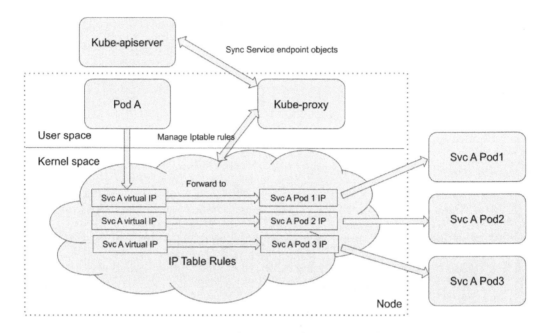

Figure 2.7 – kube-proxy iptables proxy mode

Compared to the user space proxy mode, the advantage of the iptables mode is obvious. The traffic will no longer go through the kernel space to the user space and then back to the kernel space. Instead, it will be forwarded in the kernel space directly. The overhead is much lower. The disadvantage of this mode is the error handling required. For a case where kube-proxy runs in the iptables proxy mode, if the first selected pod does not respond, the connection will fail. While in the user space mode, however, kube-proxy would detect that the connection to the first pod had failed and then automatically retry with a different backend pod.

IPVS proxy mode

The `kube-proxy` component in the **IP Virtual Server** (**IPVS**) proxy mode manages and leverages the IPVS rule to forward the targeted service traffic to the backend pods. Just as with iptables rules, IPVS rules also work in the kernel. IPVS is built on top of `netfilter`. It implements transport-layer load balancing as part of the Linux kernel, incorporated into **Linux Virtual Server** (**LVS**). LVS runs on a host and acts as a load balancer in front of a cluster of real servers, and any **Transmission Control Protocol** (**TCP**)- or **User Datagram Protocol** (**UDP**)-based traffic to the IPVS service will be forwarded to the real servers. This makes the IPVS service of the real servers appear as virtual services on a single IP address. IPVS is a perfect match with the Kubernetes service. The following diagram from the Kubernetes documentation illustrates this:

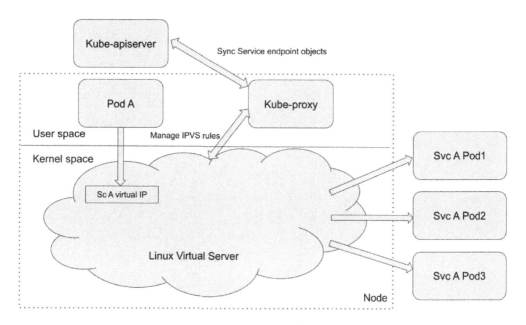

Figure 2.8 – kube-proxy IPVS proxy mode

Compared to the iptables proxy mode, both IPVS rules and iptables rules work in the kernel space. However, iptables rules are evaluated sequentially for each incoming packet. The more rules there are, the longer the process. The IPVS implementation is different from iptables: it uses a hash table managed by the kernel to store the destination of a packet so that it has lower latency and faster rules synchronization than iptables rules. IPVS mode also provides more options for load balancing. The only limitation for using IPVS mode is that you must have IPVS Linux available on the node for `kube-proxy` to consume.

Introducing the Kubernetes service

Kubernetes deployments create and destroy pods dynamically. For a general three-tier web architecture, this can be a problem if the frontend and backend are different pods. Frontend pods don't know how to connect to the backend. Network service abstraction in Kubernetes resolves this problem.

The Kubernetes service enables network access for a logical set of pods. The logical set of pods are usually defined using labels. When a network request is made for a service, it selects all the pods with a given label and forwards the network request to one of the selected pods.

A Kubernetes service is defined using a **YAML Ain't Markup Language** (**YAML**) file, as follows:

```
apiVersion: v1
kind: Service
metadata:
  name: service-1
spec:
  type: NodePort
  selector:
    app: app-1
  ports:
    - nodePort: 29763
      protocol: TCP
      port: 80
      targetPort: 9376
```

In this YAML file, the following applies:

1. The `type` property defines how the service is exposed to the network.

2. The `selector` property defines the label for the Pods.

3. The `port` property is used to define the port exposed internally in the cluster.

4. The `targetPort` property defines the port on which the container is listening.

Services are usually defined with a selector, which is a label attached to pods that need to be in the same service. A service can be defined without a selector. This is usually done to access external services or services in a different namespace. Services without selectors are mapped to a network address and a port using an endpoint object, as follows:

```
apiVersion: v1
kind: Endpoints
subsets:
  - addresses:
      - ip: 192.123.1.22
    ports:
      - port: 3909
```

This endpoint object will route traffic for 192:123.1.22:3909 to the attached service.

Service discovery

To find Kubernetes services, developers either use environment variables or the **Domain Name System (DNS)**, detailed as follows:

1. **Environment variables**: When a service is created, a set of environment variables of the form [NAME]_SERVICE_HOST and [NAME]_SERVICE_PORT are created on the nodes. These environment variables can be used by other pods or applications to reach out to the service, as illustrated in the following code snippet:

    ```
    DB_SERVICE_HOST=192.122.1.23
    DB_SERVICE_PORT=3909
    ```

2. **DNS**: The DNS service is added to Kubernetes as an add-on. Kubernetes supports two add-ons: CoreDNS and Kube-DNS. DNS services contain a mapping of the service name to IP addresses. Pods and applications use this mapping to connect to the service.

Clients can locate the service IP from environment variables as well as through a DNS query, and there are different types of services to serve different types of client.

Service types

A service can have four different types, as follows:

- **ClusterIP**: This is the default value. This service is only accessible within the cluster. A Kubernetes proxy can be used to access the ClusterIP services externally. Using `kubectl` proxy is preferable for debugging but is not recommended for production services as it requires `kubectl` to be run as an authenticated user.

- **NodePort**: This service is accessible via a static port on every node. NodePorts expose one service per port and require manual management of IP address changes. This also makes NodePorts unsuitable for production environments.

- **LoadBalancer**: This service is accessible via a load balancer. A node balancer per service is usually an expensive option.

- **ExternalName**: This service has an associated **Canonical Name Record (CNAME)** that is used to access the service.

There are a few types of service to use and they work on layer 3 and layer 4 of the OSI model. None of them is able to route a network request at layer 7. For routing requests to applications, it would be ideal if the Kubernetes service supported such a feature. Let's see, then, how an ingress object can help here.

Ingress for routing external requests

Ingress is not a type of service but is worth mentioning here. Ingress is a smart router that provides external **HTTP/HTTPS** (short for **HyperText Transfer Protocol Secure**) access to a service in a cluster. Services other than HTTP/HTTPS can only be exposed for the NodePort or LoadBalancer service types. An Ingress resource is defined using a YAML file, like this:

```
apiVersion: extensions/v1beta1
kind: Ingress
spec:
  rules:
  - http:
      paths:
      - path: /testpath
        backend:
          serviceName: service-1
          servicePort: 80
```

This minimal ingress spec forwards all traffic from the `testpath` route to the `service-1` route.

Ingress objects have five different variations, listed as follows:

- **Single-service Ingress**: This exposes a single service by specifying a default backend and no rules, as illustrated in the following code block:

```
apiVersion: extensions/v1beta1
kind: Ingress
spec:
  backend:
    serviceName: service-1
    servicePort: 80
```

This ingress exposes a dedicated IP address for `service-1`.

- **Simple fanout**: A fanout configuration routes traffic from a single IP to multiple services based on the **Uniform Resource Locator** (**URL**), as illustrated in the following code block:

```
apiVersion: extensions/v1beta1
kind: Ingress
spec:
  rules:
  - host: foo.com
    http:
      paths:
      - path: /foo
        backend:
          serviceName: service-1
          servicePort: 8080
      - path: /bar
        backend:
          serviceName: service-2
          servicePort: 8080
```

This configuration allows requests to `foo.com/foo` to reach out to `service-1` and for `foo.com/bar` to connect to `service-2`.

- **Name-based virtual hosting**: This configuration uses multiple hostnames for a single IP to reach out to different services, as illustrated in the following code block:

```
apiVersion: extensions/v1beta1
kind: Ingress
spec:
  rules:
  - host: foo.com
    http:
      paths:
      - backend:
          serviceName: service-1
          servicePort: 80
  - host: bar.com
    http:
      paths:
      - backend:
          serviceName: service-2
          servicePort: 80
```

This configuration allows requests to foo.com to connect to service-1 and requests to bar.com to connect to service-2. The IP address allocated to both services is the same in this case.

- **Transport Layer Security (TLS)**: A secret can be added to the ingress spec to secure the endpoints, as illustrated in the following code block:

```
apiVersion: extensions/v1beta1
kind: Ingress
spec:
  tls:
  - hosts:
    - ssl.foo.com
    secretName: secret-tls
  rules:
  - host: ssl.foo.com
    http:
      paths:
      - path: /
```

```
      backend:
            serviceName: service-1
            servicePort: 443
```

With this configuration, the `secret-tls` secret provides the private key and certificate for the endpoint.

- **Load balancing**: A load balancing ingress provides a load balancing policy, which includes the load balancing algorithm and weight scheme for all ingress objects.

In this section, we introduced the basic concept of the Kubernetes service, including ingress objects. These are all Kubernetes objects. However, the actual network communication magic is done by several components, such as `kube-proxy`. Next, we will introduce the CNI and CNI plugins, which is the foundation that serves the network communication of a Kubernetes cluster.

Introducing the CNI and CNI plugins

In Kubernetes, **CNI** stands for the **Container Network Interface**. CNI is a **Cloud Native Computing Foundation** (**CNCF**) project—you can find further information on GitHub here: `https://github.com/containernetworking/cni`. Basically, there are three things in this project: a specification, libraries for writing plugins to configure network interfaces in Linux containers, and some supported plugins. When people talk about the CNI, they usually make reference to either the specification or the CNI plugins. The relationship between the CNI and CNI plugins is that the CNI plugins are executable binaries that implement the CNI specification. Now, let's look into the CNI specification and plugins at a high level, and then we will give a brief introduction to one of the CNI plugins, Calico.

CNI specification and plugins

The CNI specification is only concerned with the network connectivity of containers and removing allocated resources when the container is deleted. Let me elaborate more on this. First, from a container runtime's perspective, the CNI spec defines an interface for the **Container Runtime Interface** (**CRI**) component (such as Docker) to interact with—for example, add a container to a network interface when a container is created, or delete the network interface when a container dies. Secondly, from a Kubernetes network model's perspective, since CNI plugins are actually another flavor of Kubernetes network plugins, they have to comply with Kubernetes network model requirements, detailed as follows:

1. Pods on a node can communicate with all pods in all the nodes without using NAT.

2. Agents such as `kubelet` can communicate with pods in the same node.

There are a handful of CNI plugins available to choose—just to name a few: Calico, Cilium, WeaveNet, Flannel, and so on. The CNI plugins' implementation varies, but in general, what CNI plugins do is similar. They carry out the following tasks:

- Manage network interfaces for containers

- Allocate IP addresses for pods. This is usually done via calling other **IP Address Management (IPAM)** plugins such as `host-local`

- Implement network policies (optional)

The network policy implementation is not required in the CNI specification, but when DevOps choose which CNI plugins to use, it is important to take security into consideration. Alexis Ducastel's article (`https://itnext.io/benchmark-results-of-kubernetes-network-plugins-cni-over-10gbit-s-network-36475925a560`) did a good comparison of the mainstream CNI plugins with the latest update in April 2019. The security comparison is notable, as can be seen in the following screenshot:

CNI	ENCRYPTION		NETWORK POLICIES	
Calico	😐	No	😃	Ingress + Egress
Canal	😐	No	😃	Ingress + Egress
Cilium	😃	Yes	😃	Ingress + Egress
Flannel	😐	No	😞	No
Kube-router	😐	No	😐	Ingress only
WeaveNet	😃	Yes	😃	Ingress + Egress

Figure 2.9 – CNI plugins comparison

You may notice that the majority of the CNI plugins on the list don't support encryption. Flannel does not support Kubernetes network policies, while `kube-router` supports ingress network policies only.

As Kubernetes comes with the default `kubenet` plugin, in order to use CNI plugins in a Kubernetes cluster, users must pass the `--network-plugin=cni` command-line option and specify a configuration file via the `--cni-conf-dir` flag or in the `/etc/cni/net.d` default directory. The following is a sample configuration defined within the Kubernetes cluster so that `kubelet` may know which CNI plugin to interact with:

```
{
    'name': 'k8s-pod-network',
    'cniVersion': '0.3.0',
    'plugins': [
        {
            'type': 'calico',
            'log_level': 'info',
            'datastore_type': 'kubernetes',
            'nodename': '127.0.0.1',
            'ipam': {
                'type': 'host-local',
                'subnet': 'usePodCidr'
            },
            'policy': {
                'type': 'k8s'
            },
            'kubernetes': {
                'kubeconfig': '/etc/cni/net.d/calico-kubeconfig'
            }
        },
        {
            'type': 'portmap',
            'capabilities': {'portMappings': true}
        }
    ]
}
```

The CNI configuration file tells `kubelet` to use Calico as a CNI plugin and use `host-local` to allocate IP addresses to pods. In the list, there is another CNI plugin called `portmap` that is used to support `hostPort`, which allows container ports to be exposed on the host IP.

When creating a cluster with **Kubernetes Operations (kops)**, you can also specify the CNI plugin you would like to use, as illustrated in the following code block:

```
export NODE_SIZE=${NODE_SIZE:-m4.large}
export MASTER_SIZE=${MASTER_SIZE:-m4.large}
export ZONES=${ZONES:-'us-east-1d,us-east-1b,us-east-1c'}
export KOPS_STATE_STORE='s3://my-state-store'
kops create cluster k8s-clusters.example.com \
--node-count 3 \
--zones $ZONES \
--node-size $NODE_SIZE \
--master-size $MASTER_SIZE \
--master-zones $ZONES \
--networking calico \
--topology private \
--bastion='true' \
--yes
```

In this example, the cluster is created using the `calico` CNI plugin.

Calico

Calico is an open source project that enables cloud-native application connectivity and policy. It integrates with major orchestration systems such as Kubernetes, Apache Mesos, Docker, and OpenStack. Compared to other CNI plugins, here are a few things about Calico worth highlighting:

1. Calico provides a flat IP network, which means there will be no IP encapsulation appended to the IP message (no overlays). Also, this means that each IP address assigned to the pod is fully routable. The ability to run without an overlay provides exceptional throughput characteristics.

2. Calico has better performance and less resource consumption, according to Alexis Ducastel's experiments.

3. Calico offers a more comprehensive network policy compared to Kubernetes' built-in network policy. Kubernetes' network policy can only define whitelist rules, while Calico network policies can define blacklist rules (deny).

When integrating Calico into Kubernetes, you will see three components running inside the Kubernetes cluster, as follows:

- The `calico/node` is a DaemonSet service, which means that it runs on every node in the cluster. It is responsible for programming and routing kernel routes to local workloads, and enforces the local filtering rules required by the current network policies in the cluster. It is also responsible for broadcasting the routing tables to other nodes to keep the IP routes in sync across the cluster.

- The CNI plugin binaries. This includes two binary executables (`calico` and `calico-ipam`) and a configuration file that integrates directly with the Kubernetes `kubelet` process on each node. It watches the pod creation event and then adds pods to the Calico networking.

- The Calico Kubernetes controllers, running as a standalone pod, monitor the Kubernetes **application programming interface (API)** to keep Calico in sync.

Calico is a popular CNI plugin and also the default CNI plugin in **Google Kubernetes Engine (GKE)**. Kubernetes administrators have full freedom to choose whatever CNI plugin fits their requirement. Just keep in mind that security is essential and is one of the decision factors. We've talked a lot about the Kubernetes network in the previous sections. Let's quickly review this again before you forget.

Wrapping up

In a Kubernetes cluster, every pod gets an IP address assigned, but this is an internal IP address and not accessible externally. Containers inside the same pod can communicate with each other via the name network interface, as they share the same network namespace. Containers inside the same pod also need to resolve the port resource conflict problem; however, this is quite unlikely to happen as applications run in different containers grouped in the same pod for a specific purpose. Also, it is worth noting that containers inside the same pod can communicate beyond the network through shared volume, IPC channel, and process signals.

The Kubernetes service helps pod-to-pod communication to be stabilized, as pods are usually ephemeral. The service also gets an IP address assigned but this is virtual, meaning no network interface is created for the service. The `kube-proxy` network magician actually routes all traffic to the target service to the backend pods. There are three different modes of `kube-proxy`: user space proxy, iptables proxy, and IPVS proxy. The Kubernetes service not only provides support for pod-to-pod communication but also enables communication from external sources.

There are a few ways to expose services so that they are accessible from external sources such as NodePort, LoadBalancer, and ExternalName. Also, you can create an Ingress object to achieve the same goal. Finally, though it is hard, we'll use the following single diagram to try to consolidate most of the knowledge we want to highlight in this chapter:

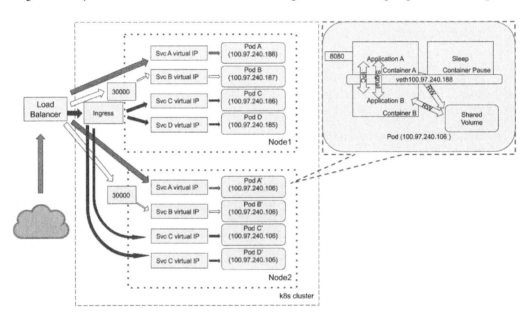

Figure 2.10 – Communications: inside pod, among pods, and from external sources

There is nearly always a load balancer sitting in front of a Kubernetes cluster. With the different service types we mentioned previously, this could be a single service that is exposed via the load balancer (this is service **A**), or it could be exposed via a NodePort. This is service **B** using node port **30000** in both nodes to accept external traffic. Though ingress is not a service type, it is powerful and cost-efficient compared to a LoadBalancer-type service. Service **C** and service **D** routing is controlled by the same ingress object. Every pod in the cluster may have an internal communication topology in the preceding callout diagram.

Summary

In this chapter, we started by discussing the typical port resource conflict problem and how the Kubernetes network model tries to avoid this while maintaining good compatibility for migrating applications from the VM to Kubernetes pods. Then, we talked about the communication inside a pod, among pods, and from external sources to pods.

Last but not least, we covered the basic concept of CNI and introduced how Calico works in the Kubernetes environment. After the first two chapters, we hope you have a basic understanding of how Kubernetes components work and how things communicate with each other.

In the next chapter, we're going to talk about threat modeling a Kubernetes cluster.

Questions

1. In a Kubernetes cluster, is the IP address assigned to a pod or a container?
2. What are the Linux namespaces that will be shared among containers inside the same pod?
3. What is a pause container and what is it for?
4. What are the types of Kubernetes services?
5. What is the advantage of using Ingress other than the LoadBalancer type service?

Further reading

If you want to build your own CNI plugin or evaluate Calico more, do check out the following links:

- `https://github.com/containernetworking/cni`
- `https://docs.projectcalico.org/v3.11/reference/architecture/`
- `https://docs.projectcalico.org/v3.11/getting-started/kubernetes/installation/integration`

3
Threat Modeling

Kubernetes is a large ecosystem comprising multiple components such as `kube-apiserver`, `etcd`, `kube-scheduler`, `kubelet`, and more. In the first chapter, we highlighted the basic functionality of different Kubernetes components. In the default configuration, interactions between Kubernetes components result in threats that developers and cluster administrators should be aware of. Additionally, deploying applications in Kubernetes introduces new entities that the application interacts with, adding new threat actors and attack surfaces to the threat model of the application.

In this chapter, we will start with a brief introduction to threat modeling and discuss component interactions within the Kubernetes ecosystem. We will look at the threats in the default Kubernetes configuration. Finally, we will talk about how threat modeling an application in the Kubernetes ecosystem introduces additional threat actors and attack surfaces.

The goal of this chapter is to help you understand that the default Kubernetes configuration is not sufficient to protect your deployed application from attackers. Kubernetes is a constantly evolving and community-maintained platform, so some of the threats that we are going to highlight in this chapter do not have mitigations because the severity of the threats varies with every environment.

This chapter aims to highlight the threats in the Kubernetes ecosystem, which includes the Kubernetes components and workloads in a Kubernetes cluster, so developers and DevOps engineers understand the risks of their deployments and have a risk mitigation plan in place for the known threats. In this chapter, we will cover the following topics:

- Introduction to threat modeling
- Component interactions
- Threat actors in the Kubernetes environment
- The Kubernetes components/objects threat model
- Threat modeling applications in Kubernetes

Introduction to threat modeling

Threat modeling is a process of analyzing the system as a whole during the design phase of the **software development life cycle** (**SDLC**) to identify risks to the system proactively. Threat modeling is used to think about security requirements early in the development cycle to reduce the severity of risks from the start. Threat modeling involves identifying threats, understanding the effects of each threat, and finally developing a mitigation strategy for every threat. Threat modeling aims to highlight the risks in an ecosystem as a simple matrix with the likelihood and impact of the risk and a corresponding risk mitigation strategy if it exists.

After a successful threat modeling session, you're able to define the following:

1. **Asset**: A property of an ecosystem that you need to protect.

2. **Security control**: A property of a system that protects the asset against identified risks. These are either safeguards or countermeasures against the risk to the asset.

3. **Threat actor**: A threat actor is an entity or organization including script kiddies, nation-state attackers, and hacktivists who exploit risks.

4. **Attack surface**: The part of the system that the threat actor is interacting with. It includes the entry point of the threat actor into the system.

5. **Threat**: The risk to the asset.

6. **Mitigation**: Mitigation defines how to reduce the likelihood and impact of a threat to an asset.

The industry usually follows one of the following approaches to threat modeling:

- **STRIDE**: The STRIDE model was published by Microsoft in 1999. It is an acronym for Spoofing, Tampering, Repudiation, Information Disclosure, Denial of Service, and Escalation of Privilege. STRIDE models threats to a system to answer the question, 'What can go wrong with the system?'

- **PASTA**: Process for Attack Simulation and Threat Analysis is a risk-centric approach to threat modeling. PASTA follows an attacker-centric approach, which is used by the business and technical teams to develop asset-centric mitigation strategies.

- **VAST**: Visual, Agile, and Simple Threat modeling aims to integrate threat modeling across application and infrastructure development with SDLC and agile software development. It provides a visualization scheme that provides actionable outputs to all stakeholders such as developers, architects, security researchers, and business executives.

There are other approaches to threat modeling, but the preceding three are the most used within the industry.

Threat modeling can be an infinitely long task if the scope for the threat model is not well defined. Before starting to identify threats in an ecosystem, it is important that the architecture and workings of each component, and the interactions between components, are clearly understood.

In previous chapters, we have already looked in detail at the basic functionality of every Kubernetes component. Now, we will look at the interactions between different components in Kubernetes before investigating the threats within the Kubernetes ecosystem.

Component interactions

Kubernetes components work collaboratively to ensure the microservices running inside the cluster are functioning as expected. If you deploy a microservice as a DaemonSet, then the Kubernetes components will make sure there will be one pod running the microservice in every node, no more, no less. So what happens behind the scenes? Let's look at a diagram to show the components' interaction at a high level:

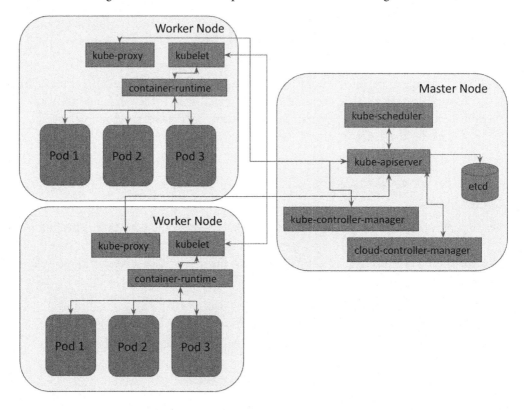

Figure 3.1 – Interactions between Kubernetes components

A quick recap on what these components do:

- **kube-apiserver**: The Kubernetes API server (kube-apiserver) is a control plane component that validates and configures data for objects.

- **etcd**: etcd is a high-availability key-value store used to store data such as configuration, state, and metadata.

- **kube-scheduler**: kube-scheduler is a default scheduler for Kubernetes. It watches for newly created pods and assigns the pods to nodes.

- **kube-controller-manager**: The Kubernetes controller manager is a combination of the core controllers that watch for state updates and make changes to the cluster accordingly.

- **cloud-controller-manager**: The cloud controller manager runs controllers to interact with the underlying cloud providers.

- **kubelet**: kubelet registers the node with the API server and monitors the pods created using Podspecs to ensure that the pods and containers are healthy.

It is worth noting that only kube-apiserver communicates with etcd. Other Kubernetes components such as kube-scheduler, kube-controller-manager, and cloud-controller manager interact with kube-apiserver running in the master nodes in order to fulfill their responsibilities. On the worker nodes, both kubelet and kube-proxy communicate with kube-apiserver.

Let's use a DaemonSet creation as an example to show how these components talk to each other:

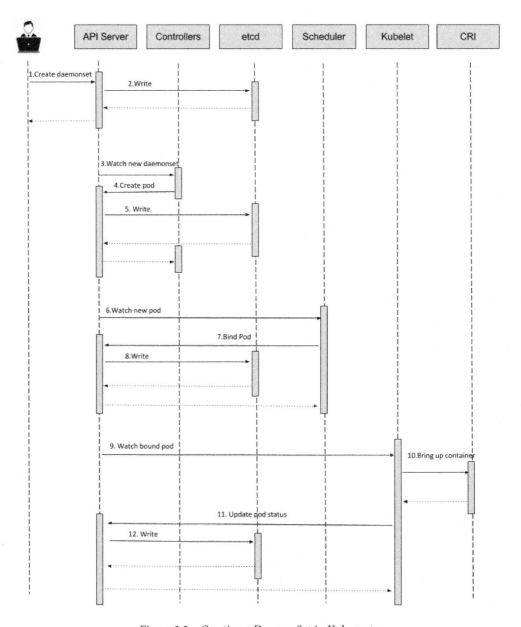

Figure 3.2 – Creating a DaemonSet in Kubernetes

To create a DaemonSet, we use the following steps:

1. The user sends a request to `kube-apiserver` to create a DaemonSet workload via HTTPS.

2. After authentication, authorization, and object validation, `kube-apiserver` creates the workload object information for the DaemonSet in the `etcd` database. Neither data in transit nor at rest is encrypted by default in `etcd`.

3. The DaemonSet controller watches that a new DaemonSet object is created, and then sends a pod creation request to `kube-apiserver`. Note that the DaemonSet basically means the microservice will run inside a pod in every node.

4. `kube-apiserver` repeats the actions in *step 2* and creates the workload object information for pods in the `etcd` database.

5. `kube-scheduler` watches as a new pod is created, then decides which node to run the pod on based on the node selection criteria. After that, `kube-scheduler` sends a request to `kube-apiserver` for which node the pod will be running on.

6. `kube-apiserver` receives the request from `kube-scheduler` and then updates `etcd` with the pod's node assignment information.

7. The `kubelet` running on the worker node watches the new pod that is assigned to this node, then sends request to the **Container Runtime Interface (CRI)** components, such as Docker, to start a container. After that, the `kubelet` will send the pod's status back to `kube-apiserver`.

8. `kube-apiserver` receives the pod's status information from the `kubelet` on the target node, then updates the `etcd` database with the pod status.

9. Once the pods (from the DaemonSet) are created, the pods are able to communicate with other Kubernetes components and the microservice should be up and running.

Note that *not* all communication between components is secure by default. It depends on the configuration of those components. We will cover this in more detail in *Chapter 6, Securing Cluster Components.*

Threat actors in Kubernetes environments

A threat actor is an entity or code executing in the system that the asset should be protected from. From a defense standpoint, you first need to understand who your potential enemies are, or your defense strategy will be too vague. Threat actors in Kubernetes environments can be broadly classified into three categories:

1. **End user**: An entity that can connect to the application. The entry point for this actor is usually the load balancer or ingress. Sometimes, pods, containers, or NodePorts may be directly exposed to the internet, adding more entry points for the end user.

2. **Internal attacker**: An entity that has limited access inside the Kubernetes cluster. Malicious containers or pods spawned within the cluster are examples of internal attackers.

3. **Privileged attacker**: An entity that has administrator access inside the Kubernetes cluster. Infrastructure administrators, compromised `kube-apiserver` instances, and malicious nodes are all examples of privileged attackers.

Examples of threat actors include script kiddies, hacktivists, and nation-state actors. All these actors fall into the three aforementioned categories, depending on where in the system the actor exists.

The following diagram highlights the different actors in the Kubernetes ecosystem:

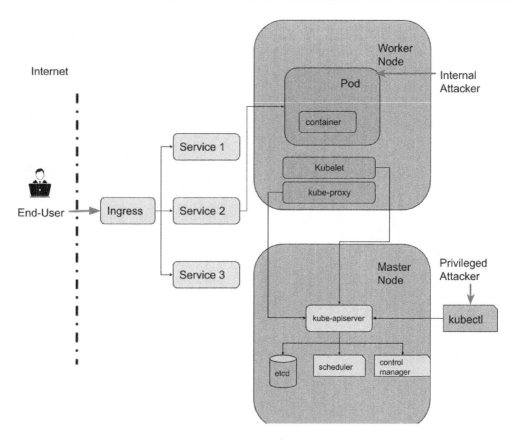

Figure 3.3 – Threat actors in Kubernetes environments

As you can see in this diagram, the end user generally interacts with the HTTP/HTTPS routes exposed by the ingress controller, the load balancer, or the pods. The end user is the least privileged. The internal attacker on the other hand has limited access to resources within the cluster. The privileged attacker is most privileged and has the ability to modify the cluster. These three categories of attackers help determine the severity of a threat. A threat involving an end user has a higher severity compared to a threat involving a privileged attacker. Although these roles seem isolated in the diagram, an attacker can change from an end user to an internal attacker using an elevation of privilege attack.

Threats in Kubernetes clusters

With our new understanding of Kubernetes components and threat actors, we're moving on to the journey of threat modeling a Kubernetes cluster. In the following table, we cover the major Kubernetes components, nodes, and pods. Nodes and pods are the fundamental Kubernetes objects that run workloads. Note that all these components are assets and should be protected from threats. Any of these components getting compromised could lead to the next step of an attack, such as privilege escalation. Also, note that `kube-apiserver` and `etcd` are the brain and heart of a Kubernetes cluster. If either of them were to get compromised, that would be game over.

The following table highlights the threats in the default Kubernetes configuration. This table also highlights how developers and cluster administrators can protect their assets from these threats:

Assets	Threat	Security control	Mitigation strategy
`kube-apiserver`	No default audit policy. This prevents forensic analysis after an attack.	Audit policy	Enable audit policy. The metadata level is recommended across the ecosystem.
	`--anonymous-auth` is set to `true` by default, which basically allows any connection to `kube-apisever`.	Authentication/ authorization	Ensure `--anonymous-auth` is not set to `false`.
	Weak authentication because of the use of self-signed certificates.	Enable client CA using `--client-ca-file`	Monitor ingress connections to `kube-apiserver` to check for anomalies.
`etcd`	Data is not encrypted at rest by default.	Encrypt data using `--encryption-provider-config`	Pass the configuration parameter `--encryption-provider-config` to kube-apiserver by default.
	Authentication is not enabled by default.	Authentication/ authorization	Ensure authentication is enabled and use TLS to avoid access to `etcd` by malicious components or objects in the cluster.

Assets	Threat	Security control	Mitigation strategy
	Can be accessed by any component in the Kubernetes ecosystem	mTLS	mTLS will reject all connections to `etcd` except `kube-apiserver`. mTLS generates a CA certificate and key. It also generates corresponding server and client certificate and key pairs. These certificates are used by the API server and `etcd` on startup.
`kube-scheduler`	Can be accessed by any component in the Kubernetes ecosystem. This can be used to map out the Kubernetes cluster.	N/A	Flag any connection to `kube-scheduler` except `kube-apiserver` as malicious.
Controller manager	A lack of component isolation can lead to privilege escalation attacks.	N/A	N/A
	Controller managers handle secrets such as environment variables, command-line arguments, and Kubernetes secrets, but each component has minimal protection for those secrets.	Secret rotation and use of Kubernetes secrets	Kubernetes secrets provide a standardized way of handling secrets. Secrets should be configured to be encrypted on startup. Secret vaults like HashiCorp can also be used instead of secrets.
`kubelet`	`kubelet` writes bootstrap certificates to disk unencrypted.	N/A	Certificates should be deleted after the cluster is up and running. Also, full disk encryption should be enabled.
	`kubelet` endpoints can be used to compromise nodes and containers. These endpoints are unauthenticated.	Authentication/authorization	Provide the CA bundle with `kubelet` to ensure authentication.

Assets	Threat	Security control	Mitigation strategy
Container runtime	Having no egress filters for a container runtime can cause malicious images to be fetched in the ecosystem.	`ImagePolicyWebhook` admission controller and image scanning tools such as Clair	Use the `ImagePolicyWebhook` admission controller to ensure images from approved sources are run within the ecosystem. Scanning images with tools such as Clair can also help here.
Nodes	Compromised nodes can inject kernel modules to compromise the pods.	`/etc/modprobe.d/ kubernetes- blacklist.conf`	A blacklist of kernel modules can be provided to protect container compromise.
	Vulnerable binaries and services on nodes can lead to pod/cluster compromise.	Minimized OS	Minimized OSes such as Alpine that have minimal binaries and libraries to support the container runtime should be used.
	Access to Kubernetes data including `kubeconfig` and private keys.	N/A	Host Intrusion Detection System (HIDS) and File Integrity Monitoring (FIM) can help notify if `kubeconfig` and private keys are accessed.
Pods	Pods can run as root users and compromise the host.	PodSecurityPolicy	Rarely do pods need root privileges in the regular workflow. Pod security policies can ensure pods are not run as privileged users.
	Network isolation in pods can be implemented by using network policies. Network policies fail silently without error.	N/A	It is advisable to create some network traffic to validate whether policies are applied correctly.

Assets	Threat	Security control	Mitigation strategy
	By default, all pods are associated with a `default` service account. Compromised pods can invoke API calls in the cluster if RBAC is not enabled.	N/A	The `kubectl` patch `serviceaccount` default `-p "automountServiceAccountToken: false"` disables the automatic mounting of the default service account token.

This table only highlights some of the threats. There are more threats, which will be covered in later chapters. We hope the preceding table will inspire you to think out loud about what needs to be protected and how to protect it in your Kubernetes cluster.

Threat modeling application in Kubernetes

Now that we have looked at threats in a Kubernetes cluster, let's move on to discuss how threat modeling will differ for an application deployed on Kubernetes. Deployment in Kubernetes adds additional complexities to the threat model. Kubernetes adds additional considerations, assets, threat actors, and new security controls that need to be considered before investigating the threats to the deployed application.

Let's look at a simple example of a three-tier web application:

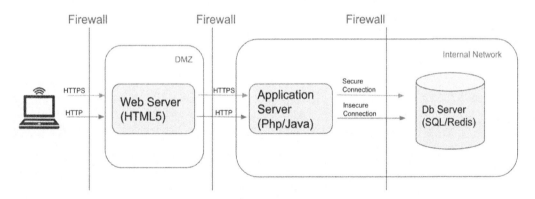

Figure 3.4 – Threat model of a traditional web application

The same application looks a little different in the Kubernetes environment:

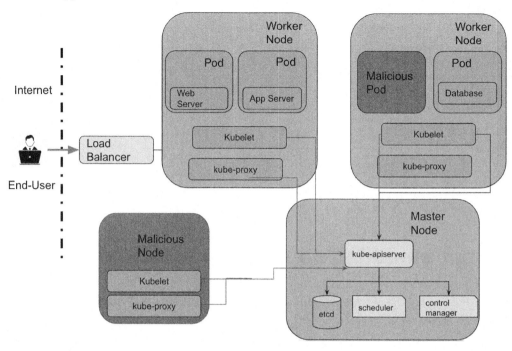

Figure 3.5 – Threat model of the three-tier web application in Kubernetes

As shown in the previous diagram, the web server, application server, and databases are all running inside pods. Let's do a high-level comparison of threat modeling between traditional web architecture and cloud-native architecture:

	Traditional web architecture	Web application on Kubernetes
Assets	Web server	Web server
	Application server	Application server
	Database server	Database server
	Hosts	Nodes (worker and master)
		Pods
		Persistent volumes
		Kubernetes components (`api-server`, `etcd`, `proxy`, `kubelet`, `scheduler`, `controller-manager`)

	Traditional web architecture	**Web application on Kubernetes**
Threat Actors	Internet/end users	Internet/end users
	Internal attackers	Internal attackers
	Admins	Admins
		Malicious/compromised nodes
		Malicious/compromised pods
		Compromised Kubernetes components
		Applications running inside the cluster
Security Controls	Firewall	Network policies
	DMZ	TLS, mTLS
	Internal network	Pod security policy
	Web application firewall	Web application firewall
	TLS connections	Pod isolation
	File encryption	File encryption
	Database authorization	Database authorization
	Database encryption	Database encryption
		Admission controllers
		Kubernetes authorization

To summarize the preceding comparison, you will find that more assets need to be protected in a cloud-native architecture, and you will face more threat actors in this space. Kubernetes provides more security controls, but it also adds more complexity. More security controls doesn't necessarily mean more security. Remember: complexity is the enemy of security.

Summary

In this chapter, we started by introducing the basic concepts of threat modeling. We discussed the important assets, threats, and threat actors in Kubernetes environments. We discussed different security controls and mitigation strategies to improve the security posture of your Kubernetes cluster.

Then we walked through application threat modeling, taking into consideration applications deployed in Kubernetes, and compared it to the traditional threat modeling of monolithic applications. The complexity introduced by the Kubernetes design makes threat modeling more complicated, as we've shown: more assets to be protected and more threat actors. And more security control doesn't necessarily mean more safety.

You should keep in mind that although threat modeling can be a long and complex process, it is worth doing to understand the security posture of your environment. It's quite necessary to do both application threat modeling and infrastructure threat modeling together to better secure your Kubernetes cluster.

In the next chapter, to help you learn about securing your Kubernetes cluster to the next level, we will talk about the principle of least privilege and how to implement it in the Kubernetes cluster.

Questions

1. When do you start threat modeling your application?
2. What are the different threat actors in Kubernetes environments?
3. Name one of the most severe threats to the default Kubernetes deployment.
4. Why is threat modeling more difficult in a Kubernetes environment?
5. How does the attack surface of deployments in Kubernetes compare to deployments in traditional architectures?

Further reading

Trail of Bits and Atredis Partners have done a good job on Kubernetes components' threat modeling. Their whitepaper highlights in detail the threats in each Kubernetes component. You can find the whitepaper at `https://github.com/kubernetes/community/blob/master/wg-security-audit/findings/Kubernetes%20Threat%20Model.pdf`.

Note that the intent, scope, and approach of threat modeling was different for the preceding whitepaper. So, the results will look a little different.

4
Applying the Principle of Least Privilege in Kubernetes

The principle of least privilege states that each component of an ecosystem should have minimal access to data and resources for it to function. In a multitenant environment, multiple resources can be accessed by different users or objects. The principle of least privilege ensures that damage to the cluster is minimal if users or objects misbehave in such environments.

In this chapter, we will first introduce the principle of least privilege. Given the complexity of Kubernetes, we will first look into the Kubernetes subjects, and then the privileges available for the subjects. Then, we will talk about the privileges of Kubernetes objects and possible ways to restrict them. The goal of this chapter is to help you understand a few critical concepts, such as the principle of least privilege and **Role-Based Access Control (RBAC)**. In this chapter, we will talk about different Kubernetes objects, such as namespaces, service accounts, Roles, and RoleBindings, and Kubernetes security features, such as the security context, the PodSecurityPolicy, and the NetworkPolicy, which can be leveraged to implement the principle of least privilege for your Kubernetes cluster.

In this chapter, we will cover the following topics:

- The principle of least privilege
- Least privilege of Kubernetes subjects
- Least privilege of Kubernetes workloads

The principle of least privilege

Privilege is the authority to perform an action such as accessing a resource or processing some data. The principle of least privilege is the idea that any subject, user, program, process, and so on should only have the minimum required privileges to perform its function. For example, Alice, a regular Linux user, is able to create a file under her own home directory. In other words, Alice at least has the privilege or permission to create a file under her home directory. However, Alice may not be able to create a file under another user's directory because she doesn't have the privilege or permission to do so. If none of Alice's daily tasks actually exercises the privilege to create a file in the home directory, but she does have the privilege to do so, then the administrator for the machine is not complying with the principle of least privilege. In this section, we will first introduce the concept of the authorization model from which the concept of least privilege derived, and then, we will talk about the benefits of implementing the principle of least privilege.

Authorization model

When we talk about least privilege, most of the time we talk in the context of authorization, and in different environments, there will be different authorization models. For example, an **Access Control List** (**ACL**) is widely used in Linux and network firewalls, while RBAC is used in database systems. It is also up to the administrator of the environment to define authorization policies to ensure least privilege based on authorization models available in the system. The following list defines some popular authorization models:

- **ACL**: An ACL defines a list of permissions associated with objects. It specifies which subjects are granted access to objects, as well as what operations are allowed on given objects. For example, the `-rw` file permission is read-write-only by the file owner.

- **RBAC**: The authorization decision is based on a subject's roles, which contain a group of permissions or privileges. For example, in Linux, a user is added to different groups (such as `staff`) to grant access to some folders instead of individually being granted access to folders on the filesystem.

- **Attribute-Based Access Control (ABAC)**: The authorization decision is based on a subject's attributes, such as labels or properties. An attribute-based rule checks user attributes such as `user.id="12345"`, `user.project="project"`, and `user.status="active"` to decide whether a user is able to perform a task.

Kubernetes supports both ABAC and RBAC. Though ABAC is powerful and flexible, the implementation in Kubernetes makes it difficult to manage and understand. Thus, it is recommended to enable RBAC instead of ABAC in Kubernetes. Besides RBAC, Kubernetes also provides multiple ways to restrict resource access. Before we look into RBAC and ABAC in Kubernetes in the next sections, let's discuss the benefits of ensuring least privilege.

Rewards of the principle of least privilege

Though it might take quite some time to understand what the minimum privileges for subjects are in order to perform their functions, the rewards are also significant if the principle of least privilege has been implemented in your environment:

- **Better security**: Inside threats, malware propagation, lateral movement, and so on can be mitigated with the implementation of the principle of least privilege. The leak by Edward Snowden happened because of a lack of least privilege.

- **Better stability**: Given the subjects are properly granted with necessary privileges only, subjects' activities become more predictable. In return, system stability is bolstered.

- **Improved audit readiness**: Given the subjects are properly granted with necessary privileges only, the audit scope will be reduced dramatically. Additionally, many common regulations call for the implementation of the principle of least privilege as a compliance requirement.

Now that you have seen the benefits for implementing the principle of least privilege, I want to introduce the challenge as well: the openness and configurability of Kubernetes makes implementing the principle of least privilege cumbersome. Let's look at how to apply the principle of least privilege to Kubernetes subjects.

Least privilege of Kubernetes subjects

Kubernetes service accounts, users, and groups communicate with `kube-apiserver` to manage Kubernetes objects. With RBAC enabled, different users or service accounts may have different privileges to operate Kubernetes objects. For example, users in the `system:master` group have the `cluster-admin` role granted, meaning they can manage the entire Kubernetes cluster, while users in the `system:kube-proxy` group can only access the resources required by the `kube-proxy` component. First, let's briefly talk about what RBAC is.

Introduction to RBAC

As discussed earlier, RBAC is a model of regulating access to resources based on roles granted to users or groups. From version 1.6 onward, RBAC is enabled by default in Kubernetes. Before version 1.6, RBAC could be enabled by running the **Application Programming Interface (API)** server with the `--authorization-mode=RBAC` flag. RBAC eases the dynamic configuration of permission policies using the API server.

The core elements of RBAC include the following:

1. **Subject**: Service accounts, users, or groups requesting access to the Kubernetes API.
2. **Resources**: Kubernetes objects that need to be accessed by the subject.
3. **Verbs**: Different types of access the subject needs on a resource—for example, create, update, list, delete.

Kubernetes RBAC defines the subjects and the type of access they have to different resources in the Kubernetes ecosystem.

Service accounts, users, and groups

Kubernetes supports three types of subject, as follows:

- **Regular users**: These users are created by cluster administrators. They do not have a corresponding object in the Kubernetes ecosystem. Cluster administrators usually create users by using the **Lightweight Directory Access Protocol (LDAP)**, **Active Directory (AD)**, or private keys.
- **Service accounts**: Pods authenticate to the `kube-apiserver` object using a service account. Service accounts are created using API calls. They are restricted to namespaces and have associated credentials stored as `secrets`. By default, pods authenticate as a `default` service account.

- **Anonymous users**: Any API request that is not associated with a regular or a service account is associated with an anonymous user.

Cluster administrators can create new service accounts to be associated with pods by running the following command:

```
$ kubectl create serviceaccount new_account
```

A new_account service account will be created in the default namespace. To ensure least privilege, cluster administrators should associate every Kubernetes resource with a service account with least privilege to operate.

Role

A role is a collection of permissions—for example, a role in namespace A can allow users to create pods in namespace A and list secrets in namespace A. In Kubernetes, there are no deny permissions. Thus, a role is an addition of a set of permissions.

A role is restricted to a namespace. On the other hand, a ClusterRole works at the cluster level. Users can create a ClusterRole that spans across the complete cluster. A ClusterRole can be used to mediate access to resources that span across a cluster, such as nodes, health checks, and namespaced objects, such as pods across multiple namespaces. Here is a simple example of a role definition:

```
kind: Role
apiVersion: rbac.authorization.k8s.io/v1
metadata:
  namespace: default
  name: role-1
rules:
- apiGroups: [""]
  resources: ["pods"]
  verbs: ["get"]
```

This simple rule allows the get operation to over-resource pods in the default namespace. This role can be created using kubectl by executing the following command:

```
$ kubectl apply -f role.yaml
```

A user can only create or modify a role if either one of the following is true:

- The user has all permissions contained in the role in the same scope (namespaced or cluster-wide).

- The user is associated with an escalated role in the given scope.

This prevents users from performing privilege escalation attacks by modifying user roles and permissions.

RoleBinding

A RoleBinding object is used to associate a role with subjects. Similar to ClusterRole, ClusterRoleBinding can grant a set of permissions to subjects across namespaces. Let's see a couple of examples:

1. Create a RoleBinding object to associate a `custom-clusterrole` cluster role to the `demo-sa` service account in the default namespace, like this:

```
kubectl create rolebinding new-rolebinding-sa \
    --clusterrole=custom-clusterrole \
    --serviceaccount=default:demo-sa
```

2. Create a RoleBinding object to associate a `custom-clusterrole` cluster role to the `group-1` group, like this:

```
kubectl create rolebinding new-rolebinding-group \
    --clusterrole=custom-clusterrole \
    --group=group-1 \
    --namespace=namespace-1
```

The RoleBinding object links roles to subjects and makes roles reusable and easy to manage.

Kubernetes namespaces

A namespace is a common concept in computer science that provides a logical grouping for related resources. Namespaces are used to avoid name collisions; resources within the same namespace should have unique names, but resources across namespaces can share names. In the Linux ecosystem, namespaces allow the isolation of system resources.

In Kubernetes, namespaces allow a single cluster to be shared between teams and projects logically. With Kubernetes namespaces, the following applies:

- They allow different applications, teams, and users to work in the same cluster.
- They allow cluster administrators to use namespace resource quotas for the applications.
- They use RBAC policies to control access to specific resources within the namespaces. RoleBinding helps cluster administrators' control permissions granted to users within the namespace.
- They allow network segmentation with the network policy defined in the namespace. By default, all pods can communicate with each other across different namespaces.

By default, Kubernetes has three different namespaces. Run the following command to view them:

```
$ kubectl get namespace
NAME            STATUS    AGE
default         Active    1d
kube-system     Active    1d
kube-public     Active    1d
```

The three namespaces are described as follows:

- `default`: A namespace for resources that are not part of any other namespace.
- `kube-system`: A namespace for objects created by Kubernetes such as `kube-apiserver`, `kube-scheduler`, `controller-manager`, and `coredns`.
- `kube-public`: Resources within this namespace are accessible to all. By default, nothing will be created in this namespace.

Let's take a look at how to create a namespace.

Creating a namespace

A new namespace in Kubernetes can be created by using the following command:

```
$ kubectl create namespace test
```

Once a new namespace is created, objects can be assigned to a namespace by using the `namespace` property, as follows:

```
$ kubectl apply --namespace=test -f pod.yaml
```

Objects within the namespace can similarly be accessed by using the `namespace` property, as follows:

```
$ kubectl get pods --namespace=test
```

In Kubernetes, not all objects are namespaced. Lower-level objects such as `Nodes` and `persistentVolumes` span across namespaces.

Wrapping up least privilege for Kubernetes subjects

By now, you should be familiar with the concepts of ClusterRole/Role, ClusterRoleBinding/RoleBinding, service accounts, and namespaces. In order to implement least privilege for Kubernetes subjects, you may ask yourself the following questions before you create a Role or RoleBinding object in Kubernetes:

- Does the subject need privileges for a namespace or across namespaces?

  This is important because once the subject has cluster-level privileges it may be able to exercise the privileges across all namespaces.

- Should the privileges be granted to a user, group, or service account?

  When you grant a role to a group, it means all the users in the group will automatically get the privileges from the newly granted role. Be sure you understand the impact before you grant a role to a group. Next, a user in Kubernetes is for humans, while a service account is for microservices in pods. Be sure you know what the Kubernetes user's responsibility is and assign privileges accordingly. Also, note that some microservices do not need any privilege at all as they don't interact with `kube-apiserver` or any Kubernetes objects directly.

- What are the resources that the subjects need to access?

  When creating a role, if you don't specify the resource name or do set `*` in the `resourceNames` field, it means access is granted to all the resources of the resource type. If you know which resource name the subject is going to access, do specify the resource name when creating a role.

Kubernetes subjects interact with Kubernetes objects with the granted privileges. Understanding the actual tasks your Kubernetes subjects perform will help you grant privileges properly.

Least privilege for Kubernetes workloads

Usually, there will be a service account (default) associated with a Kubernetes workload. Thus, processes inside a pod can communicate with `kube-apiserver` using the service account token. DevOps should carefully grant necessary privileges to the service account for the purpose of least privilege. We've already covered this in the previous section.

Besides accessing `kube-apiserver` to operate Kubernetes objects, processes in a pod can also access resources on the worker nodes and other pods/microservices in the clusters (covered in *Chapter 2, Kubernetes Networking*). In this section, we will talk about the possible least privilege implementation of access to system resources, network resources, and application resources.

Least privilege for accessing system resources

Recall that a microservice running inside a container or pod is nothing but a process on a worker node isolated in its own namespace. A pod or container may access different types of resources on the worker node based on the configuration. This is controlled by the security context, which can be configured both at the pod level and the container level. Configuring the pod/container security context should be on the developers' task list (with the help of security design and review), while pod security policies—the other way to limit pod/container access to system resources at the cluster level—should be on DevOps's to-do list. Let's look into the concepts of security context, PodSecurityPolicy, and resource limit control.

Security context

A security context offers a way to define privileges and access control settings for pods and containers with regard to accessing system resources. In Kubernetes, the security context at the pod level is different from that at the container level, though there are some overlapping attributes that can be configured at both levels. In general, the security context provides the following features that allow you to apply the principle of least privilege for containers and pods:

- **Discretionary Access Control (DAC)**: This is to configure which **user ID (UID)** or **group ID (GID)** to bind to the process in the container, whether the container's root filesystem is read-only, and so on. It is highly recommended not to run your microservice as a root user ($UID = 0$) in containers. The security implication is that if there is an exploit and a container escapes to the host, the attacker gains the root user privileges on the host immediately.

- **Security Enhanced Linux (SELinux):** This is to configure the SELinux security context, which defines the level label, role label, type label, and user label for pods or containers. With the SELinux labels assigned, pods and containers may be restricted in terms of being able to access resources, especially volumes on the node.

- **Privileged mode:** This is to configure whether a container is running in privileged mode. The power of the process running inside the privileged container is basically the same as a root user on a node.

- **Linux capabilities:** This is to configure Linux capabilities for containers. Different Linux capabilities allow the process inside the container to perform different activities or access different resources on the node. For example, `CAP_AUDIT_WRITE` allows the process to write to the kernel auditing log, while `CAP_SYS_ADMIN` allows the process to perform a range of administrative operations.

- **AppArmor:** This is to configure the AppArmor profile for pods or containers. An AppArmor profile usually defines which Linux capabilities the process owns, which network resources and files can be accessed by the container, and so on.

- **Secure Computing Mode (seccomp):** This is to configure the seccomp profile for pods or containers. A seccomp profile usually defines a whitelist of system calls that are allowed to execute and/or a blacklist of system calls that will be blocked to execute inside the pod or container.

- **AllowPrivilegeEscalation:** This is to configure whether a process can gain more privileges than its parent process. Note that `AllowPrivilegeEscalation` is always true when the container is either running as privileged or has a `CAP_SYS_ADMIN` capability.

We will talk more about security context in *Chapter 8*, *Securing Pods*.

PodSecurityPolicy

The PodSecurityPolicy is a Kubernetes cluster-level resource that controls the attributes of pod specification relevant to security. It defines a set of rules. When pods are to be created in the Kubernetes cluster, the pods need to comply with the rules defined in the PodSecurityPolicy or they will fail to start. The PodSecurityPolicy controls or applies the following attributes:

- Allows a privileged container to be run

- Allows host-level namespaces to be used

- Allows host ports to be used

- Allows different types of volumes to be used

- Allows the host's filesystem to be accessed

- Requires a read-only root filesystem to be run for containers

- Restricts user IDs and group IDs for containers

- Restricts containers' privilege escalation

- Restricts containers' Linux capabilities

- Requires an SELinux security context to be used

- Applies seccomp and AppArmor profiles to pods

- Restricts sysctls that a pod can run

- Allows a `proc` mount type to be used

- Restricts an FSGroup to volumes

We will cover more about PodSecurityPolicy in *Chapter 8, Securing Kubernetes Pods.* A PodSecurityPolicy control is basically implemented as an admission controller. You can also create your own admission controller to apply your own authorization policy for your workload. **Open Policy Agent (OPA)** is another good candidate to implement your own least privilege policy for a workload. We will look at OPA more in *Chapter 7, Authentication, Authorization, and Admission Control.*

Now, let's look at the resource limit control mechanism in Kubernetes as you may not want your microservices to saturate all the resources, such as the **Central Processing Unit (CPU)** and memory, in the system.

Resource limit control

By default, a single container can use as much memory and CPU resources as a node has. A container with a crypto-mining binary running may easily consume the CPU resources on the node shared by other pods. It's always a good practice to set resource requests and limits for workload. The resource request impacts which node the pods will be assigned to by the scheduler, while the resource limit sets the condition under which the container will be terminated. It's always safe to assign more resource requests and limits to your workload to avoid eviction or termination. However, do keep in mind that if you set the resource request or limit too high, you've caused a resource waste on your cluster, and the resources allocated to your workload may not be fully utilized. We will cover this topic more in *Chapter 10, Real-Time Monitoring and Resource Management of a Kubernetes Cluster.*

Wrapping up least privilege for accessing system resources

When pods or containers run in privileged mode, unlike the non-privileged pods or containers, they have the same privileges as admin users on the node. If your workload runs in privileged mode, why is this the case? When a pod is able to assess host-level namespaces, the pod can access resources such as the network stack, process, and **Interprocess Communication (IPC)** at the host level. But do you really need to grant host-level namespace access or set privileged mode to your pods or containers? Also, if you know which Linux capabilities are required for your processes in the container, you'd better drop those unnecessary ones. And how much memory and CPU is sufficient for your workload to be fully functional? Please do think through these questions for the purpose of implementing the principle of least privilege for your Kubernetes workload. Properly set resource requests and limits, use security context for your workload, and enforce a PodSecurityPolicy for your cluster. All of this will help ensure the least privilege for your workload to access system resources.

Least privilege for accessing network resources

By default, any two pods inside the same Kubernetes cluster can communicate with other, and a pod may be able to communicate with the internet if there is no proxy rule or firewall rule configured outside the Kubernetes cluster. The openness of Kubernetes blurs the security boundary of microservices, and we mustn't overlook network resources such as API endpoints provided by other microservices that a container or pod can access.

Suppose one of your workloads (pod X) in namespace X only needs to access another microservice A in namespace NS1; meanwhile, there is microservice B in namespace NS2. Both microservice A and microservice B expose their **Representational State Transfer** (**REST**ful) endpoints. By default, your workload can access both microservice A and B assuming there is neither authentication nor authorization at the microservice level, and also no network policies enforced in namespaces NS1 and NS2. Take a look at the following diagram, which illustrates this:

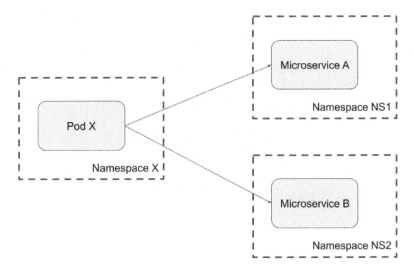

Figure 4.1 – Network access without network policy

In the preceding diagram, **Pod X** is able to access both microservices, though they reside in different namespaces. Note also that **Pod X** only requires access to **Microservice A** in namespace **NS1**. So, is there anything we can do to restrict **Pod X's** access to **Microservice A** only for the purpose of least privilege? Yes: a Kubernetes network policy can help. We will cover network policies in more detail *Chapter 5, Configuring Kubernetes Security Boundaries*. In general, a Kubernetes network policy defines rules of how a group of pods are allowed to communicate with each other and other network endpoints. You can define both ingress rules and egress rules for your workload.

> **Note**
>
> Ingress rules: Rules to define which sources are allowed to communicate with the pods under the protection of the network policy.
>
> Egress rules: Rules to define which destinations are allowed to communicate with the pods under the protection of the network policy.

In the following example, to implement the principle of least privilege in **Pod X**, you will need to define a network policy in **Namespace X** with an egress rule specifying that only **Microservice A** is allowed:

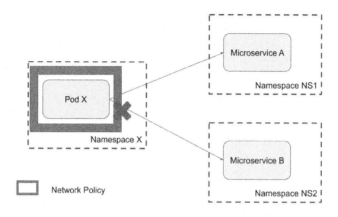

Figure 4.2 – Network policy blocks access to microservice B

In the preceding diagram, the network policy in **Namespace X** blocks any request from **Pod X** to **Microservice B**, and **Pod X** can still access **Microservice A**, as expected. Defining an egress rule in your network policy will help ensure least privilege for your workload to access network resources. Last but not least, we still need to bring your attention to the application resource level from a least-privilege standpoint.

Least privilege for accessing application resources

Though this topic falls into the category of application security, it is worth bringing up here. If there are applications that your workload accesses that support multiple users with different levels of privileges, it's better to examine whether the privileges granted to the user on your workload's behalf are necessary or not. For example, a user who is responsible for auditing does not need any write privileges. Application developers should keep this in mind when designing the application. This helps to ensure the least privilege for your workload to access application resources.

Summary

In this chapter, we went through the concept of least privilege. Then, we discussed the security control mechanism in Kubernetes that helps in implementing the principle of least privilege in two areas: Kubernetes subjects and Kubernetes workloads. It is worth emphasizing the importance of implementing the principle of the principle of least privilege holistically. If least privilege is missed in any area, this will potentially leave an attack surface wide open.

Kubernetes offers built-in security controls to implement the principle of least privilege. Note that it is a process from development to deployment: application developers should work with security architects to design the minimum privileges for the service accounts associated with the application, as well as the minimum capabilities and proper resource allocation. During deployment, DevOps should consider using a PodSecurityPolicy and a network policy to enforce least privileges across the entire cluster.

In the next chapter, we will look at the security of Kubernetes from a different angle: understanding the security boundaries of different types of resources and how to fortify them.

Questions

1. What is a Role object in Kubernetes?

2. What is a RoleBinding object in Kubernetes?

3. What is the difference between RoleBinding and ClusterRoleBinding objects?

4. By default, a pod can't access host-level namespaces. Name a few settings that allow pods to access host-level namespaces.

5. If you want to restrict pod access to external network resources (for example, the internal network or the internet), what you can do?

Further reading

You may have noticed that some of the security control mechanisms we talked about in this chapter have been around for a long time: SELinux **Multi-Category Security/ Multi-Level Security (MCS/MLS)**, AppArmor, seccomp, Linux capabilities, and so on. There are already many books or articles introducing these technologies. I would encourage you to take a look at the following materials for a better understanding of how to use them to achieve the least privilege goal in Kubernetes:

- SELinux MCS: `https://access.redhat.com/documentation/en-us/ red_hat_enterprise_linux/5/html/deployment_guide/sec-mcs- getstarted`

- AppArmor: `https://ubuntu.com/server/docs/security-apparmor`

- Linux capabilities: `http://man7.org/linux/man-pages/man7/ capabilities.7.html`

- Help defining RBAC privilege grants: `https://github.com/liggitt/ audit2rbac`

5
Configuring Kubernetes Security Boundaries

A security boundary separates security domains where a set of entities share the same security concerns and access levels, whereas a trust boundary is a dividing line where program execution and data change the level of trust. Controls in the security boundary ensure that execution moving between boundaries does not elevate the trust level without appropriate validation. As data or execution moves between security boundaries without appropriate controls, security vulnerabilities show up.

In this chapter, we'll discuss the importance of security and trust boundaries. We'll first focus on the introduction to clarify any confusion between security and trust boundaries. Then, we'll walk through the security domains and security boundaries within the Kubernetes ecosystem. Finally, we'll look at some Kubernetes features that enhance security boundaries for an application deployed in Kubernetes.

You should understand the concepts of security domain and security boundaries, and also understand the security boundaries built around Kubernetes based on the underlying container technology as well as the built-in security features, such as PodSecurityPolicy and NetworkPolicy.

We will cover the following topics in this chapter:

- Introduction to security boundaries
- Security boundaries versus trust boundaries
- Kubernetes security domains
- Kubernetes entities as security boundaries
- Security boundaries in the system layer
- Security boundaries in the network layer

Introduction to security boundaries

Security boundaries exist in the data layer, the network layer, and the system layer. Security boundaries depend on the technologies used by the IT department or infrastructure team. For example, companies use virtual machines to manage their applications – a hypervisor is the security boundary for virtual machines. Hypervisors ensure that code running in a virtual machine does not escape from the virtual machine or affect the physical node. When companies start embracing microservices and use orchestrators to manage their applications, containers are one of the security boundaries. However, compared to hypervisors, containers do not provide a strong security boundary, nor do they aim to. Containers enforce restrictions at the application layer but do not prevent attackers from bypassing these restrictions from the kernel layer.

At the network layer, traditionally, firewalls provide strong security boundaries for applications. In a microservices architecture, Pods in Kubernetes can communicate with others. Network policies are used to restrict communication among Pods and Services.

Security boundaries at the data layer are well known. Kernels limiting write access to system or bin directories to only root or system users is a simple example of security boundaries at the data layer. In containerized environments, chroot prevents containers from tampering with the filesystems of other containers. Kubernetes restructures the application deployment in a way that strong security boundaries can be enforced on both the network and system layers.

Security boundaries versus trust boundaries

Security boundary and trust boundary are often used as synonyms. Although similar, there is a subtle difference between these two terms. A **trust boundary** is where a system changes its level of trust. An execution trust boundary is where instructions need different privileges to run. For example, a database server executing code in /bin is an example of an execution crossing a trust boundary. Similarly, a data trust boundary is where data moves between entities with different trust levels. Data inserted by an end user into a trusted database is an example of data crossing a trust boundary.

Whereas a **security boundary** is a point of demarcation between different security domains, a security domain is a set of entities that are within the same access level. For example, in traditional web architecture, the user-facing applications are part of a security domain and the internal network is part of a different security domain. Security boundaries have access controls associated with it. Think of trust boundary as a wall and security boundary as a fence around the wall.

Identifying security and trust boundaries within an ecosystem is important. It helps ensure appropriate validation is done for instructions and data before it crosses the boundaries. In Kubernetes, components and objects span across different security boundaries. It is important to understand these boundaries to put risk mitigation plans in place when an attacker crosses a security boundary. CVE-2018-1002105 is a prime example of an attack caused by missing validation across trust boundaries; proxy request handling in the API server allowed an unauthenticated user to get admin privileges to the cluster. Similarly, CVE-2018-18264 allows users to skip the authentication process on the dashboard to allow unauthenticated users to access sensitive cluster information.

Now let's look at different Kubernetes security domains.

Kubernetes security domains

A Kubernetes cluster can be broadly split into three security domains:

- **Kubernetes master components**: Kubernetes master components define the control plane for the Kubernetes ecosystem. The master components are responsible for decisions required for the smooth operation of the cluster, such as scheduling. Master components include kube-apiserver, etcd, the kube-controller manager, DNS server, and kube-scheduler. A breach in the Kubernetes master components can compromise the entire Kubernetes cluster.

- **Kubernetes worker components**: Kubernetes worker components are deployed on every worker node and ensure that Pods and containers are running nicely. Kubernetes worker components use authorization and TLS tunneling for communicating with the master components. A cluster can function with compromised worker components. It is analogous to a rogue node within the environment, which can be removed from the cluster when identified.

- **Kubernetes objects**: Kubernetes objects are persistent entities that represent the state of the cluster: deployed applications, volumes, and namespaces. Kubernetes objects include Pods, Services, volumes, and namespaces. These are deployed by developers or DevOps. Object specification defines additional security boundaries for objects: defining a Pod with a SecurityContext, network rules to communicate with other Pods, and more.

The high-level security domain division should help you focus on the key assets. Keeping that in mind, we'll start looking at Kubernetes entities and the security boundaries built around them.

Kubernetes entities as security boundaries

In a Kubernetes cluster, the Kubernetes entities (objects and components) you interact with have their own built-in security boundaries. The security boundaries are derived from the design or implementation of the entities. It is important to understand the security boundaries built within or around them:

- **Containers**: Containers are a basic component within a Kubernetes cluster. A container provides minimal isolation to the application using cgroups, Linux namespaces, AppArmor profiles, and a seccomp profile to the application running within the container.

- **Pods**: A pod is a collection of one or more containers. Pods isolate more resources compared to containers, such as a network and IPC. Features such as security SecurityContext, NetworkPolicy, and PodSecurityPolicy work at the pod level to ensure a higher level of isolation.

- **Nodes**: Nodes in Kubernetes are also a security boundary. Pods can be specified to run on specific nodes using `nodeSelectors`. Kernels and hypervisors enforce security controls for pods running on the nodes. Features such as AppArmor and SELinux can help improve the security posture along with other host-hardening mechanisms.

- **Cluster**: A cluster is a collection of pods, containers, and the components on the master node and worker nodes. A cluster provides a strong security boundary. Pods and containers running within a cluster are isolated from other clusters at the network and the system layer.

- **Namespaces**: Namespaces are virtual clusters that isolate pods and services. The LimitRanger admission controller is applied at the namespace level to control resource utilization and denial-of-service attacks. Network policies can be applied to the namespace level.

- **The Kubernetes API server**: The Kubernetes API server interacts with all Kubernetes components, including `etcd`, `controller-manager`, and `kubelet`, which is used by cluster administrators to configure a cluster. It mediates communication with master components, so cluster administrators do not have to directly interact with cluster components.

We discussed three different threat actors in *Chapter 3, Threat Modeling*: privileged attackers, internal attackers, and end users. These threat actors may also interact with the preceding Kubernetes entities. We will see what the security boundaries from these entities an attacker is facing:

- **End user**: An end user interacts with either the ingress, exposed Kubernetes services, or directly to the open ports on the node. For the end user, nodes, Pods, `kube-apiserver`, and the external firewall protect the cluster components from being compromised.

- **Internal attacker**: Internal attackers have access to Pods and containers. Namespaces and access control enforced by `kube-apiserver` prevent these attackers from escalating privileges or compromising the cluster. Network policy and RBAC controls can prevent lateral movement.

- **Privileged attacker**: `kube-apiserver` is the only security boundary that protects the master components from compromise by privileged attackers. If a privileged attacker compromises `kube-apiserver`, it's game over.

In this section, we looked at security boundaries from a user perspective and showed you how security boundaries are built in the Kubernetes ecosystem. Next, let's look at the security boundaries in the system layer, from a microservice perspective.

Security boundaries in the system layer

Microservices run inside Pods, where Pods are scheduled to run on worker nodes in a cluster. In the previous chapters, we already emphasized that a container is a process assigned with dedicated Linux namespaces. A container or Pod consumes all the necessary resources provided from the worker node. So, it is important to understand the security boundaries from the system's perspective and how to fortify it. In this section, we will talk about the security boundaries built upon Linux namespaces and Linux capabilities together for microservices.

Linux namespaces as security boundaries

Linux namespaces are a feature of the Linux kernel to partition resources for isolation purposes. With namespaces assigned, a set of processes sees one set of resources while another set of processes sees another set of resources. We've already introduced Linux namespaces in *Chapter 2, Kubernetes Networking*. By default, each Pod has its own network namespace and IPC namespace. Each container inside the same pod has its own PID namespace so that one container has no knowledge about other containers running inside the same Pod. Similarly, a Pod does not know other Pods exist in the same worker node.

In general, the default settings offer pretty good isolation for microservices from a security standpoint. However, the host namespace settings are allowed to be configured in the Kubernetes workload, and more specifically, in the Pod specification. With such settings enabled, the microservice uses host-level namespaces:

- **HostNetwork**: The Pod uses the host's network namespace.
- **HostIPC**: The Pod uses the host's IPC namespace.
- **HostPID**: The Pod uses the host's PID namespace.
- **shareProcessNamespace**: The containers inside the same Pod will share a single PID namespace.

When you try to configure your workload to use host namespaces, do ask yourself the question: why do you have to do this? When using host namespaces, pods have full knowledge of other pods' activities in the same worker node, but it also depends on what Linux capabilities are assigned to the container. Overall, the fact is, you're disarming other microservices' security boundaries. Let me give a quick example. This is a list of processes visible inside a container:

```
root@nginx-2:/# ps aux
USER         PID %CPU %MEM    VSZ    RSS TTY      STAT START
```

```
TIME COMMAND
root            1   0.1   0.0   32648   5256 ?         Ss   23:47
0:00 nginx: master process nginx -g daemon off;
nginx           6   0.0   0.0   33104   2348 ?         S    23:47
0:00 nginx: worker process
root            7   0.0   0.0   18192   3248 pts/0     Ss   23:48
0:00 bash
root           13   0.0   0.0   36636   2816 pts/0     R+   23:48
0:00 ps aux
```

As you can see, inside the nginx container, only nginx processes and bash process are visible from the container. This nginx pod doesn't use a host PID namespace. Let's a look at what happens if a pod uses host PID namespace:

```
root@gke-demo-cluster-default-pool-c9e3510c-tfgh:/# ps axu
USER          PID %CPU %MEM    VSZ    RSS TTY       STAT START
TIME COMMAND
root            1   0.2   0.0   99660   7596 ?         Ss   22:54
0:10 /usr/lib/systemd/systemd noresume noswap cros_efi
root           20   0.0   0.0       0      0 ?         I<   22:54
0:00 [netns]
root           71   0.0   0.0       0      0 ?         I    22:54
0:01 [kworker/u4:2]
root          101   0.0   0.1   28288   9536 ?         Ss   22:54
0:01 /usr/lib/systemd/systemd-journald
201           293   0.2   0.0   13688   4068 ?         Ss   22:54
0:07 /usr/bin/dbus-daemon --system --address=systemd: --nofork
--nopidfile
274           297   0.0   0.0   22520   4196 ?         Ss   22:54
0:00 /usr/lib/systemd/systemd-networkd
root          455   0.0   0.0       0      0 ?         I    22:54
0:00 [kworker/0:3]
root         1155   0.0   0.0    9540   3324 ?         Ss   22:54
0:00 bash /home/kubernetes/bin/health-monitor.sh container-
runtime
root         1356   4.4   1.5 1396748 118236 ?        Ssl  22:56
2:30 /home/kubernetes/bin/kubelet --v=2 --cloud-provider=gce
--experimental
root         1635   0.0   0.0  773444   6012 ?         Sl   22:56
0:00 containerd-shim -namespace moby -workdir /var/lib/
containerd/io.contai
```

```
root          1660  0.1  0.4 417260 36292 ?          Ssl  22:56
0:03 kube-proxy --master=https://35.226.122.194 --kubeconfig=/
var/lib/kube-
root          2019  0.0  0.1 107744  7872 ?          Ssl  22:56
0:00 /ip-masq-agent --masq-chain=IP-MASQ --nomasq-all-reserved-
ranges
root          2171  0.0  0.0  16224  5020 ?          Ss   22:57
0:00 sshd: gke-1a5c3c1c4d5b7d80adbc [priv]
root          3203  0.0  0.0   1024     4 ?          Ss   22:57
0:00 /pause
root          5489  1.3  0.4  48008 34236 ?          Sl   22:57
0:43 calico-node -felix
root          6988  0.0  0.0  32648  5248 ?          Ss   23:01
0:00 nginx: master process nginx -g daemon off;
nginx         7009  0.0  0.0  33104  2584 ?          S    23:01
0:00 nginx: worker process
```

The preceding output shows the processes running in the worker node from an `nginx` container. Among these processes are system processes, `sshd`, `kubelet`, `kube-proxy`, and so on. Besides from the Pod using the host PID namespace, you can send signals to other microservices' processes, such as `SIGKILL` to kill a process.

Linux capabilities as security boundaries

Linux capabilities are a concept evolved from the traditional Linux permission check: privileged and unprivileged. Privileged processes bypass all kernel permission checks. Then, Linux divides privileges associated with Linux superusers into distinct units – Linux capabilities. There are network-related capabilities, such as CAP_NET_ADMIN, CAP_NET_BIND_SERVICE, CAP_NET_BROADCAST, and CAP_NET_RAW. And there are audit-related capabilities: CAP_AUDIT_CONTROL, CAP_AUDIT_READ, and CAP_AUDIT_WRITE. Of course, there is still an admin-like capability: CAP_SYS_ADMIN.

As mentioned in *Chapter 4, Applying the Principle of Least Privilege in Kubernetes*, you can configure Linux capabilities for containers in a pod. By default, here is a list of capabilities that are assigned to containers in Kubernetes clusters:

- CAP_SETPCAP
- CAP_MKNOD
- CAP_AUDIT_WRITE
- CAP_CHOWN

- CAP_NET_RAW

- CAP_DAC_OVERRIDE

- CAP_FOWNER

- CAP_FSETID

- CAP_KILL

- CAP_SETGID

- CAP_SETUID

- CAP_NET_BIND_SERVICE

- CAP_SYS_CHROOT

- CAP_SETFCAP

For most of the microservices, these capabilities should be good enough to perform their daily tasks. You should drop all the capabilities and only add the required ones. Similar to host namespaces, granting extra capabilities may disarm the security boundaries of other microservices. Here is an example output when you run the tcpdump command in a container:

```
root@gke-demo-cluster-default-pool-c9e3510c-tfgh:/# tcpdump -i
cali01fb9a4e4b4 -v
tcpdump: listening on cali01fb9a4e4b4, link-type EN10MB
(Ethernet), capture size 262144 bytes
23:18:36.604766 IP (tos 0x0, ttl 64, id 27472, offset 0, flags
[DF], proto UDP (17), length 86)
    10.56.1.14.37059 > 10.60.0.10.domain: 35359+ A? www.google.
com.default.svc.cluster.local. (58)
23:18:36.604817 IP (tos 0x0, ttl 64, id 27473, offset 0, flags
[DF], proto UDP (17), length 86)
    10.56.1.14.37059 > 10.60.0.10.domain: 35789+ AAAA? www.
google.com.default.svc.cluster.local. (58)
23:18:36.606864 IP (tos 0x0, ttl 62, id 8294, offset 0, flags
[DF], proto UDP (17), length 179)
    10.60.0.10.domain > 10.56.1.14.37059: 35789 NXDomain 0/1/0
(151)
23:18:36.606959 IP (tos 0x0, ttl 62, id 8295, offset 0, flags
[DF], proto UDP (17), length 179)
    10.60.0.10.domain > 10.56.1.14.37059: 35359 NXDomain 0/1/0
(151)
```

```
23:18:36.607013 IP (tos 0x0, ttl 64, id 27474, offset 0, flags
[DF], proto UDP (17), length 78)
    10.56.1.14.59177 > 10.60.0.10.domain: 7489+ A? www.google.
com.svc.cluster.local. (50)
23:18:36.607053 IP (tos 0x0, ttl 64, id 27475, offset 0, flags
[DF], proto UDP (17), length 78)
    10.56.1.14.59177 > 10.60.0.10.domain: 7915+ AAAA? www.
google.com.svc.cluster.local. (50)
```

The preceding output shows that inside a container, there is tcpdump listening on the network interface, cali01fb9a4e4b4, which was created for another pod's network communication. With a host network namespace and CAP_NET_ADMIN granted, you are able to sniff network traffic from the entire worker node inside a container. In general, the fewer capabilities granted to containers, the more secure the boundaries are for other microservices.

Wrapping up security boundaries in the system layer

The dedicated Linux namespaces and the limited Linux capabilities assigned to a container or a Pod by default establish good security boundaries for microservices. However, users are still allowed to configure host namespaces or add extra Linux capabilities to a workload. This will disarm the security boundaries of other microservices running on the same worker node. You should be very careful of doing so. Usually, monitoring tools or security tools require access to host namespaces in order to do their monitoring job or detection job. And it is highly recommended to use PodSecurityPolicy to restrict the usage of host namespaces as well as extra capabilities so that the security boundaries of microservices are fortified.

Next, let's look at the security boundaries set up in the network layer, from a microservice's perspective.

Security boundaries in the network layer

A Kubernetes network policy defines the rules for different groups of Pods that are allowed to communicate with each other. In the previous chapter, we briefly talked about the egress rule of a Kubernetes network policy, which can be leveraged to enforce the principle of least privilege for microservices. In this section, we will go through a little more on the Kubernetes network policy and will focus on the ingress rule. We will show how the ingress rules of network policies can help to establish the trust boundaries among microservices.

Network policies

As mentioned in the previous chapter, as per the network model requirement, Pods inside a cluster can communicate with each other. But still, from a security perspective, you may want to restrict your microservice to being accessed by only a few services. How can we achieve that in Kubernetes? Let's take a quick look at the following Kubernetes network policy example:

```
apiVersion: networking.k8s.io/v1
kind: NetworkPolicy
metadata:
  name: test-network-policy
  namespace: default
spec:
  podSelector:
    matchLabels:
      role: db
  policyTypes:
  - Ingress
  - Egress
  ingress:
  - from:
    - ipBlock:
        cidr: 172.17.0.0/16
        except:
        - 172.17.1.0/24
    - namespaceSelector:
        matchLabels:
          project: myproject
    - podSelector:
        matchLabels:
          role: frontend
    ports:
    - protocol: TCP
      port: 6379
  egress:
  - to:
    - ipBlock:
```

```
      cidr: 10.0.0.0/24
  ports:
  - protocol: TCP
    port: 5978
```

The `NetworkPolicy` policy is named `test-network-policy`. A few key attributes from the network policy specification worth mentioning are listed here to help you understand what the restrictions are:

- `podSelector`: A grouping of Pods to which the policy applies based on the Pod labels.

- `Ingress`: Ingress rules that apply to the Pods specified in the top-level `podSelector`. The different elements under `Ingress` are discussed as follows:

  - `ipBlock`: IP CIDR ranges that are allowed to communicate with ingress sources

  - `namespaceSelector`: Namespaces that are allowed as ingress sources based on namespace labels

  - `podSelector`: Pods that are allowed as ingress sources based on Pod labels

  - `ports`: Ports and protocols that all pods should be allowed to communicate with

- `egress`: Egress rules that apply to the Pods specified in the top-level `podSelector`. The different elements under `Ingress` are discussed as follows:

  - `ipBlock`: IP CIDR ranges that are allowed to communicate as egress destinations

  - `namespaceSelector`: Namespaces that are allowed as egress destinations based on namespace labels

  - `podSelector`: Pods that are allowed as egress destination based on Pod labels

  - `ports`: Destination ports and protocols that all Pods should be allowed to communicate with

Usually, `ipBlock` is used to specify the external IP block that microservices are allowed to interact with in the Kubernetes cluster, while the namespace selector and Pod selector are used to restrict network communications among microservices in the same Kubernetes cluster.

To strengthen the trust boundaries for microservices from a network aspect, you might want to either specify the allowed `ipBlock` from external or allowed microservices from a specific namespace. The following is another example to restrict the ingress source from certain Pods and namespaces by using `namespaceSelector` and `podSelector`:

```
apiVersion: networking.k8s.io/v1
kind: NetworkPolicy
metadata:
  name: allow-good
spec:
  podSelector:
    matchLabels:
      app: web
  policyTypes:
  - Ingress
  ingress:
  - from:
    - namespaceSelector:
        matchLabels:
          from: good
      podSelector:
        matchLabels:
          from: good
```

Note that there is no - in front of the `podSelector` attribute. This means the ingress source can only be pods with the label `from: good` in the namespace with the label `from: good`. This network policy protects Pods with the label `app: web` in the default namespace:

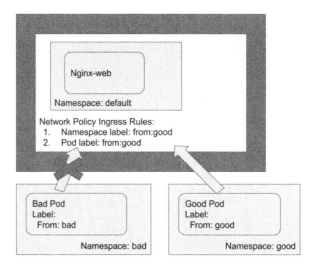

Figure 5.1 – Network policy restricting incoming traffic by Pod and namespace labels

In the preceding diagram, the `good` namespace has the label `from: good` while the `bad` namespace has the label `from: bad`. It illustrates that only Pods with the label `from: good` in the namespace with the label `from: good` can access the `nginx-web` service in the default namespace. Other Pods, no matter whether they're from the `good` namespace but without the label `from: good` or from other namespaces, cannot access the `nginx-web` service in the default namespace.

Summary

In this chapter, we discussed the importance of security boundaries. Understanding the security domains and security boundaries within the Kubernetes ecosystem helps administrators understand the blast radius of an attack and have mitigation strategies in place to limit the damage caused in the event of an attack. Knowing Kubernetes entities is the starting point of fortifying security boundaries. Knowing the security boundaries built into the system layer with Linux namespaces and capabilities is the next step. Last but not least, understanding the power of network policies is also critical to build security segmentation into microservices.

After this chapter, you should grasp the concept of the security domain and security boundaries. You should also know the security domains, common entities in Kubernetes, as well as the security boundaries built within or around Kubernetes entities. You should know the importance of using built-in security features such as PodSecurityPolicy and NetworkPolicy to fortify security boundaries and configure the security context of workloads carefully.

In the next chapter, we will talk about how to secure Kubernetes components. In particular, there are some configuration details you should pay attention to.

Questions

1. What are the security domains in Kubernetes?

2. What are the common Kubernetes entities you interact with?

3. How can you restrict a Kubernetes user to access objects in a specific namespace?

4. What does enable hostPID mean to a pod?

5. Try to configure a network policy to protect your service that only allows specific Pods as ingress sources.

Further references

- Kubernetes network policies: `https://kubernetes.io/docs/concepts/services-networking/network-policies/`

- CVE-2018-18264: `https://groups.google.com/forum/#!searchin/kubernetes-announce/CVE-2018-18264%7Csort:date/kubernetes-announce/yBrFf5nmvfI/gUO60KIlCAAJ`

- CVE-2018-1002105: `https://groups.google.com/forum/#!topic/kubernetes-announce/GVllWCg6L88`

Section 2:
Securing Kubernetes Deployments and Clusters

In this section, you will learn through hands-on exercises how to secure Kubernetes deployments/clusters in two ways: you will learn how to secure a DevOps pipeline in build, deployment, and runtime stages, and you will learn about defense in depth, looking at compliance, configuration, identity, authorization, resource management, logging and monitoring, detection, and incident response.

The following chapters are included in this section:

6
Securing Cluster Components

In previous chapters, we looked at the architecture of a Kubernetes cluster. A Kubernetes cluster consists of master components—including `kube-apiserver`, `etcd`, `kube-scheduler`, CoreDNS, `kube-controller-manager`, and `cloud-controller-manager`—and node components, including `kubelet`, `kube-proxy`, and `container-runtime`. Master components are responsible for cluster management. They form the control plane of the cluster. Node components, on the other hand, are responsible for the functioning of pods and containers on the node.

In *Chapter 3, Threat Modeling*, we briefly discussed that components in a Kubernetes cluster need to be configured to ensure the security of the cluster. A compromise of any cluster component can cause a data breach. Misconfiguration of environments is one of the primary reasons for data breaches in traditional or microservices environments. It is important to understand the configurations for each component and how each setting can open up a new attack surface. So, it's important for cluster administrators to understand different configurations.

In this chapter, we look in detail at how to secure each component in a cluster. In many cases, it will not be possible to follow all security best practices, but it is important to highlight the risks and have a mitigation strategy in place if an attacker tries to exploit a vulnerable configuration.

For each master and node component, we briefly discuss the function of components with a security-relevant configuration in a Kubernetes cluster and look in detail at each configuration. We look at the possible settings for these configurations and highlight the recommended practices. Finally, we introduce `kube-bench` and walk through how this can be used to evaluate the security posture of your cluster.

In this chapter, we will cover the following topics:

- Securing kube-apiserver
- Securing kubelet
- Securing etcd
- Securing kube-scheduler
- Securing kube-controller-manager
- Securing CoreDNS
- Benchmarking a cluster's security configuration

Securing kube-apiserver

`kube-apiserver` is the gateway to your cluster. It implements a **representational state transfer (REST) application programming interface (API)** to authorize and validate requests for objects. It is the central gateway that communicates and manages other components within the Kubernetes cluster. It performs three main functions:

- **API management**: `kube-apiserver` exposes APIs for cluster management. These APIs are used by developers and cluster administrators to modify the state of the cluster.
- **Request handling**: Requests for object management and cluster management are validated and processed.
- **Internal messaging**: The API server interacts with other components in the cluster to ensure the cluster functions properly.

A request to the API server goes through the following steps before being processed:

1. **Authentication**: `kube-apiserver` first validates the origin of the request. `kube-apiserver` supports multiple modes of authentication including client certificates, bearer tokens, and **HyperText Transfer Protocol (HTTP)** authentication.

2. **Authorization**: Once the identity of origin is validated, the API server validates that the origin is allowed to execute the request. `kube-apiserver`, by default, supports **Attribute-Based Access Control (ABAC)**, **Role-Based Access Control (RBAC)**, node authorization, and Webhooks for authorization. RBAC is the recommended mode of authorization.

3. **Admission controller**: Once `kube-apiserver` authenticates and authorizes the request, admission controllers parse the request to check if it's allowed within the cluster. If the request is rejected by any admission controller, the request is dropped.

`kube-apiserver` is the brain of the cluster. Compromise of the API server causes cluster compromise, so it's essential that the API server is secure. Kubernetes provides a myriad of settings to configure the API server. Let's look at some of the security-relevant configurations next.

To secure the API server, you should do the following:

- **Disable anonymous authentication**: Use the `anonymous-auth=false` flag to set anonymous authentication to `false`. This ensures that requests rejected by all authentication modules are not treated as anonymous and are discarded.

- **Disable basic authentication**: Basic authentication is supported for convenience in `kube-apiserver` and should not be used. Basic authentication passwords persist indefinitely. `kube-apiserver` uses the `--basic-auth-file` argument to enable basic authentication. Ensure that this argument is not used.

- **Disable token authentication**: `--token-auth-file` enables token-based authentication for your cluster. Token-based authentication is not recommended. Static tokens persist forever and need a restart of the API server to update. Client certificates should be used for authentication.

- **Ensure connections with kubelet use HTTPS**: By default, `--kubelet-https` is set to `true`. Ensure that this argument is not set to `false` for `kube-apiserver`.

- **Disable profiling**: Enabling profiling using `--profiling` exposes unnecessary system and program details. Unless you are experiencing performance issues, disable profiling by setting `--profiling=false`.

- **Disable AlwaysAdmit**: `--enable-admission-plugins` can be used to enable admission control plugins that are not enabled by default. `AlwaysAdmit` accepts the request. Ensure that the plugin is not in the `--enabled-admission-plugins` list.

- **Use AlwaysPullImages**: The `AlwaysPullImages` admission control ensures that images on the nodes cannot be used without correct credentials. This prevents malicious pods from spinning up containers for images that already exist on the node.

- **Use SecurityContextDeny**: This admission controller should be used if `PodSecurityPolicy` is not enabled. `SecurityContextDeny` ensures that pods cannot modify `SecurityContext` to escalate privileges.

- **Enable auditing**: Auditing is enabled by default in `kube-apiserver`. Ensure that `--audit-log-path` is set to a file in a secure location. Additionally, ensure that the `maxage`, `maxsize`, and `maxbackup` parameters for auditing are set to meet compliance expectations.

- **Disable AlwaysAllow authorization**: Authorization mode ensures that requests from users with correct privileges are parsed by the API server. Do not use `AlwaysAllow` with `--authorization-mode`.

- **Enable RBAC authorization**: RBAC is the recommended authorization mode for the API server. ABAC is difficult to use and manage. The ease of use, and easy updates to, RBAC roles and role bindings makes RBAC suitable for environments that scale often.

- **Ensure requests to kubelet use valid certificates**: By default, `kube-apiserver` uses HTTPS for requests to `kubelet`. Enabling `--kubelet-certificate-authority`, `--kubelet-client-key`, and `--kubelet-client-key` ensures that the communication uses valid HTTPS certificates.

- **Enable service-account-lookup**: In addition to ensuring that the service account token is valid, `kube-apiserver` should also verify that the token is present in `etcd`. Ensure that `--service-account-lookup` is not set to `false`.

- **Enable PodSecurityPolicy**: `--enable-admission-plugins` can be used to enable `PodSecurityPolicy`. As we have seen in *Chapter 5, Configuring Kubernetes Security Boundaries*, `PodSecurityPolicy` is used to define the security-sensitive criteria for a pod. We will dive deep into creating pod security policies in *Chapter 8, Securing Kubernetes Pods*.

- **Use a service account key file**: Use of `--service-account-key-file` enables rotation of keys for service accounts. If this is not specified, `kube-apiserver` uses the private key from the **Transport Layer Security** (**TLS**) certificates to sign the service account tokens.

- **Enable authorized requests to etcd**: `--etcd-certfile` and `--etcd-keyfile` can be used to identify requests to `etcd`. This ensures that any unidentified requests can be rejected by `etcd`.

- **Do not disable the ServiceAccount admission controller**: This admission control automates service accounts. Enabling ServiceAccount ensures that custom ServiceAccount with restricted permissions can be used with different Kubernetes objects.

- **Do not use self-signed certificates for requests**: If HTTPS is enabled for kube-apiserver, a --tls-cert-file and a --tls-private-key-file should be provided to ensure that self-signed certificates are not used.

- **Secure connections to etcd**: Setting --etcd-cafile allows kube-apiserver to verify itself to etcd over **Secure Sockets Layer** (**SSL**) using a certificate file.

- **Use secure TLS connections**: Set --tls-cipher-suites to strong ciphers only. --tls-min-version is used to set the minimum-supported TLS version. TLS 1.2 is the recommended minimum version.

- **Enable advanced auditing**: Advanced auditing can be disabled by setting the --feature-gates to AdvancedAuditing=false. Ensure that this field is present and is set to true. Advanced auditing helps in an investigation if a breach happens.

On Minikube, the kube-apiserver configuration looks like this:

```
$ps aux | grep kube-api
root       4016  6.1 17.2 495148 342896 ?       Ssl   01:03
0:16 kube-apiserver --advertise-address=192.168.99.100 --allow-
privileged=true --authorization-mode=Node,RBAC --client-ca-
file=/var/lib/minikube/certs/ca.crt --enable-admission-plugin
s=NamespaceLifecycle,LimitRanger,ServiceAccount,DefaultSto
rageClass,DefaultTolerationSeconds,NodeRestriction,Mutatin
gAdmissionWebhook,ValidatingAdmissionWebhook,ResourceQuota
--enable-bootstrap-token-auth=true --etcd-cafile=/var/
lib/minikube/certs/etcd/ca.crt --etcd-certfile=/var/lib/
minikube/certs/apiserver-etcd-client.crt --etcd-keyfile=/
var/lib/minikube/certs/apiserver-etcd-client.key --etcd-
servers=https://127.0.0.1:2379 --insecure-port=0 --kubelet-
client-certificate=/var/lib/minikube/certs/apiserver-
kubelet-client.crt --kubelet-client-key=/var/lib/minikube/
certs/apiserver-kubelet-client.key --kubelet-preferred-
address-types=InternalIP,ExternalIP,Hostname --proxy-client-
cert-file=/var/lib/minikube/certs/front-proxy-client.crt
--proxy-client-key-file=/var/lib/minikube/certs/front-proxy-
client.key --requestheader-allowed-names=front-proxy-client
--requestheader-client-ca-file=/var/lib/minikube/certs/
front-proxy-ca.crt --requestheader-extra-headers-prefix=X-
```

```
Remote-Extra- --requestheader-group-headers=X-Remote-Group
--requestheader-username-headers=X-Remote-User --secure-
port=8443 --service-account-key-file=/var/lib/minikube/certs/
sa.pub --service-cluster-ip-range=10.96.0.0/12 --tls-cert-
file=/var/lib/minikube/certs/apiserver.crt --tls-private-key-
file=/var/lib/minikube/certs/apiserver.key
```

As you can see, by default on Minikube, kube-apiserver does not follow all security best practices. For example, PodSecurityPolicy is not enabled by default, and strong cipher suites and the tls minimum version are not set by default. It's the responsibility of the cluster administrator to ensure that the API server is securely configured.

Securing kubelet

kubelet is the node agent for Kubernetes. It manages the life cycle of objects within the Kubernetes cluster and ensures that the objects are in a healthy state on the node.

To secure kubelet, you should do the following:

- **Disable anonymous authentication**: If anonymous authentication is enabled, requests that are rejected by other authentication methods are treated as anonymous. Ensure that --anonymous-auth=false is set for each instance of kubelet.

- **Set the authorization mode**: The authorization mode for kubelet is set using config files. A config file is specified using the --config parameter. Ensure that the authorization mode does not have AlwaysAllow in the list.

- **Rotate kubelet certificates**: kubelet certificates can be rotated using a RotateCertificates configuration in the kubelet configuration file. This should be used in conjunction with RotateKubeletServerCertificate to auto-request rotation of server certificates.

- **Provide a Certificate Authority (CA) bundle**: A CA bundle is used by kubelet to verify client certificates. This can be set using the ClientCAFile parameter in the config file.

- **Disable the read-only port**: The read-only port is enabled for kubelet by default, and should be disabled. The read-only port is served with no authentication or authorization.

- **Enable the NodeRestriction admission controller**: The NodeRestriction admission controller only allows kubelet to modify the node and pod objects on the node it is bound to.

- **Restrict access to the Kubelet API**: Only the kube-apiserver component interacts with the kubelet API. If you try to communicate with the kubelet API on the node, it is forbidden. This is ensured by using RBAC for kubelet.

On Minikube, the kubelet configuration looks like this:

```
root       4286  2.6  4.6 1345544 92420 ?         Ssl  01:03
0:18 /var/lib/minikube/binaries/v1.17.3/kubelet
--authorization-mode=Webhook --bootstrap-kubeconfig=/etc/
kubernetes/bootstrap-kubelet.conf --cgroup-driver=cgroupfs
--client-ca-file=/var/lib/minikube/certs/ca.crt --cluster-
domain=cluster.local --config=/var/lib/kubelet/config.yaml
--container-runtime=docker --fail-swap-on=false --hostname-
override=minikube --kubeconfig=/etc/kubernetes/kubelet.conf
--node-ip=192.168.99.100 --pod-manifest-path=/etc/kubernetes/
manifests
```

Similar to the API server, not all secure configurations are used by default on a kubelet—for example, disabling the read-only port. Next, we talk about how cluster administrators can secure etcd.

Securing etcd

etcd is a key-value store that is used by Kubernetes for data storage. It stores the state, configuration, and secrets of the Kubernetes cluster. Only kube-apiserver should have access to etcd. Compromise of etcd can lead to a cluster compromise.

To secure etcd, you should do the following:

- **Restrict node access**: Use Linux firewalls to ensure that only nodes that need access to etcd are allowed access.

- **Ensure the API server uses TLS**: --cert-file and --key-file ensure that requests to etcd are secure.

- **Use valid certificates**: --client-cert-auth ensures that communication from clients is made using valid certificates, and setting --auto-tls to false ensures that self-signed certificates are not used.

- **Encrypt data at rest**: --encryption-provider-config is passed to the API server to ensure that data is encrypted at rest in etcd.

On Minikube, the `etcd` configuration looks like this:

```
$ ps aux | grep etcd
root       3992  1.9  2.4 10612080 48680 ?       Ssl  01:03
0:18 etcd --advertise-client-urls=https://192.168.99.100:2379
--cert-file=/var/lib/minikube/certs/etcd/server.crt --client-
cert-auth=true --data-dir=/var/lib/minikube/etcd --initial-
advertise-peer-urls=https://192.168.99.100:2380 --initial-
cluster=minikube=https://192.168.99.100:2380 --key-file=/var/
lib/minikube/certs/etcd/server.key --listen-client-urls=ht
tps://127.0.0.1:2379,https://192.168.99.100:2379 --listen-
metrics-urls=http://127.0.0.1:2381 --listen-peer-urls=ht
tps://192.168.99.100:2380 --name=minikube --peer-cert-file=/
var/lib/minikube/certs/etcd/peer.crt --peer-client-cert-
auth=true --peer-key-file=/var/lib/minikube/certs/etcd/peer.
key --peer-trusted-ca-file=/var/lib/minikube/certs/etcd/ca.crt
--snapshot-count=10000 --trusted-ca-file=/var/lib/minikube/
certs/etcd/ca.crt
```

`etcd` stores sensitive data of a Kubernetes cluster, such as private keys and secrets. Compromise of `etcd` is compromise of the `api-server` component. Cluster administrators should pay special attention while setting up `etcd`.

Securing kube-scheduler

Next, we look at `kube-scheduler`. As we have already discussed in *Chapter 1*, *Kubernetes Architecture*, `kube-scheduler` is responsible for assigning a node to a pod. Once the pod is assigned to a node, the `kubelet` executes the pod. `kube-scheduler` first filters the set of nodes on which the pod can run, then, based on the scoring of each node, it assigns the pod to the filtered node with the highest score. Compromise of the `kube-scheduler` component impacts the performance and availability of the pods in the cluster.

To secure `kube-scheduler`, you should do the following:

- **Disable profiling**: Profiling of `kube-scheduler` exposes system details. Setting `--profiling` to `false` reduces the attack surface.

- **Disable external connections to kube-scheduler**: External connections should be disabled for `kube-scheduler`. `AllowExtTrafficLocalEndpoints` is set to `true`, enabling external connections to `kube-scheduler`. Ensure that this feature is disabled using `--feature-gates`.

- **Enable AppArmor**: By default, `AppArmor` is enabled for `kube-scheduler`. Ensure that `AppArmor` is not disabled for `kube-scheduler`.

On Minikube, the `kube-scheduler` configuration looks like this:

```
$ps aux | grep kube-scheduler
root      3939  0.5  2.0 144308 41640 ?          Ssl  01:03
0:02 kube-scheduler --authentication-kubeconfig=/etc/
kubernetes/scheduler.conf --authorization-kubeconfig=/etc/
kubernetes/scheduler.conf --bind-address=0.0.0.0 --kubeconfig=/
etc/kubernetes/scheduler.conf --leader-elect=true
```

Similar to `kube-apiserver`, the scheduler also does not follow all security best practices such as disabling profiling.

Securing kube-controller-manager

`kube-controller-manager` manages the control loop for the cluster. It monitors the cluster for changes through the API server and aims to move the cluster from the current state to the desired state. Multiple controller managers are shipped by default with `kube-controller-manager`, such as a replication controller and a namespace controller. Compromise of `kube-controller-manager` can result in updates to the cluster being rejected.

To secure `kube-controller-manager`, you should use `--use-service-account-credentials` which, when used with RBAC ensures that control loops run with minimum privileges.

On Minikube, the `kube-controller-manager` configuration looks like this:

```
$ps aux | grep kube-controller-manager
root      3927  1.8  4.5 209520 90072 ?          Ssl  01:03
0:11 kube-controller-manager --authentication-kubeconfig=/
etc/kubernetes/controller-manager.conf --authorization-
kubeconfig=/etc/kubernetes/controller-manager.conf --bind-
address=0.0.0.0 --client-ca-file=/var/lib/minikube/certs/ca.crt
--cluster-signing-cert-file=/var/lib/minikube/certs/ca.crt
--cluster-signing-key-file=/var/lib/minikube/certs/ca.key
--controllers=*,bootstrapsigner,tokencleaner --kubeconfig=/
etc/kubernetes/controller-manager.conf --leader-elect=true
--requestheader-client-ca-file=/var/lib/minikube/certs/front-
proxy-ca.crt --root-ca-file=/var/lib/minikube/certs/ca.crt
--service-account-private-key-file=/var/lib/minikube/certs/
sa.key --use-service-account-credentials=true
```

Next, let's talk about securing CoreDNS.

Securing CoreDNS

kube-dns was the default **Domain Name System (DNS)** server for a Kubernetes cluster. The DNS server helps internal objects such as services, pods, and containers locate each other. kube-dns is comprised of three containers, detailed as follows:

- kube-dns: This container uses SkyDNS to perform DNS resolution services.

- dnsmasq: A lightweight DNS resolver. It caches responses from SkyDNS.

- sidecar: This monitors health and handles metrics reporting for DNS.

kube-dns has been superseded by CoreDNS since version 1.11 because of security vulnerabilities in dnsmasq and performance issues in SkyDNS. CoreDNS is a single container that provides all the functions of kube-dns.

To edit the configuration file for CoreDNS, you can use kubectl, like this:

```
$ kubectl -n kube-system edit configmap coredns
```

By default, the CoreDNS config file on Minikube looks like this:

```
# Please edit the object below. Lines beginning with a '#'
# will be ignored, and an empty file will abort the edit.
# If an error occurs while saving this file will be
# reopened with the relevant failures.
apiVersion: v1
data:
  Corefile: |
    .:53 {
        errors
        health {
            lameduck 5s
        }
        ready
        kubernetes cluster.local in-addr.arpa ip6.arpa {
            pods insecure
            fallthrough in-addr.arpa ip6.arpa
            ttl 30
        }
        prometheus :9153
        forward . /etc/resolv.conf
```

```
        cache 30
        loop
        reload
        loadbalance
    }
```

To secure CoreDNS, do the following:

- **Ensure that the health plugin is not disabled**: The `health` plugin monitors the status of CoreDNS. It is used to confirm if CoreDNS is up and running. It is enabled by adding `health` to the list of plugins to be enabled in `Corefile`.

- **Enable istio for CoreDNS**: `istio` is a service mesh that is used by Kubernetes to provide service discovery, load balancing, and authentication. It is not available by default in Kubernetes and needs to be added as an external dependency. You can add `istio` to your cluster by starting the `istio` service and adding a proxy for the `istio` service to the config file, like this:

```
global:53 {
        errors
        proxy . {cluster IP of this istio-core-dns
    service}
    }
```

Now that we have looked at different configurations of cluster components, it is important to realize that as the components become more sophisticated, more configuration parameters will be added. It's not possible for a cluster administrator to remember these configurations. So, next, we talk about a tool that helps cluster administrators monitor the security posture of cluster components.

Benchmarking a cluster's security configuration

The **Center for Internet Security (CIS)** released a benchmark of Kubernetes that can be used by cluster administrators to ensure that the cluster follows the recommended security configuration. The published Kubernetes benchmark is more than 200 pages.

`kube-bench` is an automated tool written in Go and published by Aqua Security that runs tests documented in the CIS benchmark. The tests are written in **YAML Ain't Markup Language (YAML)**, making it easy to evolve.

kube-bench can be run on a node directly using the kube-bench binary, as follows:

```
$kube-bench node --benchmark cis-1.4
```

For clusters hosted on gke, eks, and aks, kube-bench is run as a pod. Once the pod finishes running, you can look at the logs to see the results, as illustrated in the following code block:

```
$ kubectl apply -f job-gke.yaml
$ kubectl get pods
NAME                 READY    STATUS       RESTARTS    AGE
kube-bench-2p1pm     0/1      Completed    0           5m20s
$ kubectl logs kube-bench-2p1pm
[INFO] 4 Worker Node Security Configuration
[INFO] 4.1 Worker Node Configuration Files
[WARN] 4.1.1 Ensure that the kubelet service file permissions
are set to 644 or more restrictive (Not Scored)
[WARN] 4.1.2 Ensure that the kubelet service file ownership is
set to root:root (Not Scored)
[PASS] 4.1.3 Ensure that the proxy kubeconfig file permissions
are set to 644 or more restrictive (Scored)
[PASS] 4.1.4 Ensure that the proxy kubeconfig file ownership is
set to root:root (Scored)
[WARN] 4.1.5 Ensure that the kubelet.conf file permissions are
set to 644 or more restrictive (Not Scored)
[WARN] 4.1.6 Ensure that the kubelet.conf file ownership is set
to root:root (Not Scored)
[WARN] 4.1.7 Ensure that the certificate authorities file
permissions are set to 644 or more restrictive (Not Scored)
......
== Summary ==
0 checks PASS
0 checks FAIL
37 checks WARN
0 checks INFO
```

It is important to investigate the checks that have a FAIL status. You should aim to have zero checks that fail. If this is not possible for any reason, you should have a risk mitigation plan in place for the failed check.

kube-bench is a helpful tool for monitoring cluster components that are following security best practices. It is recommended to add/modify kube-bench rules to suit your environment. Most developers run kube-bench while starting a new cluster, but it's important to run it regularly to monitor that the cluster components are secure.

Summary

In this chapter, we looked at different security-sensitive configurations for each master and node component: kube-apiserver, kube-scheduler, kube-controller-manager, kubelet, CoreDNS, and etcd. We learned how each component can be secured. By default, components might not follow all the security best practices, so it is the responsibility of the cluster administrators to ensure that the components are secure. Finally, we looked at kube-bench, which can be used to understand the security baseline for your running cluster.

It is important to understand these configurations and ensure that the components follow these checklists to reduce the chance of a compromise.

In the next chapter, we'll look at authentication and authorization mechanisms in Kubernetes. We briefly talked about some admission controllers in this chapter. We'll dive deep into different admission controllers and, finally, talk about how they can be leveraged to provide a finer-grained access control.

Questions

1. What is token-based authentication?
2. What is a NodeRestriction admission controller?
3. How do you ensure data is encrypted at rest in etcd?
4. Why did CoreDNS supersede kube-dns?
5. How do you use kube-bench on an **Elastic Kubernetes Service (EKS)** cluster?

Further reading

You can refer to the following links for more information on the topics covered in this chapter:

- CIS Benchmarks: https://www.cisecurity.org/benchmark/kubernetes/
- GitHub (kube-bench): https://github.com/aquasecurity/kube-bench

7
Authentication, Authorization, and Admission Control

Authentication and authorization play a very vital role in securing applications. These two terms are often used interchangeably but are very different. Authentication validates the identity of a user. Once the identity is validated, authorization is used to check whether the user has the privileges to perform the desired action. Authentication uses something the user knows to verify their identity; in the simplest form, this is a username and password. Once the application verifies the user's identity, it checks what resources the user has access to. In most cases, this is a variation of an access control list. Access control lists for the user are compared with the request attributes to allow or deny an action.

In this chapter, we will discuss how a request is processed by authentication, authorization modules, and admission controllers before it is processed by `kube-apiserver`. We'll walk through the details of different modules and admission controllers and highlight the recommended security configurations.

We will finally look at **Open Policy Agent** (**OPA**), which is an open source tool that can be used to implement authorization across microservices. In Kubernetes, we will look at how it can be used as a validating admission controller. Many clusters require a more granular level of authorization than what is already provided by Kubernetes. With OPA, developers can define custom authorization policies that can be updated at runtime. There are several open source tools that leverage OPA, such as Istio.

In this chapter, we will discuss the following topics:

- Requesting a workflow in Kubernetes
- Kubernetes authentication
- Kubernetes authorization
- Admission controllers
- Introduction to OPA

Requesting a workflow in Kubernetes

In Kubernetes, the kube-apiserver processes all requests to modify the state of the cluster. The kube-apiserver first verifies the origin of the request. It can use one or more authentication modules, including client certificates, passwords, or tokens. The request passes serially from one module to the other. If the request is not rejected by all the modules, it is tagged as an anonymous request. The API server can be configured to allow anonymous requests.

Once the origin of the request is verified, it passes through the authorization modules to check whether the origin of the request is permitted to perform the action. The authorization modules allow the request if a policy permits the user to perform the action. Kubernetes supports multiple authorization modules, such as **Attribute-Based Access Control** (**ABAC**), **Role-Based Access Control** (**RBAC**), and webhooks. Similar to authentication modules, a cluster can use multiple authorizations:

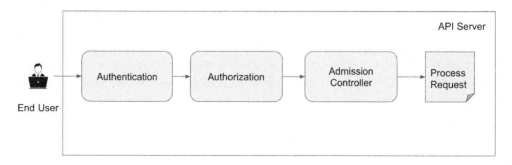

Figure 7.1 – Requesting parsing before processing with the kube-apiserver

After passing through the authorization and authentication modules, admission controllers modify or reject the requests. Admission controllers intercept requests that create, update, or delete an object in the admission controller. Admission controllers fall into two categories: mutating or validating. Mutating admission controllers run first; they modify the requests they admit. Validating admission controllers run next. These controllers cannot modify objects. If any of the admission controllers reject a request, an error is returned to the user and the request will not be processed by the API server.

Kubernetes authentication

All requests in Kubernetes originate from external users, service accounts, or Kubernetes components. If the origin of the request is unknown, it is treated as an anonymous request. Depending on the configuration of the components, anonymous requests can be allowed or dropped by the authentication modules. In v1.6+, anonymous access is allowed to support anonymous and unauthenticated users for the RBAC and ABAC authorization modes. It can be explicitly disabled by passing the --anonymous-auth=false flag to the API server configuration:

```
$ps aux | grep api
root        3701  6.1  8.7 497408 346244 ?        Ssl  21:06
0:16 kube-apiserver --advertise-address=192.168.99.111 --allow-
privileged=true --anonymous-auth=false
```

Kubernetes uses one or more of these authentication strategies. Let's discuss them one by one.

Client certificates

Using X509 **Certificate Authority (CA)** certificates is the most common authentication strategy in Kubernetes. It can be enabled by passing --client-ca-file=file_ path to the server. The file passed to the API server has a list of CAs, which creates and validates client certificates in the cluster. The common name property in the certificate is often used as the username for the request and the organization property is used to identify the user's groups:

```
kube-apiserver --advertise-address=192.168.99.104 --allow-
privileged=true --authorization-mode=Node,RBAC --client-ca-
file=/var/lib/minikube/certs/ca.crt
```

To create a new certificate, the following steps need to be taken:

1. Generate a private key. A private key can be generated using `openssl`, `easyrsa`, or `cfssl`:

```
openssl genrsa -out priv.key 4096
```

2. Generate a **Certificate Signing Request (CSR)**. Using the private key and a config file similar to the following generates a CSR. This CSR is for the `test` user, which will be part of the `dev` group:

```
[ req ]
default_bits = 2048
prompt = no
default_md = sha256
distinguished_name = dn

[ dn ]
CN = test
O = dev

[ v3_ext ]
authorityKeyIdentifier=keyid,issuer:always
basicConstraints=CA:FALSE
keyUsage=keyEncipherment,dataEncipherment
extendedKeyUsage=serverAuth,clientAuth
```

You can generate a CSR using `openssl`:

```
openssl req -config ./csr.cnf -new -key priv.key -nodes
-out new.csr
```

3. Sign the CSR. Create a Kubernetes `CertificateSigningRequest` request using the following YAML file:

```
apiVersion: certificates.k8s.io/v1beta1
kind: CertificateSigningRequest
metadata:
  name: mycsr
spec:
  groups:
```

```
  - system:authenticated
  request: ${BASE64_CSR}
  usages:
  - digital signature
  - key encipherment
  - server auth
  - client auth
```

The certificate-signing request generated earlier is used with the preceding YAML specification to generate a new Kubernetes certificate-signing request:

```
$ export BASE64_CSR=$(cat ./new.csr | base64 | tr -d
'\n')
$ cat csr.yaml | envsubst | kubectl apply -f -
```

Once this request is created, it needs to be approved by the cluster administrators to generate the certificate:

```
kubectl certificate approve mycsr
```

4. Export the CRT. The certificate can be exported using kubectl:

```
kubectl get csr mycsr -o jsonpath='{.status.certificate}'
\
  | base64 --decode > new.crt
```

Next, we will look at static tokens, which are a popular mode of authentication in development and debugging environments but should not be used in production clusters.

Static tokens

The API server uses a static file to read the bearer tokens. This static file is passed to the API server using --token-auth-file=<path>. The token file is a comma-separated file consisting of secret, user, uid, group1, and group2.

The token is passed as an HTTP header in the request:

```
Authorization: Bearer 66e6a781-09cb-4e7e-8e13-34d78cb0dab6
```

The tokens persist indefinitely, and the API server needs to be restarted to update the tokens. This is *not* a recommended authentication strategy. These tokens can be easily compromised if the attacker is able to spawn a malicious pod in a cluster. Once compromised, the only way to generate a new token is to restart the API server.

Next, we will look at basic authentication, a variation of static tokens that has been used as a method for authentication by web services for many years.

Basic authentication

Similar to static tokens, Kubernetes also supports basic authentication. This can be enabled by using `basic-auth-file=<path>`. The authentication credentials are stored in a CSV file as `password`, `user`, `uid`, `group1`, and `group2`.

The username and password are passed as an authentication header in the request:

```
Authentication: Basic base64(user:password)
```

Similar to static tokens, basic authentication passwords cannot be changed without restarting the API server. Basic authentication should not be used in production clusters.

Bootstrap tokens

Bootstrap tokens are an improvisation over the static tokens. Bootstrap tokens are the default authentication method used in Kubernetes. They are dynamically managed and stored as secrets in `kube-system`. To enable bootstrap tokens, do the following:

1. Use `--enable-bootstrap-token-auth` in the API server to enable the bootstrap token authenticator:

```
$ps aux | grep api
root       3701 3.8  8.8 497920 347140 ?         Ssl  21:06
4:58 kube-apiserver --advertise-address=192.168.99.111
--allow-privileged=true --anonymous-auth=true
--authorization-mode=Node,RBAC --client-ca-file=/var/lib/
minikube/certs/ca.crt --enable-admission-plugins=Namesp
aceLifecycle,LimitRanger,ServiceAccount,DefaultStorageC
lass,DefaultTolerationSeconds,NodeRestriction,Mutating
AdmissionWebhook,ValidatingAdmissionWebhook,ResourceQuota
--enable-bootstrap-token-auth=true
```

2. Enable `tokencleaner` in the controller manager using the `controller` flag:

```
$ ps aux | grep controller
root       3693 1.4  2.3 211196 94396 ?          Ssl
21:06   1:55 kube-controller-manager --authentication-
kubeconfig=/etc/kubernetes/controller-manager.conf
--authorization-kubeconfig=/etc/kubernetes/controller-
manager.conf --bind-address=127.0.0.1 --client-ca-
```

```
file=/var/lib/minikube/certs/ca.crt --cluster-name=mk
--cluster-signing-cert-file=/var/lib/minikube/
ca.crt --cluster-signing-key-file=/var/lib/minikube/
certs/ca.key --controllers=*,bootstrapsigner,tokencleaner
```

3. Similar to token authentication, bootstrap tokens are passed as an HTTP header in the request:

```
Authorization: Bearer 123456.aa1234fdeffeeedf
```

The first part of the token is the `TokenId` value and the second part of it is the `TokenSecret` value. `TokenController` ensures that expired tokens are deleted from the system secrets.

Service account tokens

The service account authenticator is automatically enabled. It verifies signed bearer tokens. The signing key is specified using `--service-account-key-file`. If this value is unspecified, the Kube API server's private key is used:

```
$ps aux | grep api
root        3711 27.1 14.9 426728 296552 ?        Ssl   04:22
0:04 kube-apiserver --advertise-address=192.168.99.104 ...
--secure-port=8443 --service-account-key-file=/var/lib/
minikube/certs/sa.pub --service-cluster-ip-range=10.96.0.0/12
--tls-cert-file=/var/lib/minikube/certs/apiserver.crt
--tls-private-key-file=/var/lib/minikube/certs/apiserver.key
docker      4496 0.0  0.0  11408    544 pts/0     S+    04:22
0:00 grep api
```

Service accounts are created by the `kube-apiserver` and are associated with the pods. This is similar to instance profiles in AWS. The default service account is associated with a pod if no service account is specified.

To create a service account test, you can use the following:

```
kubectl create serviceaccount test
```

The service account has associated secrets, which includes the CA of the API server and a signed token:

```
$ kubectl get serviceaccounts test -o yaml
apiVersion: v1
```

```
kind: ServiceAccount
metadata:
  creationTimestamp: "2020-03-29T04:35:58Z"
  name: test
  namespace: default
  resourceVersion: "954754"
  selfLink: /api/v1/namespaces/default/serviceaccounts/test
  uid: 026466f3-e2e8-4b26-994d-ee473b2f36cd
secrets:
- name: test-token-sdq2d
```

If we enumerate the details, we can see the certificate and the token:

```
$ kubectl get secret test-token-sdq2d -o yaml
apiVersion: v1
data:
  ca.crt: base64(crt)
  namespace: ZGVmYXVsdA==
  token: base64(token)
kind: Secret
```

Next, we will talk about webhook tokens. Some enterprises have a remote authentication and authorization server, which is often used across all services. In Kubernetes, developers can use webhook tokens to leverage the remote services for authentication.

Webhook tokens

In webhook mode, Kubernetes makes a call to a REST API outside the cluster to determine the user's identity. Webhook mode for authentication can be enabled by passing `--authorization-webhook-config-file=<path>` to the API server.

Here is an example of a webhook configuration. In this, `authn.example.com/authenticate` is used as the authentication endpoint for the Kubernetes cluster:

```
clusters:
  - name: name-of-remote-authn-service
    cluster:
      certificate-authority: /path/to/ca.pem
      server: https://authn.example.com/authenticate
```

Let's look at another way that a remote service can be used for authentication.

Authentication proxy

`kube-apiserver` can be configured to identify users using the X-Remote request header. You can enable this method by adding the following arguments to the API server:

```
--requestheader-username-headers=X-Remote-User
--requestheader-group-headers=X-Remote-Group
--requestheader-extra-headers-prefix=X-Remote-Extra-
```

Each request has the following headers to identify them:

```
GET / HTTP/1.1
X-Remote-User: foo
X-Remote-Group: bar
X-Remote-Extra-Scopes: profile
```

The API proxy validates the requests using the CA.

User impersonation

Cluster administrators and developers can use user impersonation to debug authentication and authorization policies for new users. To use user impersonation, a user must be granted impersonation privileges. The API server uses impersonation the following headers to impersonate a user:

- Impersonate-User
- Impersonate-Group
- Impersonate-Extra-*

Once the impersonation headers are received by the API server, the API server verifies whether the user is authenticated and has the impersonation privileges. If yes, the request is executed as the impersonated user. `kubectl` can use the `--as` and `--as-group` flags to impersonate a user:

```
kubectl apply -f pod.yaml --as=dev-user --as-group=system:dev
```

Once the authentication modules verify the identity of a user, they parse the request to check whether the user is allowed to access or modify the request.

Kubernetes authorization

Authorization determines whether a request is allowed or denied. Once the origin of the request is identified, active authorization modules evaluate the attributes of the request against the authorization policies of the user to allow or deny a request. Each request passes through the authorization module sequentially and if any module provides a decision to allow or deny, it is automatically accepted or denied.

Request attributes

Authorization modules parse a set of attributes in a request to determine whether the request should be parsed, allowed, or denied:

- **User**: The originator of the request. This is validated during authentication.
- **Group**: The group that the user belongs to. This is provided in the authentication layer.
- **API**: The destination of the request.
- **Request verb**: The type of request, which can be GET, CREATE, PATCH, DELETE, and more.
- **Resource**: The ID or name of the resource being accessed.
- **Namespace**: The namespace of the resource being accessed.
- **Request path**: If the request is for a non-resource endpoint, the path is used to check whether the user is allowed to access the endpoint. This is true for the api and healthz endpoints.

Now, let's look at the different authorization modes that use these request attributes to determine whether the origin is allowed to initiate the request.

Authorization modes

Let's look at the different authorization modes available in Kubernetes.

Node

Node authorization mode grants permissions to kubelets to access services, endpoints, nodes, pods, secrets, and persistent volumes for a node. The kubelet is identified as part of the system:nodes group with a username of system:node:<name> to be authorized by the node authorizer. This mode is enabled by default in Kubernetes.

The NodeRestriction admission controller, which we'll learn about later in this chapter, is used in conjunction with the node authorizer to ensure that the kubelet can only modify objects on the node that it is running. The API server uses the --authorization-mode=Node flag to use the node authorization module:

```
$ps aux | grep api
root       3701   6.1   8.7 497408 346244 ?          Ssl   21:06
0:16 kube-apiserver --advertise-address=192.168.99.111
--allow-privileged=true --anonymous-auth=true
--authorization-mode=Node,RBAC --client-ca-file=/var/lib/
minikube/certs/ca.crt --enable-admission-plugins=Namespa
ceLifecycle,LimitRanger,ServiceAccount,DefaultStorageCla
ss,DefaultTolerationSeconds,NodeRestriction,MutatingAdm
issionWebhook,ValidatingAdmissionWebhook,ResourceQuota
```

Node authorization is used in conjunction with ABAC or RBAC, which we will look at next.

ABAC

With ABAC, requests are allowed by validating policies against the attributes of the request. ABAC authorization mode can be enabled by using --authorization-policy-file=<path> and --authorization-mode=ABAC with the API server.

The policies include a JSON object per line. Each policy consists of the following:

- **Version**: The API version for the policy format.
- **Kind**: The Policy string is used for policies.
- **Spec**: This includes the user, group, and resource properties, such as apiGroup, namespace, and nonResourcePath (such as /version, /apis, readonly) to allow requests that don't modify the resource.

An example policy is as follows:

```
{"apiVersion": "abac.authorization.kubernetes.io/v1beta1",
 "kind": "Policy", "spec": {"user": "kubelet", "namespace": "*",
 "resource": "pods", "readonly": true}}
```

This policy allows a kubelet to read any pods. ABAC is difficult to configure and maintain. It is not recommended that you use ABAC in production environments.

RBAC

With RBAC, access to resources is regulated using roles assigned to users. RBAC is enabled by default in many clusters since v1.8. To enable RBAC, start the API server with `--authorization-mode=RBAC`:

```
$ ps aux | grep api
root      14632  9.2 17.0 495148 338780 ?        Ssl  06:11
0:09 kube-apiserver --advertise-address=192.168.99.104 --allow-
privileged=true --authorization-mode=Node,RBAC ...
```

RBAC uses Role, which is a set of permissions, and RoleBinding, which grants permissions to users. Role and RoleBinding are restricted to namespaces. If a role needs to span across namespaces, ClusterRole and ClusterRoleBinding can be used to grant permissions to users across namespace boundaries.

Here is an example of a `Role` property that allows a user to create and modify pods in the default namespace:

```
kind: Role
apiVersion: rbac.authorization.k8s.io/v1beta1
metadata:
  namespace: default
  name: deployment-manager
rules:
- apiGroups: [""]
  resources: ["pods"]
  verbs: ["get", "list", "watch", "create", "update", "patch",
"delete"]
```

The corresponding `RoleBinding` can be used with `Role` to grant permissions to the user:

```
kind: RoleBinding
apiVersion: rbac.authorization.k8s.io/v1beta1
metadata:
  name: binding
  namespace: default
subjects:
- kind: User
  name: employee
```

```
    apiGroup: ""
roleRef:
  kind: Role
  name: deployment-manager
    apiGroup: ""
```

Once `RoleBinding` is applied, you can switch the context to see whether it worked correctly:

```
$ kubectl --context=employee-context get pods
NAME                            READY   STATUS    RESTARTS   AGE
hello-node-677b9cfc6b-xks5f     1/1     Running   0          12m
```

However, if you try to view the deployments, it will result in an error:

```
$ kubectl --context=employee-context get deployments
Error from server (Forbidden): deployments.apps is forbidden:
User "employee" cannot list resource "deployments" in API group
"apps" in the namespace "default"
```

Since roles and role bindings are restricted to the default namespace, accessing the pods in a different namespace will result in an error:

```
$ kubectl --context=employee-context get pods -n test
Error from server (Forbidden): pods is forbidden: User "test"
cannot list resource "pods" in API group "" in the namespace
"test"
$ kubectl --context=employee-context get pods -n kube-system
Error from server (Forbidden): pods is forbidden: User "test"
cannot list resource "pods" in API group "" in the namespace
"kube-system"
```

Next, we will talk about webhooks, which provide enterprises with the ability to use remote servers for authorization.

Webhooks

Similar to webhook mode for authentication, webhook mode for authorization uses a remote API server to check user permissions. Webhook mode can be enabled by using `--authorization-webhook-config-file=<path>`.

Let's look at a sample webhook configuration file that sets `https://authz.remote` as the remote authorization endpoint for the Kubernetes cluster:

```
clusters:
  - name: authz_service
    cluster:
      certificate-authority: ca.pem
      server: https://authz.remote/
```

Once the request is passed by the authentication and authorization modules, admission controllers process the request. Let's discuss admission controllers in detail.

Admission controllers

Admission controllers are modules that intercept requests to the API server after the request is authenticated and authorized. The controllers validate and mutate the request before modifying the state of the objects in the cluster. A controller can be both mutating and validating. If any of the controllers reject the request, the request is dropped immediately and an error is returned to the user so that the request will not be processed.

Admission controllers can be enabled by using the `--enable-admission-plugins` flag:

```
$ps aux | grep api
root       3460 17.0  8.6 496896 339432 ?        Ssl  06:53
0:09 kube-apiserver --advertise-address=192.168.99.106 --allow-
privileged=true --authorization-mode=Node,RBAC --client-ca-
file=/var/lib/minikube/certs/ca.crt --enable-admission-plugin
s=PodSecurityPolicy,NamespaceLifecycle,LimitRanger --enable-
bootstrap-token-auth=true
```

Default admission controllers can be disabled using the `--disable-admission-plugins` flag.

In the following sections, we will look at some important admission controllers.

AlwaysAdmit

This admission controller allows all the pods to exist in the cluster. This controller has been deprecated since 1.13 and should not be used in any cluster. With this controller, the cluster behaves as if no controllers exist in the cluster.

AlwaysPullImages

This controller ensures that new pods always force image pull. This is helpful to ensure updated images are used by pods. It also ensures that private images can only be used by users who have the privileges to access them since users without access cannot pull images when a new pod is started. This controller should be enabled in your clusters.

EventRateLimit

Denial-of-service attacks are common in infrastructure. Misbehaving objects can also cause high consumption of resources, such as the CPU or network, resulting in increased cost or low availability. `EventRateLimit` is used to prevent these scenarios.

The limit is specified using a config file, which can be specified by adding a `--admission-control-config-file` flag to the API server.

A cluster can have four types of limits: `Namespace`, `Server`, `User` and `SourceAndObject`. With each limit, the user can have a maximum limit for the **Queries Per Second (QPS)**, the burst and cache size.

Let's look at an example of a configuration file:

```
limits:
- type: Namespace
  qps: 50
  burst: 100
  cacheSize: 200
- type: Server
  qps: 10
  burst: 50
  cacheSize: 200
```

This adds the `qps`, `burst`, and `cacheSize` limits to all API servers and namespaces.

Next, we will talk about LimitRanger, which prevents the overutilization of resources available in the cluster.

LimitRanger

This admission controller observes the incoming request and ensures that it does not violate any of the limits specified in the `LimitRange` object.

An example of a `LimitRange` object is as follows:

```
apiVersion: "v1"
kind: "LimitRange"
metadata:
  name: "pod-example"
spec:
  limits:
    - type: "Pod"
      max:
        memory: "128Mi"
```

With this limit range object, any pod requesting memory of more than 128 Mi will fail:

```
pods "range-demo" is forbidden maximum memory usage per Pod is
128Mi, but limit is 1073741824
```

When using LimitRanger, malicious pods cannot consume excess resources.

NodeRestriction

This admission controller restricts the pods and nodes that a kubelet can modify. With this admission controller, a kubelet gets a username in the `system:node:<name>` format and is only able to modify the node object and pods running on its own node.

PersistentVolumeClaimResize

This admission controller adds validations for the `PersistentVolumeClaimResize` requests.

PodSecurityPolicy

This admission controller runs on the creation or modification of pods to determine whether the pods should be run based on the security-sensitive configuration of the pods. The set of conditions in the policy is checked against the workload configuration to verify whether the workload creation request should be allowed. A PodSecurityPolicy can check for fields such as `privileged`, `allowHostPaths`, `defaultAddCapabilities`, and so on. You'll learn more about PodSecurityPolicy in the next chapter.

SecurityContextDeny

This is the recommended admission controller to use if PodSecurityPolicy is not enabled. It restricts the settings of security-sensitive fields, which can cause privilege escalation, such as running a privileged pod or adding Linux capabilities to a container:

```
$ ps aux | grep api
root      3763  6.7  8.7 497344 345404 ?        Ssl  23:28
0:14 kube-apiserver --advertise-address=192.168.99.112 --allow-
privileged=true --authorization-mode=Node,RBAC --client-
ca-file=/var/lib/minikube/certs/ca.crt --enable-admission-
plugins=SecurityContextDeny
```

It is recommended that PodSecurityPolicy is enabled by default in a cluster. However, due to the administrative overhead, `SecurityContextDeny` can be used until PodSecurityPolicy is configured for the cluster.

ServiceAccount

`ServiceAccount` is an identity of the pod. This admission controller implements `ServiceAccount`; it should be used if the cluster uses service accounts.

MutatingAdmissionWebhook and ValidatingAdmissionWebhook

Similar to webhook configurations for authentication and authorization, webhooks can be used as admission controllers. MutatingAdmissionWebhook modifies the workload's specifications. These hooks execute sequentially. ValidatingAdmissionWebhook parses the incoming request to verify whether it is correct. Validating hooks execute simultaneously.

Now, we have looked at authentication, authorization, and admission control of resources in Kubernetes. Let's look at how developers can implement fine-grained access control in their clusters. In the next section, we talk about OPA, an open source tool that is used extensively in production clusters.

Introduction to OPA

OPA is an open source policy engine that allows policy enforcement in Kubernetes. Several open source projects, such as Istio, utilize OPA to provide finer-grained controls. OPA is an incubating project hosted by **Cloud Native Computing Foundation** (**CNCF**).

OPA is deployed as a service alongside your other services. To make authorization decisions, the microservice makes a call to OPA to decide whether the request should be allowed or denied. Authorization decisions are offloaded to OPA, but this enforcement needs to be implemented by the service itself. In Kubernetes environments, it is often used as a validating webhook:

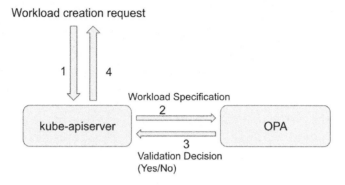

Figure 7.2 – Open Policy Agent

To make a policy decision, OPA needs the following:

- **Cluster information**: The state of the cluster. The objects and resources available in the cluster are important for OPA to make a decision about whether a request should be allowed or not.

- **Input query**: The parameters of the request being parsed by the policy agent are analyzed by the agent to allow or deny the request.

- **Policies**: The policy defines the logic that parses cluster information and input query to return the decision. Policies for OPA are defined in a custom language called Rego.

Let's look at an example of how OPA can be leveraged to deny the creation of pods with a busybox image. You can use the official OPA documentation (https://www.openpolicyagent.org/docs/latest/kubernetes-tutorial/) to install OPA on your cluster.

Here is the policy that restricts the creation and updating of pods with the busybox image:

```
$ cat pod-blacklist.rego
package kubernetes.admission


import data.kubernetes.namespaces
```

```
operations = {"CREATE", "UPDATE"}


deny [msg] {
    input.request.kind.kind == "Pod"
    operations [input.request.operation]
    image := input.request.object.spec.containers[_].image
    image == "busybox"
    msg := sprintf("image not allowed %q", [image])
}
```

To apply this policy, you can use the following:

```
kubectl create configmap pod —from-file=pod-blacklist.rego
```

Once configmap is created, kube-mgmt loads these policies out of configmap in the opa container, both kube-mgmt and opa containers are in the opa pod. Now, if you try to create a pod with the busybox image, you get the following:

```
$ cat busybox.yaml
apiVersion: v1
kind: Pod
metadata:
  name: busybox
spec:
  containers:
  - name: sec-ctx-demo
    image: busybox
    command: [ "sh", "-c", "sleep 1h" ]
```

This policy checks the request for the busybox image name and denies creation of pods with the busybox image with an image not allowed error:

```
admission webhook "validating-webhook.openpolicyagent.org"
denied the request: image not allowed "busybox"
```

Similar to the admission controller that we discussed previously, further finer-grained admission controllers can be created using OPA in the Kubernetes cluster.

Summary

In this chapter, we looked at the importance of authentication and authorization in Kubernetes. We discussed the different modules available for authentication and authorization and discussed these modules in detail, as well as going through detailed examples of how each module is used. When looking at authentication, we discussed user impersonation, which can be used by cluster administrators or developers to test permissions. Next, we talked about admission controllers, which can be used to validate or mutate requests after authentication and authorization. We also discussed some admission controllers in detail. Finally, we looked at OPA, which can be used in Kubernetes clusters to perform a more fine-grained level of authorization.

Now, you should be able to devise appropriate authentication and authorization strategies for your cluster. You should be able to figure out which admission controllers work for your environment. In many cases, you'll need more granular controls for authorization, which can be provided by using OPA.

In the next chapter, we will take a deep dive into securing pods. The chapter will cover some of the topics that we covered in this chapter in more detail, such as PodSecurityPolicy. Securing pods is essential to securing application deployment in Kubernetes.

Questions

1. Which authorization modules should not be used in a cluster?

2. How can cluster administrators test permissions granted to a new user?

3. Which authorization modes are recommended for production clusters?

4. What is the difference between the `EventRateLimit` and LimitRange admission controllers?

5. Can you write a Rego policy to deny the creation of ingress with the `test.example` endpoint?

Further reading

You can refer to the following links for more information:

- Admission controllers: `https://kubernetes.io/docs/reference/access-authn-authz/admission-controllers/#what-does-each-admission-controller-do`

- OPA: `https://www.openpolicyagent.org/docs/latest/`

- Kubernetes RBAC: `https://rbac.dev/`

- audit2RBAC: `https://github.com/liggitt/audit2rbac`

- KubiScan: `https://github.com/cyberark/KubiScan`

8
Securing Kubernetes Pods

Even though a pod is the most fine-grained unit that serves as a placeholder to run microservices, securing Kubernetes pods is a vast topic as it should cover the entire DevOps flow: build, deployment, and runtime.

In this chapter, we choose to narrow our focus to the build and runtime stages. To secure Kubernetes pods in the build stage, we will talk about how to harden a container image and configure the security attributes of pods (or pod templates) to reduce the attack surface. Although some of the security attributes of workloads, such as AppArmor and SELinux labels, take effect in the runtime stage, security control has already been defined for the workload. To clarify matters further, we're trying to secure Kubernetes workloads by configuring the runtime effect security attributes in the build stage. To secure Kubernetes pods in the runtime stage, we will introduce a PodSecurityPolicy with examples along with the facilitating tool, `kube-psp-advisor`.

Later chapters will go into more detail regarding runtime security and response. Also note that exploitation of the application may lead to pods getting compromised. However, we don't intend to cover application in this chapter.

In this chapter, we will cover the following topics:

- Hardening container images
- Configuring the security attributes of pods
- The power of PodSecurityPolicy

Hardening container images

Container image hardening means to follow security best practices or baselines to configure a container image in order to reduce the attack surface. Image scanning tools only focus on finding publicly disclosed issues in applications bundled inside the image. But, following the best practices along with secure configuration while building the image ensures that the application has a minimal attack surface.

Before we start talking about the secure configuration baseline, let's look at what a container image is, as well as a Dockerfile, and how it is used to build an image.

Container images and Dockerfiles

A **container image** is a file that bundles the microservice binary, its dependencies, and configurations of the microservice, and so on. A container is a running instance of an image. Nowadays, application developers not only write code to build microservices; they also need to build the Dockerfile to containerize the microservice. To help build a container image, Docker offers a standardized approach, known as a Dockerfile. A **Dockerfile** contains a series of instructions, such as copy files, configure environment variables, configure open ports, and container entry points, which can be understood by the Docker daemon to construct the image file. Then, the image file will be pushed to the image registry from where the image is then deployed in Kubernetes clusters. Each Dockerfile instruction will create a file layer in the image.

Before we look at an example of a Dockerfile, let's understand some basic Dockerfile instructions:

- **FROM**: Initialize a new build stage from the base image or parent image. Both mean the foundation or the file layer on which you're bundling your own image.
- **RUN**: Execute commands and commit the results on top of the previous file layer.
- **ENV**: Set environment variables for the running containers.
- **CMD**: Specify the default commands that the containers will run.
- **COPY/ADD**: Both commands copy files or directories from the local (or remote) URL to the filesystem of the image.

- **EXPOSE**: Specify the port that the microservice will be listening on during container runtime.
- **ENTRYPOINT**: Similar to CMD, the only difference is that ENTRYPOINT makes a container that will run as an executable.
- **WORKDIR**: Sets the working directory for the instructions that follow.
- **USER**: Sets the user and group ID for any CMD/ENTRYPOINT of containers.

Now, let's take a look at an example of a Dockerfile:

```
FROM ubuntu

# install dependencies
RUN apt-get install -y software-properties-common python
RUN add-apt-repository ppa:chris-lea/node.js
RUN echo "deb http://us.archive.ubuntu.com/ubuntu/ precise
universe" >> /etc/apt/sources.list
RUN apt-get update
RUN apt-get install -y nodejs

# make directory
RUN mkdir /var/www

# copy app.js
ADD app.js /var/www/app.js

# set the default command to run
CMD ["/usr/bin/node", "/var/www/app.js"]
```

From the preceding Dockerfile, we can tell that the image was built on top of ubuntu. Then, it ran a bunch of apt-get commands to install the dependencies, and created a directory called /var/www. Next, copy the app.js file from the current directory to /var/www/app.js in the filesystem of the image. Finally, configure the default command to run this Node.js application. I believe you will see how straightforward and powerful Dockerfile is when it comes to helping you build an image.

The next question is any security concern, as it looks like you're able to build any kind of image. Next, let's talk about CIS Docker benchmarks.

CIS Docker benchmarks

Center for Internet Security (CIS) put together a guideline regarding Docker container administration and management. Now, let's take a look at the security recommendations from CIS Docker benchmarks regarding container images:

- **Create a user for a container image to run a microservice**: It is good practice to run a container as non-root. Although user namespace mapping is available, it is not enabled by default. Running as root means that if an attacker were to successfully escape from the container, they would gain root access to the host. Use the USER instruction to create a user in the Dockerfile.

- **Use trusted base images to build your own image**: Images downloaded from public repositories cannot be fully trusted. It is well known that images from public repositories may contain malware or crypto miners. Hence, it is recommended that you build your image from scratch or use minimal trusted images, such as Alpine. Also, perform the image scan after your image has been built. Image scanning will be covered in the next chapter.

- **Do not install unnecessary packages in your image**: Installing unnecessary packages will increase the attack surface. It is recommended that you keep your image slim. Occasionally, you will probably need to install some tools during the process of building an image. Do remember to remove them at the end of the Dockerfile.

- **Scan and rebuild an image in order to apply security patches**: It is highly likely that new vulnerabilities will be discovered in your base image or in the packages you install in your image. It is good practice to scan your image frequently. Once you identify any vulnerabilities, try to patch the security fixes by rebuilding the image. Image scanning is a critical mechanism for identifying vulnerabilities at the build stage. We will cover image scanning in more detail in the next chapter.

- **Enable content trust for Docker**: Content trust uses digital signatures to ensure data integrity between the client and the Docker registry. It ensures the provenance of the container image. However, it is not enabled by default. You can turn it on by setting the environment variable, DOCKER_CONTENT_TRUST, to 1.

- **Add a HEALTHCHECK instruction to the container image**: A HEALTHCHECK instruction defines a command to ask Docker Engine to check the health status of the container periodically. Based on the health status check result, Docker Engine then exits the non-healthy container and initiates a new one.

- **Ensure that updates are not cached in Dockerfile**: Depending on the base image you choose, you may need to update the package repository before installing new packages. However, if you specify RUN apt-get update (Debian) in a single line in the Dockerfile, Docker Engine will cache this file layer, so, when you build your image again, it will still use the old package repository information that is cached. This will prevent you from using the latest packages in your image. Therefore, either use update along with install in a single Dockerfile instruction or use the --no-cache flag in the Docker build command.

- **Remove setuid and setgid permission from files in the image**: setuid and setgid permissions can be used for privilege escalation as files with such permissions are allowed to be executed with owners' privileges instead of launchers' privileges. You should carefully review the files with setuid and setgid permissions and remove those files that don't require such permissions.

- **Use COPY instead of ADD in the Dockerfile**: The COPY instruction can only copy files from the local machine to the filesystem of the image, while the ADD instruction can not only copy files from the local machine but also retrieve files from the remote URL to the filesystem of the image. Using ADD may introduce the risk of adding malicious files from the internet to the image.

- **Do not store secrets in the Dockerfile**: There are many tools that are able to extract image file layers. If there are any secrets stored in the image, secrets are no longer secrets. Storing secrets in the Dockerfile renders containers potentially exploitable. A common mistake is to use the ENV instruction to store secrets in environment variables.

- **Install verified packages only**: This is similar to using the trusted base image only. Observe caution as regards the packages you are going to install within your image. Make sure they are from trusted package repositories.

If you follow the security recommendations from the preceding CIS Docker benchmarks, you will be successful in hardening your container image. This is the first step in securing pods in the build stage. Now, let's look at the security attributes we need to pay attention to in order to secure a pod.

Configuring the security attributes of pods

As we mentioned in the previous chapter, application developers should be aware of what privileges a microservice must have in order to perform tasks. Ideally, application developers and security engineers work together to harden the microservice at the pod and container level by configuring the security context provided by Kubernetes.

We classify the major security attributes into four categories:

- Setting host namespaces for pods
- Security context at the container level
- Security context at the pod level
- AppArmor profile

By employing such a means of classification, you will find them easy to manage.

Setting host-level namespaces for pods

The following attributes in the pod specification are used to configure the use of host namespaces:

- **hostPID**: By default, this is `false`. Setting it to `true` allows the pod to have visibility on all the processes in the worker node.

- **hostNetwork**: By default, this is `false`. Setting it to `true` allows the pod to have visibility on all the network stacks in the worker node.

- **hostIPC**: By default, this is `false`. Setting it to `true` allows the pod to have visibility on all the IPC resources in the worker node.

The following is an example of how to configure the use of host namespaces at the pod level in an `ubuntu-1` pod `YAML` file:

```
apiVersion: v1
kind: Pod
metadata:
  name: ubuntu-1
  labels:
    app: util
spec:
  containers:
  - name: ubuntu
    image: ubuntu
    imagePullPolicy: Always
  hostPID: true
  hostNetwork: true
  hostIPC: true
```

The preceding workload YAML configured the ubuntu-1 pod to use a host-level PID namespace, network namespace, and IPC namespace. Keep in mind that you shouldn't set these attributes to true unless necessary. Setting these attributes to true also disarms the security boundaries of other workloads in the same worker node, as has already been mentioned in *Chapter 5, Configuring Kubernetes Security Boundaries*.

Security context for containers

Multiple containers can be grouped together inside the same pod. Each container can have its own security context, which defines privileges and access controls. The design of a security context at a container level provides a more fine-grained security control for Kubernetes workloads. For example, you may have three containers running inside the same pod and one of them has to run in privileged mode, while the others run in non-privileged mode. This can be done by configuring a security context for individual containers.

The following are the principal attributes of a security context for containers:

- **privileged**: By default, this is false. Setting it to true essentially makes the processes inside the container equivalent to the root user on the worker node.

- **capabilities**: There is a default set of capabilities granted to the container by the container runtime. The default capabilities granted are as follows: CAP_SETPCAP, CAP_MKNOD, CAP_AUDIT_WRITE, CAP_CHOWN, CAP_NET_RAW, CAP_DAC_OVERRIDE, CAP_FOWNER, CAP_FSETID, CAP_KILL, CAP_SETGID, CAP_SETUID, CAP_NET_BIND_SERVICE, CAP_SYS_CHROOT, and CAP_SETFCAP.

  You may add extra capabilities or drop some of the defaults by configuring this attribute. Capabilities such as CAP_SYS_ADMIN and CAP_NETWORK_ADMIN should be added with caution. For the default capabilities, you should also drop those that are unnecessary.

- **allowPrivilegeEscalation**: By default, this is true. Setting it directly controls the no_new_privs flag, which will be set to the processes in the container. Basically, this attribute controls whether the process can gain more privileges than its parent process. Note that if the container runs in privileged mode, or has the CAP_SYS_ADMN capability added, this attribute will be set to true automatically. It is good practice to set it to false.

- **readOnlyRootFilesystem**: By default, this is false. Setting it to true makes the root filesystem of the container read-only, which means that the library files, configuration files, and so on are read-only and cannot be tampered with. It is a good security practice to set it to true.

- **runAsNonRoot**: By default, this is `false`. Setting it to `true` enables validation that the processes in the container cannot run as a root user (UID=0). Validation is done by `kubelet`. With `runAsNonRoot` set to `true`, `kubelet` will prevent the container from starting if run as a root user. It is a good security practice to set it to `true`. This attribute is also available in `PodSecurityContext`, which takes effect at pod level. If this attribute is set in both `SecurityContext` and `PodSecurityContext`, the value specified at the container level takes precedence.

- **runAsUser**: This is designed to specify to the UID to run the entrypoint process of the container image. The default setting is the user specified in the image's metadata (for example, the `USER` instruction in the Dockerfile). This attribute is also available in `PodSecurityContext`, which takes effect at the pod level. If this attribute is set in both `SecurityContext` and `PodSecurityContext`, the value specified at the container level takes precedence.

- **runAsGroup**: Similar to `runAsUser`, this is designed to specify the **Group ID** or **GID** to run the entrypoint process of the container. This attribute is also available in `PodSecurityContext`, which takes effect at the pod level. If this attribute is set in both `SecurityContext` and `PodSecurityContext`, the value specified at the container level takes precedence.

- **seLinuxOptions**: This is designed to specify the SELinux context to the container. By default, the container runtime will assign a random SELinux context to the container if not specified. This attribute is also available in `PodSecurityContex`, which takes effect at the pod level. If this attribute is set in both `SecurityContext` and `PodSecurityContext`, the value specified at the container level takes precedence.

Since you now understand what these security attributes are, you may come up with your own hardening strategy aligned with your business requirements. In general, the security best practices are as follows:

- Do not run in privileged mode unless necessary.

- Do not add extra capabilities unless necessary.

- Drop unused default capabilities.

- Run containers as a non-root user.

- Enable a `runAsNonRoot` check.

- Set the container root filesystem as read-only.

Now, let's take a look at an example of configuring `SecurityContext` for containers:

```
apiVersion: v1
kind: Pod
metadata:
  name: nginx-pod
  labels:
    app: web
spec:
  hostNetwork: false
  hostIPC: false
  hostPID: false
  containers:
  - name: nginx
    image: kaizheh/nginx
    securityContext:
      privileged: false
      capabilities:
        add:
        - NETWORK_ADMIN
      readOnlyRootFilesystem: true
      runAsUser: 100
      runAsGroup: 1000
```

The `nginx` container inside `nginx-pod` runs as a user with a UID of `100` and a GID of `1000`. In addition to this, the `nginx` container gains extra `NETWORK_ADMIN` capability and the root filesystem is set to read-only. The YAML file here only shows an example of how to configure the security context. Note that adding `NETWORK_ADMIN` is not recommended for containers running in production environments.

Security context for pods

A security context is used at the pod level, which means that security attributes will be applied to all the containers inside the pod.

The following is a list of the principal security attributes at the pod level:

- **fsGroup**: This is a special supplemental group applied to all containers. The effectiveness of this attribute depends on the volume type. Essentially, it allows `kubelet` to set the ownership of the mounted volume to the pod with the supplemental GID.

- **sysctls**: `sysctls` is used to configure kernel parameters at runtime. In such a context, `sysctls` and kernel parameters are used interchangeably. These `sysctls` commands are namespaced kernel parameters that apply to the pod. The following `sysctls` commands are known to be namespaced: `kernel.shm*`, `kernel.msg*`, `kernel.sem`, and `kernel.mqueue.*`. Unsafe `sysctls` are disabled by default and should not be enabled in production environments.

- **runAsUser**: This is designed to specify the UID to run the entrypoint process of the container image. The default setting is the user specified in the image's metadata (for example, the `USER` instruction in the Dockerfile). This attribute is also available in `SecurityContext`, which takes effect at the container level. If this attribute is set in both `SecurityContext` and `PodSecurityContext`, the value specified at the container level takes precedence.

- **runAsGroup**: Similar to `runAsUser`, this is designed to specify the GID to run the entrypoint process of the container. This attribute is also available in `SecurityContext`, which takes effect at the container level. If this attribute is set in both `SecurityContext` and `PodSecurityContext`, the value specified at the container level takes precedence.

- **runAsNonRoot**: Set to `false` by default, setting it to `true` enables validation that the processes in the container cannot run as a root user (UID=0). Validation is done by `kubelet`. By setting it to `true`, `kubelet` will prevent the container from starting if run as a root user. It is a good security practice to set it to `true`. This attribute is also available in `SecurityContext`, which takes effect at the container level. If this attribute is set in both `SecurityContext` and `PodSecurityContext`, the value specified at the container level takes precedence.

- **seLinuxOptions**: This is designed to specify the SELinux context to the container. By default, the container runtime will assign a random SELinux context to the container if not specified. This attribute is also available in `SecurityContext`, which takes effect at the container level. If this attribute is set in both `SecurityContext` and `PodSecurityContext`, the value specified at the container level takes precedence.

Notice that the attributes `runAsUser`, `runAsGroup`, `runAsNonRoot`, and `seLinuxOptions` are available both in `SecurityContext` at the container level and `PodSecurityContext` at the pod level. This gives users both the flexibility and extreme importance of security control. `fsGroup` and `sysctls` are not as commonly used as the others, so only use them when you have to.

AppArmor profiles

An AppArmor profile usually defines what Linux capabilities the process owns, what network resources and files can be accessed by the container, and so on. In order to use an AppArmor profile to protect pods or containers, you will need to update the annotation of the pod. Let's look at an example, assuming you have an AppArmor profile to block any file write activities:

```
#include <tunables/global>
profile k8s-apparmor-example-deny-write flags=(attach_
disconnected) {
  #include <abstractions/base>
  file,
  # Deny all file writes.
  deny /** w,
}
```

Note that AppArmor is not a Kubernetes object, like a pod, deployment, and so on. It can't be operated through `kubectl`. You will have to SSH to each node and load the AppArmor profile into the kernel so that the pod may be able to use it.

The following is the command for loading the AppArmor profile:

```
cat /etc/apparmor.d/profile.name | sudo apparmor_parser -a
```

Then, put the profile into `enforce` mode:

```
sudo aa-enforce /etc/apparmor.d/profile.name
```

Once the AppArmor profile is loaded, you can update the annotation of the pod to use the AppArmor profile to protect your container. Here is an example of applying an AppArmor profile to containers:

```
apiVersion: v1
kind: Pod
metadata:
  name: hello-apparmor
  annotations:
    # Tell Kubernetes to apply the AppArmor profile
    # "k8s-apparmor-example-deny-write".
    container.apparmor.security.beta.kubernetes.io/hello:
      localhost/k8s-apparmor-example-deny-write
spec:
  containers:
  - name: hello
    image: busybox
    command: [ "sh", "-c", "echo 'Hello AppArmor!' && sleep 1h"
]
```

The container inside `hello-apparmor` does nothing but sleep after echoing the `Hello AppArmor!` message. When it is running, if you launch a shell from a container and write to any file, it will be blocked by AppArmor. Even though writing a robust AppArmor profile is not easy, you can still create some basic restrictions, such as denying writing to certain directories, denying accepting raw packets, and making certain files read-only. Also, test the profile first before applying it to the production cluster. Open source tools such as bane can help create AppArmor profiles for containers.

We do not intend to dive into the seccomp profile in this book since writing a seccomp profile for a microservice is not easy. Even an application developer doesn't have knowledge of what system calls are legitimate for the microservice they developed. Although you can turn the audit mode on to avoid breaking the microservice's functionality, building a robust seccomp profile is still a long way off. Another reason is that this feature is still in the alpha stage up to version 1.17. According to Kubernetes' official documentation, being alpha means it is disabled by default, perhaps buggy, and only recommended to run in a short-lived testing cluster. When there are any new updates on seccomp, we may come back to introduce seccomp in more detail at a later date.

We've covered how to secure Kubernetes pods in the build time. Next, let's look at how we can secure Kubernetes pods during runtime.

The power of PodSecurityPolicy

A Kubernetes PodSecurityPolicy is a cluster-level resource that controls security-sensitive aspects of the pod specification through which the access privileges of a Kubernetes pod are limited. As a DevOps engineer, you may want to use a PodSecurityPolicy to restrict most of the workloads run in limited access privileges, while only allowing a few workloads to be run with extra privileges.

In this section, we will first take a closer look at a PodSecurityPolicy, and then we will introduce an open source tool, kube-psp-advisor, which can help build an adaptive PodSecurityPolicy for the running Kubernetes cluster.

Understanding PodSecurityPolicy

You can think of a PodSecurityPolicy as a policy to evaluate the security attributes defined in the pod's specification. Only those pods whose security attributes meet the requirements of PodSecurityPolicy will be admitted to the cluster. For example, PodSecurityPolicy can be used to block the launch of most privileged pods, while only allowing those necessary or limited pods access to the host filesystem.

The following are the principal security attributes that are controlled by PodSecurityPolicy:

- **privileged**: Determines whether a pod can run in privileged mode.
- **hostPID**: Determines whether a pod can use a host PID namespace.
- **hostNetwork**: Determines whether a pod can use a host network namespace.
- **hostIPC**: Determines whether a pod can use a host IPC namespace. The default setting is true.
- **allowedCapabilities**: Specifies a list of capabilities that could be added to containers. The default setting is empty.
- **defaultAddCapabilities**: Specifies a list of capabilities that will be added to containers by default. The default setting is empty.
- **requiredDropCapabilities**: Specifies a list of capabilities that will be dropped from containers. Note that a capability cannot be specified in both the allowedCapabilities and requiredDropCapabilities fields. The default setting is empty.

- **readOnlyRootFilesystem**: When set to `true`, the PodSecurityPolicy will force containers to run with a read-only root filesystem. If the attribute is set to `false` explicitly in the security context of the container, the pod will be denied from running. The default setting is `false`.

- **runAsUser**: Specifies the allowable user IDs that may be set in the security context of pods and containers. The default setting allows all.

- **runAsGroup**: Specifies the allowable group IDs that may be set in the security context of pods and containers. The default setting allows all.

- **allowPrivilegeEscalation**: Determines whether a pod can submit a request to allow privilege escalation. The default setting is `true`.

- **allowedHostPaths**: Specifies a list of host paths that could be mounted by the pod. The default setting allows all.

- **volumes**: Specifies a list of volume types that can be mounted by the pod. For example, `secret`, `configmap`, and `hostpath` are the valid volume types. The default setting allows all.

- **seLinux**: Specifies the allowable `seLinux` labels that may be set in the security context of pods and containers. The default setting allows all.

- **allowedUnsafeSysctl**: Allows unsafe `sysctls` to run. The default setting allows none.

Now, let's take a look at an example of a PodSecurityPolicy:

```
apiVersion: policy/v1beta1
kind: PodSecurityPolicy
metadata:
    name: example
spec:
  allowedCapabilities:
  - NET_ADMIN
  - IPC_LOCK
  allowedHostPaths:
  - pathPrefix: /dev
  - pathPrefix: /run
  - pathPrefix: /
```

```
  fsGroup:
    rule: RunAsAny
  hostNetwork: true
  privileged: true
  runAsUser:
    rule: RunAsAny
  seLinux:
    rule: RunAsAny
  supplementalGroups:
    rule: RunAsAny
  volumes:
  - hostPath
  - secret
```

This PodSecurityPolicy allows the NET_ADMIN and IPC_LOCK capabilities, mounts /, /dev, and /run from the host and Kubernetes' secret volumes. It doesn't enforce any filesystem group ID or supplemental groups and it also allows the container to run as any user, access the host network namespace, and run as a privileged container. No SELinux policy is enforced in the policy.

To enable this Pod Security Policy, you can run the following command:

```
$ kubectl apply -f example-psp.yaml
```

Now, let's verify that the Pod Security Policy has been created successfully:

```
$ kubectl get psp
```

The output will appear as follows:

```
NAME        PRIV        CAPS                          SELINUX
RUNASUSER   FSGROUP     SUPGROUP    READONLYROOTFS    VOLUMES
example     true        NET_ADMIN, IPC_LOCK           RunAsAny
RunAsAny    RunAsAny    RunAsAny    false
hostPath,secret
```

After you have created the Pod Security Policy, there is one more step required in order to enforce it. You will have to grant the privilege of using the `PodSecurityPolicy` object to the users, groups, or service accounts. By doing so, the pod security policies are entitled to evaluate the workloads based on the associated service account. Here is an example of how to enforce a PodSecurityPolicy. First, you will need to create a cluster role that uses the PodSecurityPolicy:

```
apiVersion: rbac.authorization.k8s.io/v1
kind: ClusterRole
metadata:
  name: use-example-psp
rules:
- apiGroups: ['policy']
  resources: ['podsecuritypolicies']
  verbs:      ['use']
  resourceNames:
  - example
```

Then, create a `RoleBinding` or `ClusterRoleBinding` object to associate the preceding `ClusterRole` object created with the service accounts, users, or groups:

```
apiVersion: rbac.authorization.k8s.io/v1
kind: RoleBinding
metadata:
  name: use-example-psp-binding
roleRef:
  kind: ClusterRole
  name: use-example-psp
  apiGroup: rbac.authorization.k8s.io
subjects:
# Authorize specific service accounts:
- kind: ServiceAccount
  name: test-sa
  namespace: psp-test
```

The preceding `use-example-pspbinding.yaml` file created a `RoleBinding` object to associate the `use-example-psp` cluster role with the `test-sa` service account in the `psp-test` namespace. With all of these set up, any workloads in the `psp-test` namespace whose service account is `test-sa` will run through the PodSecurityPolicy example's evaluation. And only those that meet the requirements will be admitted to the cluster.

From the preceding example, think of there being different types of workloads running in your Kubernetes cluster, and each of them may require different privileges to access different types of resources. It would be a challenge to create and manage pod security policies for different workloads. Now, let's take a look at `kube-psp-advisor` and see how it can help create pod security policies for you.

Kubernetes PodSecurityPolicy Advisor

Kubernetes PodSecurityPolicy Advisor (also known as `kube-psp-advisor`) is an open source tool from Sysdig. It scans the security attributes of running workloads in the cluster and then, on this basis, recommends pod security policies for your cluster or workloads.

First, let's install `kube-psp-advisor` as a `kubectl` plugin. If you haven't installed `krew`, a `kubectl` plugin management tool, please follow the instructions (`https://github.com/kubernetes-sigs/krew#installation`) in order to install it. Then, install `kube-psp-advisor` with `krew` as follows:

```
$ kubectl krew install advise-psp
```

Then, you should be able to run the following command to verify the installation:

```
$ kubectl advise-psp
A way to generate K8s PodSecurityPolicy objects from a live
K8s environment or individual K8s objects containing pod
specifications

Usage:
  kube-psp-advisor [command]

Available Commands:
  convert      Generate a PodSecurityPolicy from a single K8s
Yaml file
  help         Help about any command
```

```
inspect      Inspect a live K8s Environment to generate a
PodSecurityPolicy
Flags:
 -h, --help            help for kube-psp-advisor
      --level string   Log level (default "info")
```

To generate pod security policies for workloads in a namespace, you can run the following command:

```
$ kubectl advise-psp inspect --grant --namespace psp-test
```

The preceding command generates pod security policies for workloads running inside the psp-test namespace. If the workload uses a default service account, no PodSecurityPolicy will be generated for it. This is because the default service account will be assigned to the workload that does not have a dedicated service account associated with it. And you certainly don't want to have a default service account that is able to use a PodSecurityPolicy for privileged workloads.

Here is an example of output generated by kube-psp-advisor for workloads in the psp-test namespace, including Role, RoleBinding, and PodSecurityPolicy in a single YAML file with multiple pod security policies. Let's take a look at one of the recommended PodSecurityPolicy:

```
# Pod security policies will be created for service account
'sa-1' in namespace 'psp-test' with following workloads:
#    Kind: ReplicaSet, Name: busy-rs, Image: busybox
#    Kind: Pod, Name: busy-pod, Image: busybox
apiVersion: policy/v1beta1
kind: PodSecurityPolicy
metadata:
  creationTimestamp: null
  name: psp-for-psp-test-sa-1
spec:
  allowedCapabilities:
  - SYS_ADMIN
  allowedHostPaths:
  - pathPrefix: /usr/bin
    readOnly: true
  fsGroup:
    rule: RunAsAny
```

```
hostIPC: true
hostNetwork: true
hostPID: true
runAsUser:
  rule: RunAsAny
seLinux:
  rule: RunAsAny
supplementalGroups:
  rule: RunAsAny
volumes:
- configMap
- secret
- hostPath
```

Following is the Role generated by `kube-psp-advisor`:

```
apiVersion: rbac.authorization.k8s.io/v1
kind: Role
metadata:
  creationTimestamp: null
  name: use-psp-by-psp-test:sa-1
  namespace: psp-test
rules:
- apiGroups:
  - policy
  resourceNames:
  - psp-for-psp-test-sa-1
  resources:
  - podsecuritypolicies
  verbs:
  - use
---
```

Following is the RoleBinding generated by `kube-psp-advisor`:

```
apiVersion: rbac.authorization.k8s.io/v1
kind: RoleBinding
metadata:
```

```
    creationTimestamp: null
    name: use-psp-by-psp-test:sa-1-binding
    namespace: psp-test
roleRef:
    apiGroup: rbac.authorization.k8s.io
    kind: Role
    name: use-psp-by-psp-test:sa-1
subjects:
- kind: ServiceAccount
    name: sa-1
    namespace: psp-test
---
```

The preceding section is the recommended PodSecurityPolicy, `psp-for-psp-test-sa-1`, for the `busy-rs` and `busy-pod` workloads, since these two workloads share the same service account, `sa-1`. Hence, `Role` and `RoleBinding` are created to use the Pod Security Policy, `psp-for-psp-test-sa-1`, respectively. The PodSecurityPolicy is generated based on the aggregation of the security attributes of workloads using the `sa-1` service account:

```
---
# Pod security policies will NOT be created for service account
'default' in namespace 'psp-test' with following workdloads:
#    Kind: ReplicationController, Name: busy-rc, Image: busybox
---
```

The preceding section mentions that the `busy-rc` workload uses a `default` service account, so there is no Pod Security Policy created for it. This is a reminder that if you want to generate pod security policies for workloads, don't use the default service account.

Building a Kubernetes PodSecurityPolicy is not straightforward, although it would be ideal if a single restricted PodSecurityPolicy was to apply to the entire cluster and all workloads complied with it. DevOps engineers need to be creative in order to build restricted pod security policies while not breaking workloads' functionalities. `kube-psp-advisor` makes the implementation of Kubernetes pod security policies simple, adapts to your application requirements and, specifically, is fine-grained for each one to allow only the privilege of least access.

Summary

In this chapter, we covered how to harden a container image with CIS Docker benchmarks, and then we gave a detailed introduction to the security attributes of Kubernetes workloads. Next, we looked at the PodSecurityPolicy in detail and introduced the `kube-psp-advisor` open source tool, which facilitates the establishment of pod security policies.

Securing Kubernetes workloads is not a one-shot thing. Security controls need to be applied from the build, deployment, and runtime stages. It starts with hardening container images, and then configuring security attributes of Kubernetes workloads in a secure way. This happens at the build stage. It is also important to build adaptive pod security policies for different Kubernetes workloads. The goal is to restrict most of the workloads to run with limited privileges, while allowing only a few workloads to run with extra privileges, and without breaking workload availability. This happens at the runtime stage. `kube-psp-advisor` is able to help build adaptive pod security policies.

In the next chapter, we will talk about image scanning. It is critical in helping to secure Kubernetes workloads in the DevOps workflow.

Questions

1. What does `HEALTHCHECK` do in a Dockerfile?

2. Why use `COPY` instead of `ADD` in a Dockerfile?

3. If your application doesn't listen on any port, which default capabilities can be dropped?

4. What does the `runAsNonRoot` attribute control?

5. When you create a `PodSecurityPolicy` object, what else do you need to do in order to enforce that Pod Security Policy on workloads?

Further reading

You can refer to the following links for more information on the topics covered in this chapter:

- To learn more about `kube-psp-advisor`, please visit the following link: `https://github.com/sysdiglabs/kube-psp-advisor`

- To learn more about AppArmor, please visit the following link: `https://gitlab.com/apparmor/apparmor/-/wikis/Documentation`

- To learn more about bane, please visit the following link: `https://github.com/genuinetools/bane`

9
Image Scanning in DevOps Pipelines

It is a good practice to find defects and vulnerabilities in the early stages of the development life cycle. Identifying issues and fixing them in the early stages helps improve the robustness and stability of an application. It also helps to reduce the attack surface in the production environment. Securing Kubernetes clusters has to cover the entire DevOps flow. Similar to hardening container images and restricting powerful security attributes in the workload manifest, image scanning can help improve the security posture on the development side. However, image scanning can definitely go beyond that.

In this chapter, first, we will introduce the concept of image scanning and vulnerabilities, then we'll talk about a popular open source image scanning tool called **Anchore Engine** and show you how you can use it to do image scanning. Last but not least, we will show you how image scanning can be integrated into CI/CD pipelines.

After this chapter, you should be familiar with the concept of image scanning and feel comfortable using Anchore Engine to scan images. More importantly, you need to start thinking of a strategy for integrating image scanning into your CI/CD pipeline if you haven't so far.

We will cover the following topics in this chapter:

- Introducing container images and vulnerabilities
- Scanning images with Anchore Engine
- Integrating image scanning into the CI/CD pipeline

Introducing container images and vulnerabilities

Image scanning can be used to identify vulnerabilities or violations of best practices (depending on the image scanner's capability) inside an image. Vulnerabilities may come from application libraries or tools inside the image. Before we jump into image scanning, it would be good to know a little bit more about container images and vulnerabilities.

Container images

A container image is a file that bundles the microservice binary, its dependency, configurations of the microservice, and so on. Nowadays, application developers not only write code to build microservices but also need to build an image to containerize an application. Sometimes application developers may not follow the security best practices to write code or download libraries from uncertified sources. This means vulnerabilities could potentially exist in your own application or the dependent packages that your application relies on. Still, don't forget the base image you use, which might include another set of vulnerable binaries and packages. So first, let's look at what an image looks like:

```
$ docker history kaizheh/anchore-cli
```

IMAGE SIZE	CREATED COMMENT	CREATED BY
76b8613d39bc file:92b27c0a57eddb63...	8 hours ago 678B	/bin/sh -c #(nop) COPY
38ea9049199d PATH=/.local/bin/:/us...	10 hours ago 0B	/bin/sh -c #(nop) ENV
525287c1340a anchorecli	10 hours ago 5.74MB	/bin/sh -c pip install
f0cbce9c40f4 update && apt-get install...	10 hours ago 423MB	/bin/sh -c apt-get
a2a15febcdf3 ["/bin/bash"]	7 months ago 0B	/bin/sh -c #(nop) CMD

<missing> 7 months ago run/systemd && echo 'do… 7B		/bin/sh -c mkdir -p /
<missing> 7 months ago echo '#!/bin/sh' > /… 745B		/bin/sh -c set -xe &&
<missing> 7 months ago get indextargets)"] 987kB		/bin/sh -c [-z "$(apt-
<missing> 7 months ago file:c477cb0e95c56b51e… 63.2MB		/bin/sh -c #(nop) ADD

The preceding output shows the file layer of the image kaizheh/anchore-cli (show full commands with the --no-trunc flag). You may notice that each file layer has a corresponding command that creates it. After each command, a new file layer is created, which means the content of the image has been updated, layer by layer (basically, Docker works on copy-on-write), and you can still see the size of each file layer. This is easy to understand: when you install new packages or add files to the base, the image size increases. The missing image ID is a known issue because Docker Hub only stores the digest of the leaf layer and not the intermediate ones in the parent image. However, the preceding image history does tell how the image was in the Dockerfile, as follows:

```
FROM ubuntu
RUN apt-get update && apt-get install -y python-pip jq vim
RUN pip install anchorecli
ENV PATH="$HOME/.local/bin/:$PATH"
COPY ./demo.sh /demo.sh
```

The workings of the preceding Dockerfile are described as follows:

1. To build the kaizheh/anchore-cli image, I chose to build from ubuntu.

2. Then, I installed the packages python-pip, jq, and vim.

3. Next, I installed anchore-cli using pip, which I installed in the previous step.

4. Then I configured the environment variable path.

5. Lastly, I copied a shell script, demo.sh, to the image.

The following figure shows the image file layers mapped to the Dockerfile instructions:

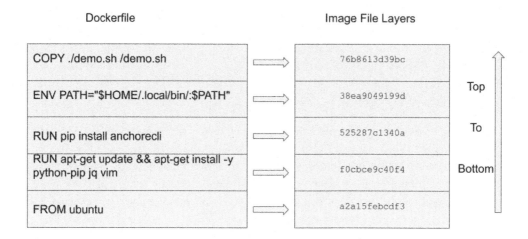

Figure 9.1 – Dockerfile instructions map to image file layers

You don't have to remember what has been added in each layer. Ultimately, a container image is a compressed file that contains all the binaries and packages required for your application. When a container is created from an image, the container runtime extracts the image and then creates a directory purposely for the extracted content of the image, then configures chroot, cgroup, Linux namespaces, Linux capabilities, and so on for the entry point application in the image before launching it.

Now you know the magic done by the container runtime to launch a container from an image. But you are still not sure whether your image is vulnerable so that it could easily be hacked. Let's look at what image scanning really does.

Detecting known vulnerabilities

People make mistakes and so do developers. If flaws in an application are exploitable, those flaws become security vulnerabilities. There are two types of vulnerability—one is those that have been discovered, while the other type remains unknown. Security researchers, penetration testers, and others work very hard to look for security vulnerabilities so that corresponding fixes reduce the potential for compromise. Once security vulnerabilities have been patched, developers apply patches as updates to the application. If these updates are not applied on time, there is a risk of the application getting compromised. It would cause huge damage to companies if these known security issues were exploited by malicious guys.

In this section, we're not going to talk about how to hunt for security vulnerabilities. Let the security researchers and ethical hackers do their job. Instead, we will talk about how to discover and manage those known vulnerabilities uncovered by image scanning tools by performing vulnerability management. In addition, we also need to know how vulnerabilities are tracked and shared in the community. So, let's talk about CVE and NVD.

Introduction to vulnerability databases

CVE stands for **Common Vulnerability and Exposure**. When a vulnerability is identified, there is a unique ID assigned to it with a description and a public reference. Usually, there is impacted version information inside the description. This is one CVE entry. Every day, there are hundreds of vulnerabilities that are identified and get a unique CVE ID assigned by MITRE.

NVD stands for **National Vulnerability Database**. It synchronizes the CVE list. Once there is a new update to the CVE list, the new CVE will show up in NVD immediately. Besides NVD, there are some other vulnerability databases available, such as Synk.

To explain the magic done by an image scanning tool in a simple way: the image scanning tool extracts the image file, then looks for all the available packages and libraries in the image and looks up their version within the vulnerability database. If there is any package whose version matches with any of the CVE's descriptions in the vulnerability database, the image scanning tool will report that there is a vulnerability in the image. You shouldn't be surprised if there are vulnerabilities found in a container image. So, what are you going to do about them? The first thing you need to do is stay calm and don't panic.

Managing vulnerabilities

When you have a vulnerability management strategy, you won't panic. In general, every vulnerability management strategy will start with understanding the exploitability and impact of the vulnerability based on the CVE detail. NVD provides a vulnerability scoring system also known as **Common Vulnerability Scoring System** (**CVSS**) to help you better understand how severe the vulnerability is.

The following information needs to be provided to calculate the vulnerability score based on your own understanding of the vulnerability:

- **Attack vector**: Whether the exploit is a network attack, local attack, or physical attack
- **Attack complexity**: How hard it is to exploit the vulnerability
- **Privileges required**: Whether the exploit requires any privileges, such as root or non-root

- **User interaction**: Whether the exploit requires any user interaction

- **Scopes**: Whether the exploit will lead to cross security domain

- **Confidentiality impact**: How much the exploit impacts the confidentiality of the software

- **Integrity impact**: How much the exploit impacts the integrity of the software

- **Availability impact**: How much the exploit impacts the availability of the software

The CVSS calculator is available at `https://nvd.nist.gov/vuln-metrics/cvss/v3-calculator`:

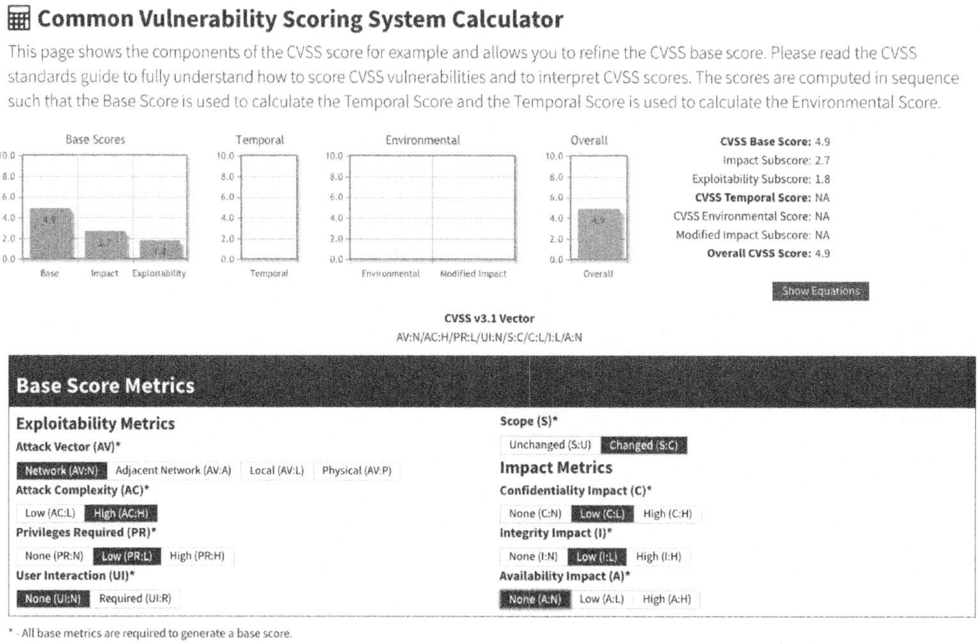

Figure 9.2 – CVSS calculator

Though the input fields in the preceding screenshot only cover the base score metrics, they serve as fundamental factors that decide how critical the vulnerability is. There are two other metrics that can be used to evaluate the criticalness of the vulnerability but we're not going to cover them in this section. According to CVSS (version 3), there are four ranges of score:

- **Low**: 0.1-3.9

- **Medium**: 4-6.9

- **High**: 7-8.9
- **Critical**: 9-10

Usually, image scanning tools will provide the CVSS score when they report any vulnerabilities in an image. There is at least one more step for the vulnerability analysis before you take any response action. You need to know that the severity of the vulnerability may be influenced by your own environment as well. Let me give you a few examples:

- The vulnerability is only exploitable in Windows, but the base OS image is not Windows.
- The vulnerability can be exploited from network access but the processes in the image only send outbound requests and never accept inbound requests.

The preceding scenarios show good examples that the CVSS score is not the only factor that matters. You should focus on the vulnerabilities that are both critical and relevant. However, our recommendation is still to prioritize vulnerabilities wisely and fix them as soon as possible.

If there is a vulnerability found in an image, it is always better to fix it early. If vulnerabilities are found in the development stage, then you should have enough time to respond. If vulnerabilities are found in a running production cluster, you should patch the images and redeploy as soon as a patch is available. If a patch is not available, having a mitigation strategy in place prevents compromise of the cluster.

This is why an image scanning tool is critical to your CI/CD pipeline. It's not realistic to cover vulnerability management in one section, but I think a basic understanding of vulnerability management will help you make the most use of any image scanning tool. There are a few popular open source image scanning tools available, such as Anchore, Clair, Trivvy, and so on. Let's look at one such image scanning tool with examples.

Scanning images with Anchore Engine

Anchore Engine is an open source image scanning tool. It not only analyzes Docker images but also allows users to define an acceptance image scanning policy. In this section, we will first give a high-level introduction to Anchore Engine, then we will show how to deploy Anchore Engine and the basic image scanning use case of Anchore Engine by using Anchore's own CLI tool, `anchore-cli`.

Introduction to Anchore Engine

When an image is submitted to Anchore Engine for analysis, Anchore Engine will first retrieve the image metadata from image registry, then download the image and queue the image for analysis. The following are the items that Anchore Engine will analyze:

- Image metadata
- Image layers
- Operating system packages such as `deb`, `rpm`, `apkg`, and so on
- File data
- Application dependency packages:
    - Ruby gems
    - Node.js NPMs
    - Java archives
    - Python packages
- File content

To deploy Anchore Engine in a Kubernetes cluster with **Helm**—CNCF project which is a package manage tool for the Kubernetes cluster, run the following command:

```
$ helm install anchore-demo stable/anchore-engine
```

Anchore Engine is composed of a few microservices. When deployed in a Kubernetes cluster, you will find the following workloads are running:

```
$ kubectl get deploy
```

NAME	READY	UP-TO-DATE
AVAILABLE AGE		
anchore-demo-anchore-engine-analyzer	1/1	1
1 3m37s		
anchore-demo-anchore-engine-api	1/1	1
1 3m37s		
anchore-demo-anchore-engine-catalog	1/1	1
1 3m37s		
anchore-demo-anchore-engine-policy	1/1	1
1 3m37s		

```
anchore-demo-anchore-engine-simplequeue    1/1       1
1            3m37s
anchore-demo-postgresql                    1/1       1
1            3m37s
```

Anchore Engine decouples image scanning services into the microservices shown in the preceding log:

- **API**: Accepts the image scan request
- **Catalog**: Maintains the states of the image scan job
- **Policy**: Loads image analysis results and performs policy evaluation
- **Analyzer**: Pulls images from image registry and performs analysis
- **Simplequeue**: Queues image scanning tasks
- **PostgreSQL**: Stores image analysis results and state

Now Anchore Engine is successfully deployed in a Kubernetes cluster, let's see how we can do image scanning with `anchore-cli`.

Scanning images with anchore-cli

Anchore Engine supports access both from the RESTful API and `anchore-cli`. `anchore-cli` is handy to use in an iterative way. `anchore-cli` does not need to run in a Kubernetes cluster. You need to configure the following environment variables to enable CLI access to Anchore Engine:

- `ANCHORE_CLI_URL`: Anchore Engine API endpoint
- `ANCHORE_CLI_USER`: Username to access Anchore Engine
- `ANCHORE_CLI_PASS`: Password to access Anchore Engine

Once you've configured the environment variables successfully, you can verify the connectivity to Anchore Engine with the following command:

```
root@anchore-cli:/# anchore-cli system status
```

And the output should be like the following:

```
Service analyzer (anchore-demo-anchore-engine-analyzer-
5fd777cfb5-jtqp2, http://anchore-demo-anchore-engine-
analyzer:8084): up
```

```
Service apiext (anchore-demo-anchore-engine-api-6dd475cf-n24xb,
http://anchore-demo-anchore-engine-api:8228): up
```

```
Service policy_engine (anchore-demo-anchore-engine-policy-
7b8f68fbc-q2dm2, http://anchore-demo-anchore-engine-
policy:8087): up
```

```
Service simplequeue (anchore-demo-anchore-engine-simplequeue-
6d4567c7f4-7sll5, http://anchore-demo-anchore-engine-
simplequeue:8083): up
```

```
Service catalog (anchore-demo-anchore-engine-catalog-949bc68c9-
np2pc, http://anchore-demo-anchore-engine-catalog:8082): up
```

```
Engine DB Version: 0.0.12
```

```
Engine Code Version: 0.6.1
```

`anchore-cli` is able to talk to Anchore Engine in a Kubernetes cluster. Now let's scan an image with the following command:

```
root@anchore-cli:/# anchore-cli image add kaizheh/nginx-docker
```

And the output should be like the following:

```
Image Digest:
sha256:416b695b09a79995b3f25501bf0c9b9620e82984132060bf7d66d877
6c1554b7
```

```
Parent Digest:
sha256:416b695b09a79995b3f25501bf0c9b9620e82984132060bf7d66d877
6c1554b7
```

```
Analysis Status: analyzed
```

```
Image Type: docker
```

```
Analyzed At: 2020-03-22T05:48:14Z
```

```
Image ID:
bcf644d78ccd89f36f5cce91d205643a47c8a5277742c5b311c9d9
6699a3af82
```

```
Dockerfile Mode: Guessed
```

```
Distro: debian
```

```
Distro Version: 10
```

```
Size: 1172316160
```

```
Architecture: amd64
Layer Count: 16


Full Tag: docker.io/kaizheh/nginx-docker:latest
Tag Detected At: 2020-03-22T05:44:38Z
```

You will get the image digest, full tag, and more from the image. It may take some time for Anchore Engine to analyze the image depending on the image size. Once it is analyzed, you will see the `Analysis Status` field has been updated to `analyzed`. Use the following command to check the image scanning status:

```
root@anchore-cli:/# anchore-cli image get kaizheh/nginx-docker
```

And the output should be like the following:

```
Image Digest:
sha256:416b695b09a79995b3f25501bf0c9b9620e82984132060bf7d66d877
6c1554b7
Parent Digest:
sha256:416b695b09a79995b3f25501bf0c9b9620e82984132060bf7d66d877
6c1554b7
Analysis Status: analyzed
Image Type: docker
Analyzed At: 2020-03-22T05:48:14Z
Image ID:
bcf644d78ccd89f36f5cce91d205643a47c8a5277742c5b311c9d96699a3a
f82
Dockerfile Mode: Guessed
Distro: debian
Distro Version: 10
Size: 1172316160
Architecture: amd64
Layer Count: 16


Full Tag: docker.io/kaizheh/nginx-docker:latest
Tag Detected At: 2020-03-22T05:44:38Z
```

We briefly mentioned Anchore Engine policies earlier; Anchore Engine policies allow you to define rules to handle vulnerabilities differently based on their severity. In the default Anchore Engine policy, you will find the following rules in the default policy with two rules. The first rule is as follows:

```
{
    "action": "WARN",
    "gate": "vulnerabilities",
    "id": "6063fdde-b1c5-46af-973a-915739451ac4",
    "params": [{
                "name": "package_type",
                "value": "all"
        },
        {
                "name": "severity_comparison",
                "value": "="
        },
        {
                "name": "severity",
                "value": "medium"
        }
    ],
    "trigger": "package"
},
```

The first rule defines that any package that has medium-level vulnerability will still set the policy evaluation result to pass. The second rule is as follows:

```
{
    "action": "STOP",
    "gate": "vulnerabilities",
    "id": "b30e8abc-444f-45b1-8a37-55be1b8c8bb5",
    "params": [{
                "name": "package_type",
                "value": "all"
        },
        {
```

```
                "name": "severity_comparison",
                "value": ">"
        },
        {
                "name": "severity",
                "value": "medium"
        }
    ],
    "trigger": "package"
},
```

The second rule defines that any package that has high or critical vulnerability will set the policy evaluation result to fail. After the image is analyzed, use the following command to check with the policy:

```
root@anchore-cli:/# anchore-cli --json evaluate check
sha256:416b695b09a79995b3f25501bf0c9b9620e82984132060bf7d66d877
6c1554b7 --tag docker.io/kaizheh/nginx-docker:latest
```

And the output should be like the following:

```
[
    {
        "sha256:416b695b09a79995b3f25501bf0c9b9620e82984132060
bf7d66d8776c1554b7": {
            "docker.io/kaizheh/nginx-docker:latest": [
                {
                    "detail": {},
                    "last_evaluation": "2020-03-22T06:19:44Z",
                    "policyId": "2c53a13c-1765-11e8-82ef-235277
61d060",
                    "status": "fail"
                }
            ]
        }
    }
]
```

So the image `docker.io/kaizheh/nginx-docker:latest` failed the default policy evaluation. This means that there must be some vulnerabilities at a high or critical level. Use the following command to list all the vulnerabilities in the image:

```
root@anchore-cli:/# anchore-cli image vuln docker.io/kaizheh/
nginx-docker:latest all
```

And the output should be like the following:

```
Vulnerability ID          Package
Severity           Fix                          CVE Refs
Vulnerability URL
CVE-2019-9636             Python-2.7.16
Critical           None                         CVE-2019-
9636               https://nvd.nist.gov/vuln/detail/CVE-2019-9636
CVE-2020-7598             minimist-0.0.8
Critical           None                         CVE-2020-
7598               https://nvd.nist.gov/vuln/detail/CVE-2020-7598
CVE-2020-7598             minimist-1.2.0
Critical           None                         CVE-2020-
7598               https://nvd.nist.gov/vuln/detail/CVE-2020-7598
CVE-2020-8116             dot-prop-4.2.0
Critical           None                         CVE-2020-
8116               https://nvd.nist.gov/vuln/detail/CVE-2020-8116
CVE-2013-1753             Python-2.7.16
High               None                         CVE-2013-
1753               https://nvd.nist.gov/vuln/detail/CVE-2013-1753
CVE-2015-5652             Python-2.7.16
High               None                         CVE-2015-
5652               https://nvd.nist.gov/vuln/detail/CVE-2015-5652
CVE-2019-13404            Python-2.7.16
High               None                         CVE-2019-
13404              https://nvd.nist.gov/vuln/detail/CVE-2019-13404
CVE-2016-8660             linux-compiler-gcc-8-x86-
4.19.67-2+deb10u1              Low              None
CVE-2016-8660             https://security-tracker.debian.org/
tracker/CVE-2016-8660
CVE-2016-8660             linux-headers-4.19.0-6-amd64-
4.19.67-2+deb10u1              Low              None
CVE-2016-8660             https://security-tracker.debian.org/
tracker/CVE-2016-8660
```

The preceding list shows all the vulnerabilities in the image with information including CVE ID, package name, severity, whether a fix is available, and references. Anchore Engine policies essentially help you filter out less severe vulnerabilities so that you can focus on the more severe ones. Then you can start engaging with the security team for vulnerability analysis.

> **Note**
>
> Sometimes, if a fix is not available for a high-level or critical-level vulnerability in a package or library, you should find an alternative instead of continuing to use the vulnerable one.

In the next section, we are going to talk about how to integrate image scanning into the CI/CD pipeline.

Integrating image scanning into the CI/CD pipeline

Image scanning can be triggered at multiple stages in the DevOps pipeline and we've already talked about the advantages of scanning an image in an early stage of the pipeline. However, new vulnerabilities will be discovered, and your vulnerability database should be updated constantly. This indicates that passing an image scan in the build stage doesn't mean it will pass at the runtime stage if there is a new critical vulnerability found that also exists in the image. You should stop the workload deployment when it happens and apply mitigation strategies accordingly. Before we dive into integration, let's look at a rough definition of the DevOps stages that are applicable for image scanning:

- **Build**: When the image is built in the CI/CD pipeline
- **Deployment**: When the image is about to be deployed in a Kubernetes cluster
- **Runtime**: After the image is deployed to a Kubernetes cluster and the containers are up and running

Though there are many different CI/CD pipelines and many different image scanning tools for you to choose from, the notion is that integrating image scanning into the CI/CD pipeline secures Kubernetes workloads as well as Kubernetes clusters.

Scanning at the build stage

There are so many CI/CD tools, such as Jenkins, Spinnaker, and Screwdriver, for you to use. In this section, we're going to show how image scanning can be integrated into a GitHub workflow. A workflow in GitHub is a configurable automated process that contains multiple jobs. It is a similar concept to the Jenkins pipeline but defined in YAML format. A simple workflow with image scanning is like defining a trigger. Usually done when a pull request or commit is pushed, setting up the build environment, for example, Ubuntu.

Then define the steps in the workflow:

1. Check out the PR branch.

2. Build the image from the branch.

3. Push the image to the registry – this is optional. You should be able to launch the image scanner to scan the image when the image is built locally.

4. Scan the newly built or pushed image.

5. Fail the workflow if policy violations occur.

The following is a sample workflow defined in GitHub:

```
name: CI
...
  build:
    runs-on: ubuntu-latest
    steps:
    # Checks-out your repository under $GITHUB_WORKSPACE, so
your job can access it
    - uses: actions/checkout@v2
    # Runs a set of commands using the runners shell
    - name: Build and Push
      env:
        DOCKER_SECRET: ${{ secrets.DOCKER_SECRET }}
      run: |
        cd master/chapter9 && echo "Build Docker Image"
        docker login -u kaizheh -p ${DOCKER_SECRET}
```

```
        docker build -t kaizheh/anchore-cli . && docker push
kaizheh/anchore-cli
  - name: Scan
    env:
      ANCHORE_CLI_URL: ${{ secrets.ANCHORE_CLI_URL }}
      ANCHORE_CLI_USER:  ${{ secrets.ANCHORE_CLI_USER }}
      ANCHORE_CLI_PASS:  ${{ secrets.ANCHORE_CLI_PASS }}
    run: |
      pip install anchorecli        # install anchore-cli
      export PATH="$HOME/.local/bin/:$PATH"
      img="kaizheh/anchore-cli"
      anchore-cli image add $img        # add image
      sha=$(anchore-cli --json --api-version=0.2.4 image
get $img | jq .[0].imageDigest -r)                # get sha
value
      anchore-cli image wait $img       # wait for image
analyzed
      anchore-cli --json evaluate check $sha --tag $img #
evaluate
  - name: Post Scan
    run: |
      # Slack to notify developers scan result or invite new
reviewer if failed
      exit 1  # purposely ends here
```

In the first step of the build pipeline, I used the `checkout` GitHub action to check out the branch. A GitHub action to a workflow is like a function to a programming language. It encapsulates the details you don't need to know but performs tasks for you. It may take input parameters and return results. In the second step, we ran a few commands to build the image `kaizheh/anchore-cli` and push the image to the registry. In the third step, we used `anchore-cli` to scan the image (yes, we use Anchore Engine to scan our own `anchore-cli` image).

Note that I configured the GitHub secrets to store sensitive information such as the Docker Hub access token, Anchore username, and password. In the last step, we failed purposely for demo purposes. But usually, the last step comes with a notification and response to the image scanning result as the comments suggest. And you will find the result details of the workflow in GitHub, as follows:

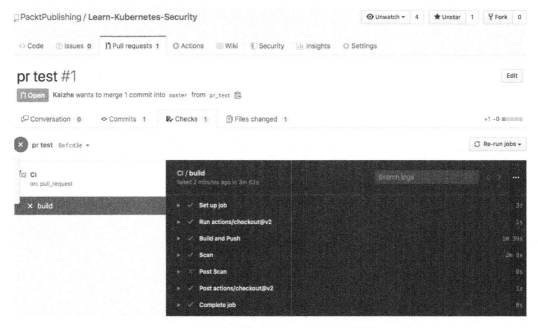

Figure 9.3 – GitHub image scanning workflow

The preceding screenshot shows the status of each step in the workflow, and you will find the detail of each step when you click into it. Anchore also offers an image scan GitHub action called **Anchore Container Scan**. It launches the Anchore Engine scanner on the newly built image and returns the vulnerabilities, manifests, and a pass/fail policy evaluation that can be used to fail the build if desired.

Scanning at the deployment stage

Though deployment is a seamless process, I want to bring it up in a separate section about conducting image scanning at the deployment stage for two reasons:

- New vulnerabilities may be found when you deploy applications to a Kubernetes cluster, even though they passed the image scanning check when they were built. It is better to block them before you find the vulnerabilities when they are running in a Kubernetes cluster.

- Image scanning can be part of the validation admission process in Kubernetes.

We've already introduced the concept of ValidatingAdmissionWebhook in *Chapter 7, Authentication, Authorization, and Admission Control*. Now, let's see how image scanning can help validate the workload by scanning its images before the workload is admitted to run in the Kubernetes cluster. Image scanning admission controller is an open source project from Sysdig. It scans images from the workload that is about to be deployed. If an image fails the image scanning policy, the workload will be rejected. The following is the workflow diagram:

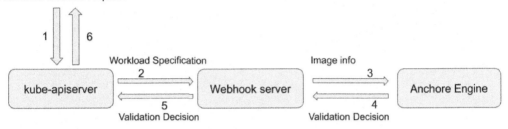

Figure 9.4 – Image scanning admission workflow

The preceding diagram shows the workload admission process validated based on image scanning:

1. There is a workload creation request sent to kube-apiserver.

2. kube-apiserver forwards the request to the registered validating webhook server based on the validating webhook configurations.

3. The validating webhook server extracts image information from the workload's specification and sends it to the Anchore Engine API server.

4. Based on the image scanning policy, Anchore Engine will return the policy evaluation result as a validation decision back to the server.

5. The validating webhook server forwards the validation decision to kube-apiserver.

6. kube-apiserver either admits or rejects the workload based on the validation decision from the image scan policy evaluation result.

To deploy the image scanning admission controller, first check out the GitHub repository (https://github.com/sysdiglabs/image-scanning-admission-controller) and then run the following command:

```
$ make deploy
```

And you should find the webhook servers and services are created:

```
NAME                                                      READY
STATUS     RESTARTS    AGE
pod/image-scan-k8s-webhook-controller-manager-0    1/1
Running    1           16s


NAME
TYPE            CLUSTER-IP        EXTERNAL-IP    PORT(S)    AGE
service/image-scan-k8s-webhook-controller-manager-service
ClusterIP       100.69.225.172    <none>         443/TCP    16s
service/webhook-server-service
ClusterIP       100.68.111.117    <none>         443/TCP    8s


NAME
READY    AGE
statefulset.apps/image-scan-k8s-webhook-controller-manager
1/1      16s
```

Besides the webhook server deployment, the script also creates a
ValidatingWebhookConfiguration object to register the image scan admission
webhook server, which is defined in generic-validatingewebhookconfig.yaml
to the kube-apiserver:

```
apiVersion: admissionregistration.k8s.io/v1beta1
kind: ValidatingWebhookConfiguration
metadata:
  name: validating-webhook-configuration
webhooks:
- name: validating-create-pods.k8s.io
  clientConfig:
    service:
      namespace: image-scan-k8s-webhook-system
      name: webhook-server-service
      path: /validating-create-pods
    caBundle: {{CA_BUNDLE}}
  rules:
  - operations:
    - CREATE
```

```
    apiGroups:
    - ""
    apiVersions:
    - "v1"
    resources:
    - pods
  failurePolicy: Fail
```

The validating webhook configuration object basically tells `kube-apiserver` to forward any pod creation request to `webhook-server-service` in the `image-scan-webhook-system` namespace using the `/validating-create-pod` URL path.

You can use the test cases provided by image scanning admission controller to verify your setup as follows:

```
$ make test
```

In the test, three different pods will be deployed in the Kubernetes cluster. One of them has a critical vulnerability that violates the image scanning policy. So, the workload with the critical vulnerability is rejected as follows:

```
+ kubectl run --image=bitnami/nginx --restart=Never nginx
pod/nginx created
+ kubectl run --image=kaizheh/apache-struts2-cve-2017-5638
--restart=Never apache-struts2
Error from server (Image failed policy check: kaizheh/apache-
struts2-cve-2017-5638): admission webhook "validating-create-
pods.k8s.io" denied the request: Image failed policy check:
kaizheh/apache-struts2-cve-2017-5638
+ kubectl run --image=alpine:3.2 --restart=Never alpine
pod/alpine created
```

The preceding output shows that the workload with image `kaizheh/apache-struts2-cve-2017-5638` is rejected. The image runs the Apache Struts 2 service, which contains a critical vulnerability with a CVSS score of 10 (`https://nvd.nist.gov/vuln/detail/CVE-2017-5638`). Though the CVE in the test is old, you should be able to discover it at an earlier stage. However, new vulnerabilities will be found, and the vulnerability database keeps updating. It's critical to set a gatekeeper for any workload that is going to be deployed in a Kubernetes cluster. Image scanning as validating admission is a good security practice for Kubernetes deployment. Now, let's talk about image scanning at the runtime stage in a Kubernetes cluster.

Scanning at the runtime stage

Good job! The workload's image passed the image scanning policy evaluation in the build and deployment stages. But it still doesn't mean the image is vulnerability free. Remember, new vulnerabilities will be discovered. Usually, the vulnerability database that the image scanner uses will update every few hours. Once the vulnerability database is updated, you should trigger the image scanner to scan images that are actively running in the Kubernetes cluster. There are a couple of ways to do it:

- Scan images pulled on each worker node directly. To scan images on the worker nodes, you can use tools such as `secure-inline-scan` from Sysdig (`https://github.com/sysdiglabs/secure-inline-scan`).

- Scan images in the registry regularly, directly after the vulnerability database has been updated.

Again, once you identify impactful vulnerabilities in the images in use, you should patch vulnerable images and redeploy them to reduce the attack surface.

Summary

In this chapter, we first briefly talked about container images and vulnerabilities. Then we introduced an open source image scanning tool, Anchore Engine, and showed how to use `anchore-cli` to do image scanning. Last but not least, we talked about how to integrate image scanning into a CI/CD pipeline at three different stages: build, deployment, and runtime. Image scanning showed great value in securing the DevOps flow. A secure Kubernetes cluster requires securing the entire DevOps flow.

You should now feel comfortable deploying Anchore Engine and using `anchore-cli` to trigger image scanning. Once you find any vulnerabilities in an image, filter them out by using an Anchore Engine policy and understand their real impact. I know it's going to take time, but it is necessary and awesome to set up image scanning as gatekeepers in your CI/CD pipeline. By doing so, you'll make your Kubernetes cluster more secure.

In the next chapter, we will talk about resource management and real-time monitoring in a Kubernetes cluster.

Questions

Let's use some questions to help you understand this chapter better:

1. Which Docker command can be used to list image file layers?

2. According to the CVSS3 standard, what vulnerability score range is considered high?

3. What is the `anchore-cli` command to start scanning an image?

4. What is the `anchore-cli` command to list an image's vulnerabilities?

5. What is the `anchore-cli` command to evaluate an image with an Anchore Engine policy?

6. Why is it so important to integrate image scanning into CI/CD pipelines?

Further references

- To learn more about Anchore Engine, read: `https://docs.anchore.com/current/docs/engine/general/`

- To learn more about the Anchore scan action: `https://github.com/marketplace/actions/anchore-container-scan`

- To learn more about Sysdig's image scanning admission controller: `https://github.com/sysdiglabs/image-scanning-admission-controller`

- To learn more about GitHub actions: `https://help.github.com/en/actions`

10
Real-Time Monitoring and Resource Management of a Kubernetes Cluster

The availability of services is one of the critical components of the **Confidentiality, Integrity and Availability (CIA)** triad. There have been many instances of malicious attackers using different techniques to disrupt the availability of services for users. Some of these attacks on critical infrastructure such as the electricity grid and banks have resulted in significant losses to the economy. One of the most significant attacks was an attack on Amazon AWS Route 53 infrastructure that resulted in the disruption of core IT services all over the world. To avoid such issues, infrastructure engineers monitor resource usage and application health in real time to ensure the availability of services offered by an organization. Real-time monitoring is often plugged into an alert system that notifies the stakeholders when symptoms of service disruption are observed.

In this chapter, we will look at how you can ensure that services in the Kubernetes cluster are always up and running. We will begin by discussing monitoring and resource management in monolith environments. Next, we will discuss resource requests and resource limits, two concepts at the heart of resource management in Kubernetes. We will then look at tools such as `LimitRanger`, which Kubernetes provides for resource management, before shifting our focus to resource monitoring. We will look at built-in monitors, such as Kubernetes Dashboard and Metrics Server. Finally, we will look at open source tools, such as Prometheus and Grafana, that can be used to monitor the state of a Kubernetes cluster.

In this chapter, we will discuss the following:

- Real-time monitoring and management in monolith environments
- Managing resources in Kubernetes
- Monitoring resources in Kubernetes

Real-time monitoring and management in monolith environments

Resource management and monitoring are important in monolith environments as well. In monolith environments, infrastructure engineers often pipe the output of Linux tools such as `top`, `ntop`, and `htop` to data visualization tools in order to monitor the state of VMs. In managed environments, built-in tools such as Amazon CloudWatch and Azure Resource Manager help to monitor resource usage.

In addition to resource monitoring, infrastructure engineers proactively allocate minimum resource requirements and usage limits for processes and other entities. This ensures that sufficient resources are available to services. Furthermore, resource management ensures that misbehaving or malicious processes do not hog resources and prevent other processes from working. For monolith deployments, resources such as CPU, memory, and spawned processes are capped for different processes. On Linux, process limits can be capped using `prlimit`:

```
$prlimit --nproc=2 --pid=18065
```

This command sets the limit of child processes that a parent process can spawn to 2. With this limit set, if a process with a PID of `18065` tries to spawn more than 2 child processes, it will be denied.

Similar to monolith environments, a Kubernetes cluster runs multiple pods, deployments, and services. If an attacker is able to spawn up Kubernetes objects such as pods or deployments, the attacker can cause a denial-of-service attack by depleting resources available in the Kubernetes cluster. Without adequate resource monitoring and resource management in place, unavailability of the services running in the cluster can cause an economic impact to the organization.

Managing resources in Kubernetes

Kubernetes provides the ability to proactively allocate and limit resources available to Kubernetes objects. In this section, we will discuss resource requests and limits, which form the basis for resource management in Kubernetes. Next, we explore namespace resource quotas and limit ranges. Using these two feature, clusters, administrators can cap the compute and storage limits available to different Kubernetes objects.

Resource requests and limits

`kube-scheduler`, as we discussed in *Chapter 1, Kubernetes Architecture*, is the default scheduler and runs on the master node. `kube-scheduler` finds the most optimal node for the unscheduled pods to run on. It does that by filtering the nodes based on the storage and compute resources requested for the pod. If the scheduler is not able to find a node for the pod, the pod will remain in a pending state. Additionally, if all the resources of the node are being utilized by the pods, `kubelet` on the node will clean up dead pods – unused images. If the cleanup does not reduce the stress, `kubelet` will start evicting those pods that consume more resources.

Resource requests specify what a Kubernetes object is guaranteed to get. Different Kubernetes variations or cloud providers have different defaults for resource requests. Custom resource requests for Kubernetes objects can be specified in the workload's specifications. Resource requests can be specified for CPU, memory, and HugePages. Let's look at an example of resource requests.

Let's create a pod without a resource request in the `yaml` specification, as follows:

```
apiVersion: v1
kind: Pod
metadata:
  name: demo
spec:
  containers:
  - name: demo
```

The pod will use the default resource request for deployment:

```
$kubectl get pod demo —output=yaml
apiVersion: v1
kind: Pod
metadata:
  annotations:
    kubectl.kubernetes.io/last-applied-configuration: |
      {"apiVersion":"v1","kind":"Pod","metadata":{"annotations"
:{},"name":"demo","namespace":"default"},"spec":{"containers":
[{"image":"nginx","name":"demo"}]}}
      kubernetes.io/limit-ranger: 'LimitRanger plugin set: cpu
request for container
      demo'
  creationTimestamp: "2020-05-07T21:54:47Z"
  name: demo
  namespace: default
  resourceVersion: "3455"
  selfLink: /api/v1/namespaces/default/pods/demo
  uid: 5e783495-90ad-11ea-ae75-42010a800074
spec:
  containers:
  - image: nginx
    imagePullPolicy: Always
    name: demo
    resources:
      requests:
        cpu: 100m
```

For the preceding example, the default resource request is for 0.1 CPU cores for the pod. Let's now add a resource request to the .yaml specification and see what happens:

```
apiVersion: v1
kind: Pod
metadata:
  name: demo
spec:
```

```
containers:
- name: demo
  image: nginx
  resources:
    limits:
        hugepages-2Mi: 100Mi
    requests:
      cpu: 500m
      memory: 300Mi
      hugepages-2Mi: 100Mi
```

This specification creates a pod with a resource request of 0.5 CPU cores, 300 MB, and hugepages-2Mi of 100 MB. You can check the resource request for a pod using the following command:

```
$kubectl get pod demo —output=yaml
apiVersion: v1
kind: Pod
metadata:
  creationTimestamp: "2020-05-07T22:02:16Z"
  name: demo-1
  namespace: default
  resourceVersion: "5030"
  selfLink: /api/v1/namespaces/default/pods/demo-1
  uid: 6a276dd2-90ae-11ea-ae75-42010a800074
spec:
  containers:
  - image: nginx
    imagePullPolicy: Always
    name: demo
    resources:
      limits:
        hugepages-2Mi: 100Mi
      requests:
        cpu: 500m
        hugepages-2Mi: 100Mi
        memory: 300Mi
```

As you can see from the output, the pod uses a custom resource request of 0.5 CPU cores, 300 MB of `memory`, and 100 MB of 2 MB `hugepages`, instead of the default 1 MB.

Limits, on the other hand, are hard limits on the resources that the pod can use. Limits specify the maximum resources that a pod should be allowed to use. Pods are restricted if more resources are required than are specified in the limit. Similar to resource requests, you can specify limits for CPU, memory, and HugePages. Let's look at an example of limits:

```
$ cat stress.yaml
apiVersion: v1
kind: Pod
metadata:
  name: demo
spec:
  containers:
  - name: demo
    image: polinux/stress
    command: ["stress"]
    args: ["--vm", "1", "--vm-bytes", "150M", "--vm-hang", "1"]
```

This pod initiates a stress process that tries to allocate memory of `150M` at startup. If no limits are specified in the `.yaml` specification, the pod runs without any issues:

```
$ kubectl create -f stress.yaml
pod/demo created
$ kubectl get pods
NAME          READY     STATUS         RESTARTS     AGE
demo          1/1       Running        0            3h
```

Limits are added to the container section of the `yaml` specification for the pod:

```
containers:
  - name: demo
    image: polinux/stress
    resources:
      limits:
        memory: "150Mi"
    command: ["stress"]
args: ["--vm", "1", "--vm-bytes", "150M", "--vm-hang", "1"]
```

The stress process fails to run and the pod runs into `CrashLoopBackOff`:

```
$ kubectl get pods
NAME      READY    STATUS             RESTARTS    AGE
demo      1/1      Running            0           44s
demo-1    0/1      CrashLoopBackOff   1           5s
```

You can see that the pod was terminated with an `OOMKilled` error when you described the pod:

```
$ kubectl describe pods demo
Name:         demo
Namespace:    default
...
Containers:
  demo:
    Container ID:   docker://a43de56a456342f7d53fa9752aa4fa7366
cd4b8c395b658d1fc607f2703750c2
    Image:          polinux/stress
    Image ID:       docker-pullable://polinux/stress@sha256:b61
44f84f9c15dac80deb48d3a646b55c7043ab1d83ea0a697c09097aaad21aa
...
    Command:
      stress
    Args:
      --vm
      1
      --vm-bytes
      150M
      --vm-hang
      1
    State:        Waiting
      Reason:     CrashLoopBackOff
    Last State:   Terminated
      Reason:     OOMKilled
      Exit Code:  1
      Started:    Mon, 04 May 2020 10:48:14 -0700
      Finished:   Mon, 04 May 2020 10:48:14 -0700
```

Resource requests and limits are converted, mapped to `docker` arguments `--cpu-shares` and `—memory` flags – and passed to the container runtime.

We looked at examples of how resource requests and limits work for pods, but the same examples apply to DaemonSet, Deployments, and StatefulSets. Next, we look at how namespace resource quotas can help set an upper limit for the resources that can be used by namespaces.

Namespace resource quotas

Resource quotas for namespaces help define the resource requests and limits available to all objects within the namespace. Using resource quotas, you can limit the following:

- `request.cpu`: The maximum resource request for CPU for all objects in the namespace.

- `request.memory`: The maximum resource request for memory for all objects in the namespace.

- `limit.cpu`: The maximum resource limit for CPU for all objects in the namespace.

- `limit.memory`: The maximum resource limit for memory for all objects in the namespace.

- `requests.storage`: The sum of storage requests in a namespace cannot exceed this value.

- `count`: Resource quotas can also be used to limit the count of different Kubernetes objects in a cluster, including pods, services, PersistentVolumeClaims, and ConfigMaps.

By default, cloud providers or different variations have standard limits applied to the namespace. On **Google Kubernetes Engine** (**GKE**), the `cpu` request is set to 0.1 CPU cores:

```
$ kubectl describe namespace default
Name:          default
Labels:        <none>
Annotations:   <none>
Status:        Active


Resource Quotas
  Name:                        gke-resource-quotas
```

Resource	Used	Hard
--------	---	---
count/ingresses.extensions	0	100
count/jobs.batch	0	5k
pods	2	1500
services	1	500

Resource Limits

Type	Resource	Min	Max	Default Request	Default Limit	Max Limit/Request Ratio
----	--------	---	---	---------------	-------------	--------------------
Container	cpu	-	-	100m	-	-

Let's see an example of what happens when resource quotas are applied to a namespace:

1. Create a namespace demo:

    ```
    $ kubectl create namespace demo
    namespace/demo created
    ```

2. Define a resource quota. In this example, the quota limits the resource request CPU to 1 CPU:

    ```
    $ cat quota.yaml
    apiVersion: v1
    kind: ResourceQuota
    metadata:
      name: compute-resources
    spec:
      hard:
        requests.cpu: "1"
    ```

3. Apply the quota to the namespace by using the following command:

    ```
    $ kubectl apply -f quota.yaml --namespace demo
    resourcequota/compute-resources created
    ```

4. You can check whether the resource quota is applied successfully to the namespace by executing the following command:

```
$ kubectl describe namespace demo
Name:          demo
Labels:        <none>
Annotations:   <none>
Status:        Active


Resource Quotas
  Name:                compute-resources
  Resource       Used  Hard
  --------       ---   ---
  requests.cpu   0     1


  Name:                            gke-resource-quotas
  Resource                   Used  Hard
  --------                   ---   ---
  count/ingresses.extensions  0    100
  count/jobs.batch            0    5k
  pods                        0    1500
  services                    0    500
```

5. Now, if we try to create two pods that use 1 CPU, the second request will fail with the following error:

```
$ kubectl apply -f nginx-cpu-1.yaml --namespace demo
Error from server (Forbidden): error when creating
"nginx-cpu-1.yaml": pods "demo-1" is forbidden: exceeded
quota: compute-resources, requested: requests.cpu=1,
used: requests.cpu=1, limited: requests.cpu=1
```

Resource quotas ensure quality of service for namespaced Kubernetes objects.

LimitRanger

We discussed the LimitRanger admission controller in *Chapter 7, Authentication, Authorization, and Admission Control.* Cluster administrators can leverage limit ranges to ensure that misbehaving pods, containers, or PersistentVolumeClaims don't consume all available resources.

To use limit ranges, enable the `LimitRanger` admission controller:

```
$ ps aux | grep kube-api
root        3708  6.7  8.7 497216 345256 ?       Ssl   01:44
0:10 kube-apiserver --advertise-address=192.168.99.116 --allow-
privileged=true --authorization-mode=Node,RBAC --client-ca-
file=/var/lib/minikube/certs/ca.crt --enable-admission-plugin
s=NamespaceLifecycle,LimitRanger,ServiceAccount,DefaultStora
geClass,DefaultTolerationSeconds,NodeRestriction,MutatingAdm-
issionWebhook,ValidatingAdmissionWebhook,ResourceQuota
```

Using LimitRanger, we can enforce `default`, `min`, and `max` limits on storage and compute resources. Cluster administrators create a limit range for objects such as pods, containers, and PersistentVolumeClaims. For any request for object creation or update, the LimitRanger admission controller verifies that the request does not violate any limit ranges. If the request violates any limit ranges, a 403 Forbidden response is sent.

Let's look at an example of a simple limit range:

1. Create a namespace in which a limit range will be applied:

    ```
    $kubectl create namespace demo
    ```

2. Define a `LimitRange` for the namespace:

    ```
    $ cat limit_range.yaml
    apiVersion: "v1"
    kind: "LimitRange"
    metadata:
      name: limit1
      namespace: demo
    spec:
      limits:
      - type: "Container"
        max:
          memory: 512Mi
          cpu: 500m
        min:
          memory: 50Mi
          cpu: 50m
    ```

3. Verify that the `limitrange` was applied:

```
$ kubectl get limitrange -n demo
NAME       CREATED AT
limit1     2020-04-30T02:06:18Z
```

4. Create a pod that violates the limit range:

```
$cat nginx-bad.yaml
apiVersion: v1
kind: Pod
metadata:
  name: nginx-bad
spec:
  containers:
  - name: nginx-bad
    image: nginx-bad
    resources:
      limits:
        memory: "800Mi"
        cpu: "500m"
```

This request will be denied:

```
$ kubectl apply -f nginx-bad.yaml -n demo
Error from server (Forbidden): error when creating
"nginx-bad.yaml": pods "nginx-bad" is forbidden: maximum
memory usage per Container is 512Mi, but limit is 800M
```

If a LimitRanger specifies a CPU or memory, all pods and containers should have the CPU or memory request or limits. LimitRanger works when the request to create or update the object is received by the API Server but not at runtime. If a pod has a violating limit before the limit is applied, it will keep running. Ideally, limits should be applied to the namespace when it is created.

Now that we have looked at a couple of features that can be used for proactive resource management, we switch gears and look at tools that can help us monitor the cluster and notify us before matters deteriorate.

Monitoring resources in Kubernetes

As we discussed earlier, resource monitoring is an essential step for ensuring the availability of your services in your cluster. Resource monitoring uncovers early signs or symptoms of service unavailability in your clusters. Resource monitoring is often complemented with alert management to ensure that stakeholders are notified as soon as any problems, or symptoms associated with any problems, in the cluster are observed.

In this section, we first look at some built-in monitors provided by Kubernetes, including Kubernetes Dashboard and Metrics Server. We look at how we can set it up and discuss how to use these tools efficiently. Next, we look at some open source tools that can plug into your Kubernetes cluster and provide far more in-depth insight than the built-in tools.

Built-in monitors

Let's look at some tools provided by Kubernetes that are used for monitoring Kubernetes resources and objects – Metrics Server and Kubernetes Dashboard.

Kubernetes Dashboard

Kubernetes Dashboard provides a web UI for cluster administrators to create, manage, and monitor cluster objects and resources. Cluster administrators can also create pods, services, and DaemonSets using the dashboard. The dashboard shows the state of the cluster and any errors in the cluster.

Kubernetes Dashboard provides all the functionality a cluster administrator requires in order to manage resources and objects within the cluster. Given the functionality of the dashboard, access to the dashboard should be limited to cluster administrators. The dashboard has a login functionality starting v1.7.0. In 2018, a privilege escalation vulnerability (CVE-2018-18264) was identified in the dashboard that allowed unauthenticated users to log in to the dashboard. There were no known in-the-wild exploits for this issue, but this simple vulnerability could have wreaked havoc on many Kubernetes distributions.

Current login functionality allows logging in using a service account and `kubeconfig`. It is recommended that service account tokens should be used to access Kubernetes Dashboard:

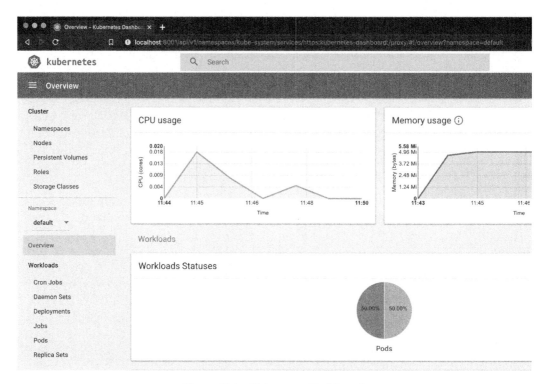

Figure 10.1 – Kubernetes Dashboard

To allow a service account to use the Kubernetes dashboard, you need to add the `cluster-admin` role to the service account. Let's look at an example of how a service account can be used to access the Kubernetes dashboard:

1. Create a service account in the default namespace:

```
$kubectl create serviceaccount dashboard-admin-sa
```

2. Associate the `cluster-admin` role with the service account:

```
$kubectl create clusterrolebinding dashboard-
admin-sa --clusterrole=cluster-admin
--serviceaccount=default:dashboard-admin-sa
```

3. Fetch the token for the service account:

```
$ kubectl describe serviceaccount dashboard-admin-sa
Name:                  dashboard-admin-sa
Namespace:             default
Labels:                <none>
Annotations:           <none>
Image pull secrets:    <none>
Mountable secrets:     dashboard-admin-sa-token-5zwpw
Tokens:                dashboard-admin-sa-token-5zwpw
Events:                <none>
```

4. Use the following command to fetch the token for the service account:

```
$ kubectl describe secrets dashboard-admin-sa-token-5zwpw
Name:        dashboard-admin-sa-token-5zwpw
Namespace:   default
Labels:      <none>
Annotations: kubernetes.io/service-account.name:
dashboard-admin-sa

             kubernetes.io/service-account.uid:
83218a92-915c-11ea-b763-42010a800022
Type:   kubernetes.io/service-account-token
Data
====
ca.crt:      1119 bytes
namespace:   7 bytes
token:       <token>
```

5.   Use the service account token to log in to the dashboard:

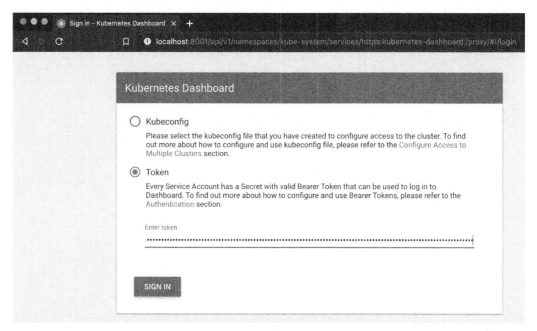

Figure 10.2 – Kubernetes dashboard login

Using Kubernetes Dashboard, administrators have insight into resource availability, resource allocation, Kubernetes objects, and event logs:

Figure 10.3 – Kubernetes Dashboard – resource allocation

The preceding screenshot shows resource allocation on a node for resource requests and limits. The following screenshot highlights the events for a node on the Kubernetes dashboard:

Events

	Message	Source	Sub-object	Count	First seen	Last seen
	Successfully assigned default/nginx-bad to gke-cluster-2-default-pool-cff7b1b9-jv79	default-scheduler	-	1	2020-05-01T04:42 UTC	2020-05-01T04:42 UTC
	Pulling image "nginx-bad"	kubelet gke-cluster-2-default-pool-cff7b1b9-jv79	spec.containers{nginx-bad}	4	2020-05-01T04:42 UTC	2020-05-01T04:44 UTC
⚠	Failed to pull image "nginx-bad": rpc error: code = Unknown desc = Error response from daemon: pull access denied for nginx-bad, repository does not exist or may require 'docker login'	kubelet gke-cluster-2-default-pool-cff7b1b9-jv79	spec.containers{nginx-bad}	4	2020-05-01T04:42 UTC	2020-05-01T04:44 UTC
⚠	Error: ErrImagePull	kubelet gke-cluster-2-default-pool-cff7b1b9-jv79	spec.containers{nginx-bad}	4	2020-05-01T04:42 UTC	2020-05-01T04:44 UTC
	Back-off pulling image "nginx-bad"	kubelet gke-cluster-2-default-pool-cff7b1b9-jv79	spec.containers{nginx-bad}	43	2020-05-01T04:42 UTC	2020-05-01T04:52 UTC
⚠	Error: ImagePullBackOff	kubelet gke-cluster-2-default-pool-cff7b1b9-jv79	spec.containers{nginx-bad}	65	2020-05-01T04:42 UTC	2020-05-01T04:57 UTC

Figure 10.4 – Kubernetes Dashboard – event logs

Kubernetes Dashboard runs as a container on the master node. You can see this by enumerating the Docker containers on the master node:

```
$ docker ps | grep dashboard
a963e6e6a54b        3b08661dc379              "/metrics-
sidecar"        4 minutes ago        Up 4 minutes
k8s_dashboard-metrics-scraper_dashboard-metrics-scraper-
84bfdf55ff-wfxdm_kubernetes-dashboard_5a7ef2a8-b3b4-4e4c-ae85-
11cc8b61c1c1_0
c28f0e2799c1        cdc71b5a8a0e              "/
dashboard --insecu…"    4 minutes ago        Up 4 minutes
k8s_kubernetes-dashboard_kubernetes-dashboard-bc446cc64-czmn8_
kubernetes-dashboard_40630c71-3c6a-447b-ae68-e23603686ede_0
10f0b024a13f        k8s.gcr.io/pause:3.2      "/
pause"        4 minutes ago        Up 4 minutes
k8s_POD_dashboard-metrics-scraper-84bfdf55ff-wfxdm_kubernetes-
dashboard_5a7ef2a8-b3b4-4e4c-ae85-11cc8b61c1c1_0
f9c1e82174d8        k8s.gcr.io/pause:3.2      "/
pause"        4 minutes ago        Up 4 minutes
k8s_POD_kubernetes-dashboard-bc446cc64-czmn8_kubernetes-
dashboard_40630c71-3c6a-447b-ae68-e23603686ede_0
```

The dashboard process runs with a set of arguments on the master node:

```
$ ps aux | grep dashboard
dbus      10727  0.9  1.1 136752 46240 ?           Ssl   05:46
0:02 /dashboard --insecure-bind-address=0.0.0.0 --bind-
address=0.0.0.0 --namespace=kubernetes-dashboard --enable-skip-
login --disable-settings-authorizer
docker    11889  0.0  0.0  11408    556 pts/0      S+    05:51
0:00 grep dashboard
```

Ensure that the dashboard container is running with the following arguments:

- **Disable insecure port**: `--insecure-port` enables Kubernetes Dashboard to receive requests over HTTP. Ensure that it is disabled in production environments.

- **Disable insecure address**: `--insecure-bind-address` should be disabled to avoid a situation where Kubernetes Dashboard is accessible via HTTP.

- **Bind address to localhost**: `--bind-address` should be set to `127.0.0.1` to prevent hosts from being connected over the internet.

- **Enable TLS**: Use `tls-cert-file` and `tls-key-file` to access the dashboard over secure channels.

- **Ensure token authentication mode is enabled**: Authentication mode can be specified using the `--authentication-mode` flag. By default, it is set to `token`. Ensure that basic authentication is not used with the dashboard.

- **Disable insecure login**: Insecure login is used when the dashboard is available via HTTP. This should be disabled by default.

- **Disable skip login**: Skip login allows unauthenticated users to access the Kubernetes dashboard. `--enable-skip-login` enables skip login; this should not be present in production environments.

- **Disable settings authorizer**: `--disable-settings-authorizer` allows unauthenticated users to access the settings page. This should be disabled in production environments.

Metrics Server

Metrics Server aggregates cluster usage data using the Summary API exposed by each `kubelet` on each node. It is registered with `kube-apiserver` using `kube-aggregator`. Metrics Server exposes the collected metrics through the Metrics API, which are used by the horizontal pod autoscalar and the vertical pod autoscalar. `kubectl top`, which is used to debug clusters, also uses the Metrics API. Metrics Server is specifically designed for autoscaling.

Metrics Server is enabled by default on some Kubernetes distributions. You can enable it on `minikube` by using the following command:

```
$ minikube addons enable metrics-server
```

You can check whether Metrics Server is enabled by using the following command:

```
$ kubectl get apiservices | grep metrics
v1beta1.metrics.k8s.io                      kube-system/metrics-
server     True           7m17s
```

Once Metrics Server is enabled, it takes some time to query the Summary API and co-relate the data. You can see the current metrics by using `kubectl top node`:

```
$ kubectl top node
NAME          CPU(cores)     CPU%     MEMORY(bytes)     MEMORY%
minikube      156m           7%       1140Mi            30%


$ kubectl top pod
NAME           CPU(cores)     MEMORY(bytes)
nginx-good     0m             2Mi
```

Similar to other services and components, Metrics Server also has configuration parameters. In production clusters, make sure that Metrics Server does not use the `--kubelet-insecure-tls` flag, which allows Metrics Server to skip verification of certificates by the CA.

Third-party monitoring tools

Third-party monitoring tools integrate in Kubernetes to provide many more features and insights into the health of Kubernetes resources. In this section, we will discuss Prometheus and Grafana, which are the most popular monitoring tools in the open source community.

Prometheus and Grafana

Prometheus is an open source instrumentation and data collection framework developed by SoundCloud and adopted by CNCF. Prometheus can be used to see time series data for different data points. Prometheus uses a pull system. It sends an HTTP request called a scrape, which fetches data from the system components, including API Server, `node-exporter`, and `kubelet`. The response to the scrape and the metrics are stored in a custom database on the Prometheus server.

Let's see how Prometheus can be set up to monitor a namespace in Kubernetes:

1. Create a namespace:

   ```
   $kubectl create namespace monitoring
   ```

2. Define a cluster role to read Kubernetes objects such as pods, nodes, and services and add the role binding to a service account. In this example, we are using the default service account:

   ```
   $ cat prometheus-role.yaml
   apiVersion: rbac.authorization.k8s.io/v1beta1
   kind: ClusterRole
   metadata:
     name: prometheus
   rules:
   - apiGroups: [""]
     resources:
     - nodes
     - nodes/proxy
     - services
     - endpoints
     - pods
     verbs: ["get", "list", "watch"]
   - apiGroups:
     - extensions
     resources:
     - ingresses
     verbs: ["get", "list", "watch"]
   - nonResourceURLs: ["/metrics"]
     verbs: ["get"]
   ```

```
$ kubectl create -f prometheus-role.yaml
clusterrole.rbac.authorization.k8s.io/prometheus created
```

Now, we create a role binding to associate the role with the default service account:

```
$ cat prometheus-rolebinding.yaml
apiVersion: rbac.authorization.k8s.io/v1beta1
kind: ClusterRoleBinding
metadata:
  name: prometheus
roleRef:
  apiGroup: rbac.authorization.k8s.io
  kind: ClusterRole
  name: prometheus
subjects:
- kind: ServiceAccount
  name: default
  namespace: monitoring
```

3. Prometheus uses ConfigMap to specify the scrape rule. The following rule-scrapes the `kube-apiserver`. Multiple scraps can be defined to fetch metrics:

```
$ cat config_prometheus.yaml
apiVersion: v1
kind: ConfigMap
metadata:
  name: prometheus-server-conf
  labels:
    name: prometheus-server-conf
  namespace: monitoring
data:
  prometheus.yml: |-
    global:
      scrape_interval: 5s
      evaluation_interval: 5s
    scrape_configs:
      - job_name: 'kubernetes-apiservers'
        kubernetes_sd_configs:
        - role: endpoints
```

```
scheme: https
tls_config:
    ca_file: /var/run/secrets/kubernetes.io/
serviceaccount/ca.crt
    bearer_token_file: /var/run/secrets/kubernetes.io/
serviceaccount/token
    relabel_configs:
    - source_labels: [__meta_kubernetes_namespace, __
meta_kubernetes_service_name, __meta_kubernetes_endpoint_
port_name]
        action: keep
        regex: default;kubernetes;https
```

4. Create a deployment for Prometheus:

```
spec:
    containers:
    - name: prometheus
        image: prom/prometheus:v2.12.0
        args:
            - "--config.file=/etc/prometheus/prometheus.
yml"
            - "--storage.tsdb.path=/prometheus/"
        ports:
            - containerPort: 9090
        volumeMounts:
        - name: prometheus-config-volume
            mountPath: /etc/prometheus/
        - name: prometheus-storage-volume
            mountPath: /prometheus/
    volumes:
    - name: prometheus-config-volume
        configMap:
        defaultMode: 420
        name: prometheus-server-conf

    - name: prometheus-storage-volume
        emptyDir: {}
```

5. Once deployment is successful, port forwarding or Kubernetes services can be used to access the dashboard:

```
$ kubectl port-forward <prometheus-pod> 8080:9090 -n
monitoring
```

This enables port forwarding for the Prometheus pod. Now, you can access it using the cluster IP on port 8080:

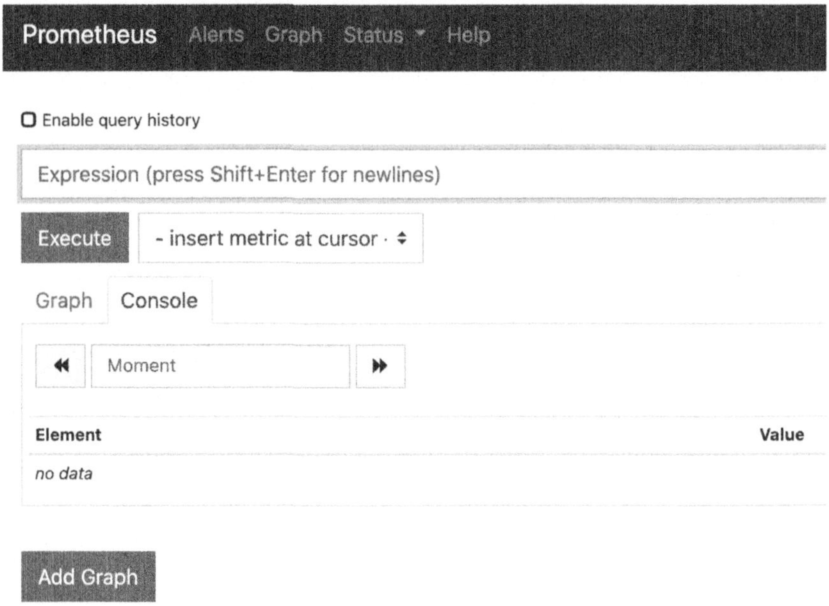

Figure 10.5 – Prometheus Dashboard

Queries can be entered as expressions and the results viewed as **Graph** or **Console** messages. Using Prometheus queries, cluster administrators can view the status of clusters, nodes, and services that are being monitored by Prometheus.

Let's look at some examples of Prometheus queries that will be helpful for cluster administrators:

- Kubernetes CPU usage:

```
sum(rate(container_cpu_usage_seconds_total{container_
name!="POD",pod_name!=""}[5m]))
```

- Kubernetes CPU usage by namespace:

```
sum(rate(container_cpu_usage_seconds_total{container_
name!="POD",namespace!=""}[5m])) by (namespace)
```

- CPU requests by pod:

```
sum(kube_pod_container_resource_requests_cpu_cores) by
(pod)
```

Let's look at CPU usage by namespace for the demo cluster:

Figure 10.6 – CPU usage by namespace

Prometheus also allows cluster administrators to set alerts using ConfigMaps:

```
prometheus.rules: |-
    groups:
    - name: Demo Alert
      rules:
      - alert: High Pod Memory
        expr: sum(container_memory_usage_bytes{pod!=""})  by
(pod) > 1000000000
        for: 1m
        labels:
          severity: high
        annotations:
          summary: High Memory Usage
```

This alert triggers an alert with a label severity of `high` when container memory usage is greater than `1000` MB for `1` minute:

Alerts

☐ Show annotations

/etc/prometheus/prometheus.rules > demo alert

High Pod Memory (1 active)

```
alert: High
  Pod Memory
expr: sum
  by(pod) (container_memory_usage_bytes{pod!=""}) > 1e+09
for: 1m
labels:
  severity: high
annotations:
  summary: High Memory Usage
```

Labels	State	Active Since	Value
alertname="High Pod Memory" pod="prod" severity="high"	PENDING	2020-06-28 21:52:02.544330682 +0000 UTC	2.105532416e+09

Figure 10.7 – Prometheus Alerts

Using `Alertmanager` with Prometheus helps deduplicate, group, and route alerts from applications such as Prometheus and route it to integrated clients, including email, OpsGenie, and PagerDuty.

Prometheus integrates well with other third-party tools that enhance data visualization and alert management. Grafana is one such tool. Grafana allows visualization, querying, and alerting on data retrieved from Prometheus.

Let's now look at how we set up Grafana with Prometheus:

1. Grafana needs a data source for ingestion; in this case, it is Prometheus. The data source can be added using the UI or can be specified using a ConfigMap:

```
$ cat grafana-data.yaml
apiVersion: v1
kind: ConfigMap
metadata:
  name: grafana-datasources
  namespace: monitoring
data:
  prometheus.yaml: |-
```

```json
{
    "apiVersion": 1,
    "datasources": [
        {
            "access":"proxy",
            "editable": true,
            "name": "prometheus",
            "orgId": 1,
            "type": "prometheus",
            "url": "http://192.168.99.128:30000",
            "version": 1
        }
    ]
}
```

2. Create a deployment for Grafana:

```yaml
apiVersion: apps/v1
kind: Deployment
metadata:
  name: grafana
  namespace: monitoring
spec:
  replicas: 1
  selector:
    matchLabels:
      app: grafana
  template:
    metadata:
      name: grafana
      labels:
        app: grafana
    spec:
      containers:
      - name: grafana
        image: grafana/grafana:latest
        ports:
```

```
        - name: grafana
          containerPort: 3000
        volumeMounts:
          - mountPath: /var/lib/grafana
            name: grafana-storage
          - mountPath: /etc/grafana/provisioning/
datasources
            name: grafana-datasources
            readOnly: false
      volumes:
        - name: grafana-storage
          emptyDir: {}
        - name: grafana-datasources
          configMap:
            name: grafana-datasources
```

3. Port forwarding or Kubernetes services can then be used to access the dashboard:

```
apiVersion: v1
kind: Service
metadata:
  name: grafana
  namespace: monitoring
  annotations:
      prometheus.io/scrape: 'true'
      prometheus.io/port:    '3000'
spec:
  selector:
    app: grafana
  type: NodePort
  ports:
    - port: 3000
      targetPort: 3000
      nodePort: 32000
```

4. The dashboard, by default, has `admin` as a username and password. Once logged in, you can either set up a new dashboard or import one from Grafana. To import one, you can click **+ > Import**, where you will be presented with the following screen. Enter `315` in the first textbox to import dashboard 315 from Grafana:

Figure 10.8 – Importing a dashboard in Grafana

5. This dashboard was created by Instrumentisto Team. On import, all fields on the next screen will be filled up automatically:

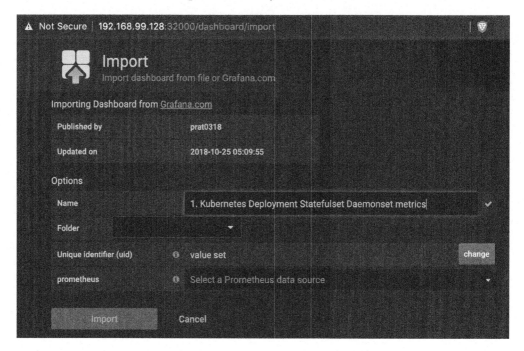

Figure 10.9 – Grafana Dashboard – 315

6. A new dashboard can also be created with custom Prometheus queries:

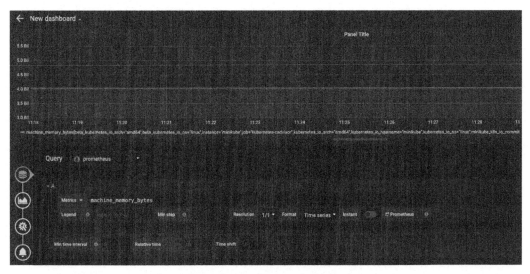

Figure 10.10 – Custom dashboard

7. Similar to Prometheus, you can set up alerts on each dashboard:

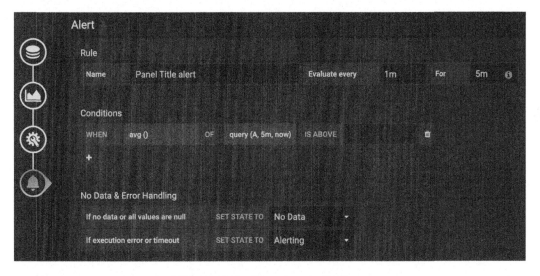

Figure 10.11 – New alerts in Grafana

There are other tools that integrate with Prometheus that make it such a valuable tool for DevOps and cluster administrators.

Summary

In this chapter, we discussed availability as an important part of the CIA triad. We discussed the importance of resource management and real-time resource monitoring from a security standpoint. We then introduced resource requests and limits, core concepts for resource management in Kubernetes. Next, we discussed resource management and how cluster administrators can proactively ensure that Kubernetes objects can be prevented from misbehaving.

We dived deep into the details of namespace resource quotas and limit ranges and looked at examples on how to set it up. We then shifted gears to resource monitoring. We looked at some built-in monitors that are available as part of Kubernetes, including Dashboard and Metrics Server. Finally, we looked at a number of third-party tools – Prometheus and Grafana – that are much more powerful and preferred by most cluster administrators and DevOps engineers.

Using resource management, cluster administrators can ensure that services in a Kubernetes cluster have sufficient resources available for operation and that malicious or misbehaving entities don't hog all the resources. Resource monitoring, on the other hand, helps to identify issues and the symptoms in real time. With alert management used in conjunction with resource monitoring, stakeholders are notified of symptoms, such as reduced disk space or high memory consumption, as soon as they occur, ensuring that downtime is minimal.

In the next chapter, we will discuss Defense in Depth in detail. We will look at how cluster administrators and DevOps engineers can supplement secure configuration, resource management, and resource monitoring with a layered approach to security. Defense in Depth will introduce more toolkits to ensure that attacks are easily detected and mitigated in production environments.

Questions

1. What is the difference between a resource request and limits?
2. Define a resource quota that limits the memory limit to 500 mi.
3. How does limit-range differ from resource-quotas?
4. What is the recommended authentication method for Kubernetes Dashboard?
5. Which is the most widely recommended resource monitoring tool?

Further references

You can refer to the following links for more information on topics covered in this chapter:

- Denial-of-service attacks on electrical systems: `https://www.cnbc.com/2019/05/02/ddos-attack-caused-interruptions-in-power-system-operations-doe.html`

- Amazon Route53 DDoS: `https://www.cpomagazine.com/cyber-security/ddos-attack-on-amazon-web-services-raises-cloud-safety-concerns/`

- Limit Ranger design documentation: `https://github.com/kubernetes/community/blob/master/contributors/design-proposals/resource-management/admission_control_limit_range.md`

- Kubernetes Dashboard: `https://github.com/kubernetes/dashboard/blob/master/docs/README.md`

- Privilege escalation using Kubernetes Dashboard: `https://sysdig.com/blog/privilege-escalation-kubernetes-dashboard/`

- Metrics Server: `https://github.com/kubernetes-sigs/metrics-server`

- Aggregated API servers: `https://github.com/kubernetes/community/blob/master/contributors/design-proposals/api-machinery/aggregated-api-servers.md`

- Prometheus queries: `https://prometheus.io/docs/prometheus/latest/querying/examples/`

- Grafana documentation: `https://grafana.com/docs/grafana/latest/`

11
Defense in Depth

Defense in depth is an approach in cybersecurity that applies multiple layers of security controls to protect valuable assets. In a traditional or monolithic IT environment, we can list quite a few: authentication, encryption, authorization, logging, intrusion detection, antivirus, a **virtual private network** (**VPN**), firewalls, and so on. You may find that these security controls also exist in the Kubernetes cluster (and they should).

We've discussed topics such as authentication, authorization, admission controllers, securing Kubernetes components, securing a configuration, hardening images, and Kubernetes workloads in the previous chapters. All these build up different security control layers to protect your Kubernetes cluster. In this chapter, we're going to discuss topics that build up additional security control layers, and these are most related to runtime defense in a Kubernetes cluster. These are the questions we're going to address in this chapter: Does your cluster expose any sensitive data? If an attack happens in the Kubernetes cluster, can you detect the attack? Can your Kubernetes cluster sustain the attack? How do you respond to the attack?

In this chapter, we will talk about Kubernetes auditing, then we will introduce the concept of high availability and talk about how we can apply high availability in the Kubernetes cluster. Next, we will introduce Vault, a handy secrets management product for the Kubernetes cluster. Then, we will talk about how to use Falco to detect anomalous activities in the Kubernetes cluster. Last but not least, we will introduce Sysdig Inspect and **Checkpoint and Resource In Userspace** (also known as **CRIU**) for forensics.

The following topics will be covered in this chapter:

- Introducing Kubernetes auditing

- Enabling high availability in a Kubernetes cluster

- Managing secrets with Vault

- Detecting anomalies with Falco

- Conducting forensics with Sysdig Inspect and CRIU

Introducing Kubernetes auditing

Kubernetes auditing was introduced in the 1.11 version. Kubernetes auditing records events such as creating a deployment, patching pods, deleting namespaces, and more in a chronological order. With auditing, a Kubernetes cluster administrator is able to answer questions such as the following:

- What happened? (A pod is created and what kind of pod it is)

- Who did it? (From user/admin)

- When did it happen? (The timestamp of the event)

- Where did it happen? (In which namespace is the pod created?)

From a security standpoint, auditing enables DevOps and the security team to do better anomaly detection and prevention by tracking events happening inside the Kubernetes cluster.

In a Kubernetes cluster, it is `kube-apiserver` that does the auditing. When a request (for example, create a namespace) is sent to `kube-apiserver`, the request may go through multiple stages. There will be an event generated per stage. The following are the known stages:

- `RequestReceived`: The event is generated as soon as the request is received by the audit handler without processing it.

- `RequestStarted`: The event is generated between the time that the response header is sent and the response body is sent, and only applies for long-running requests such as `watch`.

- `RequestComplete`: The event is generated when the response body is sent.

- `Panic`: The event is generated when panic occurs.

In this section, we will first introduce the Kubernetes audit policy, and then show you how to enable a Kubernetes audit and a couple of ways to persist audit records.

Kubernetes audit policy

As it is not realistic to record everything happening inside the Kubernetes cluster, an audit policy allows users to define rules about what kind of event should be recorded and how much detail of the event should be recorded. When an event is processed by `kube-apiserver`, it compares the list of rules in the audit policy in order. The first matching rules also dictate the audit level of the event. Let's take a look at what an audit policy looks like. Here is an example:

```
apiVersion: audit.k8s.io/v1 # This is required.
kind: Policy
# Skip generating audit events for all requests in
RequestReceived stage. This can be either set at the policy
level or rule level.
omitStages:
  - "RequestReceived"
rules:
  # Log pod changes at RequestResponse level
  - level: RequestResponse
    verbs: ["create", "update"]
    namespace: ["ns1", "ns2", "ns3"]
    resources:
    - group: ""
# Only check access to resource "pods", not the sub-resource of
pods which is consistent with the RBAC policy.
      resources: ["pods"]
# Log "pods/log", "pods/status" at Metadata level
  - level: Metadata
    resources:
    - group: ""
      resources: ["pods/log", "pods/status"]
# Don't log authenticated requests to certain non-resource URL
paths.
  - level: None
    userGroups: ["system:authenticated"]
    nonResourceURLs: ["/api*", "/version"]
```

```
# Log configmap and secret changes in all other namespaces at
the Metadata level.
  - level: Metadata
    resources:
    - group: "" # core API group
      resources: ["secrets", "configmaps"]
```

You can configure multiple audit rules in the audit policy. Each audit rule will be configured by the following fields:

- `level`: The audit level that defines the verbosity of the audit event.

- `resources`: The Kubernetes objects under audit. Resources can be specified by an **Application Programming Interface (API)** group and an object type.

- `nonResourcesURL`: A non-resource **Uniform Resource Locator (URL)** path that is not associated with any resources under audit.

- `namespace`: Decides which Kubernetes objects from which namespaces will be under audit. An empty string will be used to select non-namespaced objects, and an empty list implies every namespace.

- `verb`: Decides the specific operation of Kubernetes objects that will be under audit—for example, `create`, `update`, or `delete`.

- `users`: Decides the authenticated user the audit rule applies to

- `userGroups`: Decides the authenticated user group the audit rule applies to.

- `omitStages`: Skips generating events on the given stages. This can also be set at the policy level.

The audit policy allows you to configure a policy at a fine-grained level by specifying `verb`, `namespace`, `resources`, and more. It is the audit level of the rule that defines how much detail of the event should be recorded. There are four audit levels, detailed as follows:

- `None`: Do not log events that match the audit rule.

- `Metadata`: When an event matches the audit rule, log the metadata (such as `user`, `timestamp`, `resource`, `verb`, and more) of the request to `kube-apiserver`.

- `Request`: When an event matches the audit rule, log the metadata as well as the request body. This does not apply for the non-resource URL.

- `RequestResponse`: When an event matches the audit rule, log the metadata, request-and-response body. This does not apply for the non-resource request.

The request-level event is more verbose than the metadata level events, while the `RequestResponse` level event is more verbose than the request-level event. The high verbosity requires more **input/output (I/O)** throughputs and storage. It is quite necessary to understand the differences between the audit levels so that you can define audit rules properly, both for resource consumption and security. With an audit policy successfully configured, let's take a look at what audit events look like. The following is a metadata-level audit event:

```
{
  "kind": "Event",
  "apiVersion": "audit.k8s.io/v1",
  "level": "Metadata",
  "auditID": "05698e93-6ad7-4f4e-8ae9-046694bee469",
  "stage": "ResponseComplete",
  "requestURI": "/api/v1/namespaces/ns1/pods",
  "verb": "create",
  "user": {
    "username": "admin",
    "uid": "admin",
    "groups": [
      "system:masters",
      "system:authenticated"
    ]
  },
  "sourceIPs": [
    "98.207.36.92"
  ],
  "userAgent": "kubectl/v1.17.4 (darwin/amd64) kubernetes/8d8aa39",
  "objectRef": {
    "resource": "pods",
    "namespace": "ns1",
    "name": "pod-1",
    "apiVersion": "v1"
  },
  "responseStatus": {
    "metadata": {},
```

```
    "code": 201
  },
  "requestReceivedTimestamp": "2020-04-09T07:10:52.471720Z",
  "stageTimestamp": "2020-04-09T07:10:52.485551Z",
  "annotations": {
    "authorization.k8s.io/decision": "allow",
    "authorization.k8s.io/reason": ""
  }
}
```

The preceding audit event shows the user, timestamp, the object being accessed, the authorization decision, and so on. A request-level audit event provides extra information within the requestObject field in the audit event. You will find out the specification of the workload in the requestObject field, as follows:

```
"requestObject": {
  "kind": "Pod",
  "apiVersion": "v1",
  "metadata": {
    "name": "pod-2",
    "namespace": "ns2",
    "creationTimestamp": null,
    ...
  },
  "spec": {
    "containers": [
      {
        "name": "echo",
        "image": "busybox",
        "command": [
          "sh",
          "-c",
          "echo 'this is echo' && sleep 1h"
        ],
        ...
        "imagePullPolicy": "Always"
```

```
        }
      ],
      ...
      "securityContext": {},
    },
```

The RequestResponse-level audit event is the most verbose. The responseObject instance in the event is almost the same as requestObject, with extra information such as resource version and creation timestamp, as shown in the following code block:

```
{
  "responseObject": {
    ...
    "selfLink": "/api/v1/namespaces/ns3/pods/pod-3",
    "uid": "3fd18de1-7a31-11ea-9e8d-0a39f00d8287",
    "resourceVersion": "217243",
    "creationTimestamp": "2020-04-09T07:10:53Z",
    "tolerations": [
      {
        "key": "node.kubernetes.io/not-ready",
        "operator": "Exists",
        "effect": "NoExecute",
        "tolerationSeconds": 300
      },
      {
        "key": "node.kubernetes.io/unreachable",
        "operator": "Exists",
        "effect": "NoExecute",
        "tolerationSeconds": 300
      }
    ],
    ...
  },
}
```

Please do choose the audit level properly. More verbose logs provide deeper insight into the activities being carried out. However, it does cost more in storage and time to process the audit events. One thing worth mentioning is that if you set a request or a `RequestResponse` audit level on Kubernetes secret objects, the secret content will be recorded in the audit events. If you set the audit level to be more verbose than metadata for Kubernetes objects containing sensitive data, you should use a sensitive data redaction mechanism to avoid secrets being logged in the audit events.

The Kubernetes auditing functionality offers a lot of flexibility to audit Kubernetes objects by object kind, namespace, operations, user, and so on. As Kubernetes auditing is not enabled by default, next, let's look at how to enable Kubernetes auditing and store audit records.

Configuring the audit backend

In order to enable Kubernetes auditing, you need to pass the `--audit-policy-file` flag with your audit policy file when starting `kube-apiserver`. There are two types of audit backends that can be configured to use process audit events: a log backend and a webhook backend. Let's have a look at them.

Log backend

The log backend writes audit events to a file on the master node. The following flags are used to configure the log backend within `kube-apiserver`:

- `--log-audit-path`: Specify the log path on the master node. This is the flag to turn ON or OFF the log backend.

- `--audit-log-maxage`: Specify the maximum number of days to keep the audit records.

- `--audit-log-maxbackup`: Specify the maximum number of audit files to keep on the master node.

- `--audit-log-maxsize`: Specify the maximum size in megabytes of an audit log file before it gets rotated.

Let's take a look at the webhook backend.

Webhook backend

The webhook backend writes audit events to the remote webhook registered to `kube-apiserver`. To enable the webhook backend, you need to set the `--audit-webhook-config-file` flag with the webhook configuration file. This flag is also specified when starting `kube-apiserver`. The following is an example of a webhook configuration to register a webhook backend for the Falco service, which will be introduced later in more detail:

```
apiVersion: v1
kind: Config
clusters:
- name: falco
  cluster:
    server: http://$FALCO_SERVICE_CLUSTERIP:8765/k8s_audit
contexts:
- context:
    cluster: falco
    user: ""
  name: default-context
current-context: default-context
preferences: {}
users: []
```

The URL specified in the `server` field (`http://$FALCO_SERVICE_CLUSTERIP:8765/k8s_audit`) is the remote endpoint that the audit events will be sent to. Since version 1.13 of Kubernetes, the webhook backend can be configured dynamically via the `AuditSink` object, which is still in the alpha stage.

In this section, we talked about Kubernetes auditing by introducing the audit policy and audit backends. In the next section, we will talk about high availability in the Kubernetes cluster.

Enabling high availability in a Kubernetes cluster

Availability refers to the ability of the user to access the service or system. The high availability of a system ensures an agreed level of uptime of the system. For example, if there is only one instance to serve the service and the instance is down, users can no longer access the service. A service with high availability is served by multiple instances. When one instance is down, the standby instance or backup instance can still provide the service. The following diagram describes services with and without high availability:

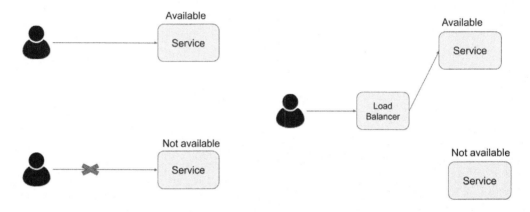

Figure 11.1 – Services with and without high availability

In a Kubernetes cluster, there will usually be more than one worker node. The high availability of the cluster is guaranteed as even if one worker node is down, there are some other worker nodes to host the workload. However, high availability is more than running multiple nodes in the cluster. In this section, we will look at high availability in Kubernetes clusters from three levels: workloads, Kubernetes components, and cloud infrastructure.

Enabling high availability of Kubernetes workloads

For Kubernetes workloads such as a deployment and a StatefulSet, you can specify the `replicas` field in the specification for how many replicated pods are running for the microservice, and controllers will ensure there will be x number of pods running on different worker nodes in the cluster, as specified in the `replicas` field. A DaemonSet is a special workload; the controller will ensure there will be one pod running on every node in the cluster, assuming your Kubernetes cluster has more than one node. So, specifying more than one replica in the deployment or the StatefulSet, or using a DaemonSet, will ensure the high availability of your workload. In order to ensure the high availability of the workload, the high availability of Kubernetes components needs to be ensured as well.

Enabling high availability of Kubernetes components

High availability also applies to the Kubernetes components. Let's review a few critical Kubernetes components, as follows:

- `kube-apiserver`: The Kubernetes API server (`kube-apiserver`) is a control plane component that validates and configures data for objects such as pods, services, and controllers. It interacts with the objects using **REepresentational State Transfer** (**REST**) requests.

- `etcd`: `etcd` is a high-availability key-value store used to store data such as configuration, state, and metadata. Its `watch` functionality provides Kubernetes with the ability to listen for updates to a configuration and make changes accordingly.

- `kube-scheduler`: `kube-scheduler` is a default scheduler for Kubernetes. It watches for newly created pods and assigns the pods to the nodes.

- `kube-controller-manager`: The Kubernetes controller manager is a combination of the core controllers that watch for state updates and make changes to the cluster accordingly.

If the `kube-apiserver` is down, then basically your cluster is down, as users or other Kubernetes components rely on communicating to the `kube-apiserver` to perform their tasks. If `etcd` is down, no states of the cluster and objects are available to be consumed. `kube-scheduler` and `kube-controller-manager` are also important to make sure the workloads are running properly in the cluster. All these components are running on the master node, to ensure the high availability of the components. One straightforward way is to bring up multiple master nodes for your Kubernetes cluster, either via `kops` or `kubeadm`. You will find something like this:

```
$ kubectl get pods -n kube-system
...
etcd-manager-events-ip-172-20-109-109.ec2.internal          1/1
Running   0          4h15m
etcd-manager-events-ip-172-20-43-65.ec2.internal            1/1
Running   0          4h16m
etcd-manager-events-ip-172-20-67-151.ec2.internal           1/1
Running   0          4h16m
etcd-manager-main-ip-172-20-109-109.ec2.internal            1/1
Running   0          4h15m
```

etcd-manager-main-ip-172-20-43-65.ec2.internal Running 0 4h15m	1/1
etcd-manager-main-ip-172-20-67-151.ec2.internal Running 0 4h16m	1/1
kube-apiserver-ip-172-20-109-109.ec2.internal Running 3 4h15m	1/1
kube-apiserver-ip-172-20-43-65.ec2.internal Running 4 4h16m	1/1
kube-apiserver-ip-172-20-67-151.ec2.internal Running 4 4h15m	1/1
kube-controller-manager-ip-172-20-109-109.ec2.internal Running 0 4h15m	1/1
kube-controller-manager-ip-172-20-43-65.ec2.internal Running 0 4h16m	1/1
kube-controller-manager-ip-172-20-67-151.ec2.internal Running 0 4h15m	1/1
kube-scheduler-ip-172-20-109-109.ec2.internal Running 0 4h15m	1/1
kube-scheduler-ip-172-20-43-65.ec2.internal Running 0 4h15m	1/1
kube-scheduler-ip-172-20-67-151.ec2.internal Running 0 4h16m	1/1

Now you have multiple kube-apiserver pods, etcd pods, kube-controller-manager pods, and kube-scheduler pods running in the kube-system namespace, and they're running on different master nodes. There are some other components such as kubelet and kube-proxy that are running on every node, so, their availability is guaranteed by the availability of the nodes, and kube-dns are spun up with more than one pod by default, so their high availability is ensured. No matter if your Kubernetes cluster is running on the public cloud or in a private data center—the infrastructure is the pillar to support the availability of the Kubernetes cluster. Next, we will talk about the high availability of a cloud infrastructure and use cloud providers as an example.

Enabling high availability of a cloud infrastructure

Cloud providers offers cloud services all over the world through multiple data centers located in different areas. Cloud users can choose in which region and zone (the actual data center) to host their service. Regions and zones provide isolation from most types of physical infrastructure and infrastructure software service failures. Note that the availability of a cloud infrastructure also impacts the services running on your Kubernetes cluster if the cluster is hosted in the cloud. You should leverage the high availability of the cloud and ultimately ensure the high availability of the service running on the Kubernetes cluster. The following code block provides an example of specifying zones using kops to leverage the high availability of a cloud infrastructure:

```
export NODE_SIZE=${NODE_SIZE:-t2.large}
export MASTER_SIZE=${MASTER_SIZE:-t2.medium}
export ZONES=${ZONES:-"us-east-1a,us-east-1b,us-east-1c"}
export KOPS_STATE_STORE="s3://my-k8s-state-store2/"

kops create cluster k8s-clusters.k8s-demo-zone.com \
  --cloud aws \
  --node-count 3 \
  --zones $ZONES \
  --node-size $NODE_SIZE \
  --master-size $MASTER_SIZE \
  --master-zones $ZONES \
  --networking calico \
  --kubernetes-version 1.14.3 \
  --yes \
```

The nodes of the Kubernetes clusters look like this:

```
$ kops validate cluster
...
INSTANCE GROUPS
NAME                ROLE   MACHINETYPE MIN   MAX   SUBNETS
master-us-east-1a   Master t2.medium   1     1
us-east-1a
master-us-east-1b   Master t2.medium   1     1
us-east-1b
```

master-us-east-1c us-east-1c	Master	t2.medium	1	1	
nodes 1a,us-east-1b,us-east-1c	Node	t2.large	3	3	us-east-

The preceding code block shows three master nodes running on the `us-east-1a`, `us-east-1b`, and `us-east-1c` availability zones respectively. So, as worker nodes, even if one of the data centers is down or under maintenance, both master nodes and worker nodes can still function in other data centers.

In this section, we've talked about the high availability of Kubernetes workloads, Kubernetes components, and a cloud infrastructure. Let's use the following diagram to recap on the high availability of a Kubernetes cluster:

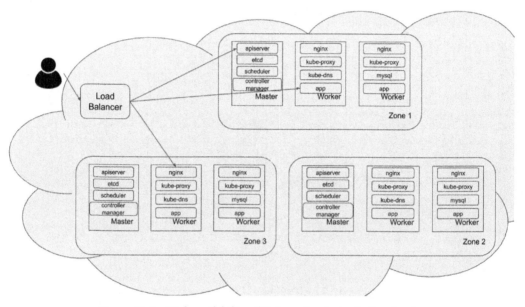

Figure 11.2 – High availability of Kubernetes cluster in the cloud

Now, let's move to the next topic about managing secrets in the Kubernetes cluster.

Managing secrets with Vault

Secrets management is a big topic, and many open source and proprietary solutions have been developed to help solve the secrets management problem on different platforms. So, in Kubernetes, its built-in `Secret` object is used to store secret data, and the actual data is stored in `etcd` along with other Kubernetes objects. By default, the secret data is stored in plaintext (encoded format) in `etcd`. `etcd` can be configured to encrypt secrets at rest. Similarly, if `etcd` is not configured to encrypt communication using **Transport Layer Security (TLS)**, secret data is transferred in plaintext too. Unless the security requirement is very low, it is recommended to use a third-party solution to manage secrets in a Kubernetes cluster.

In this section, we're going to introduce Vault, a **Cloud Native Computing Foundation (CNCF)** secrets management project. Vault supports secure storage of secrets, dynamic secrets' generation, data encryption, key revocation, and so on. In this section, we will focus on the use case of how to store and provision secrets for applications in the Kubernetes cluster using Vault. Now, let's see how to set up Vault for the Kubernetes cluster.

Setting up Vault

You can deploy Vault in the Kubernetes cluster using `helm`, as follows:

```
helm install vault --set='server.dev.enabled=true' https://
github.com/hashicorp/vault-helm/archive/v0.4.0.tar.gz
```

Note that `server.dev.enabled=true` is set. This is good for a development environment but is not recommended to be set in a production environment. You should see two pods are running, as follows:

```
$ kubectl get pods
NAME                                      READY    STATUS
RESTARTS      AGE
vault-0                                   1/1      Running    0
80s
vault-agent-injector-7fd6b9588b-fgsnj     1/1      Running    0
80s
```

The `vault-0` pod is the one to manage and store secrets, while the `vault-agent-injector-7fd6b9588b-fgsnj` pod is responsible for injecting secrets into pods with special vault annotation, which we will show in more detail in the *Provisioning and rotating secrets* section. Next, let's create an example secret for a `postgres` database connection, like this:

```
vault kv put secret/postgres username=alice password=pass
```

Note that the preceding command needs to be executed inside the `vault-0` pod. Since you want to restrict only the relevant application in the Kubernetes cluster to access the secret, you may want to define a policy to achieve that, as follows:

```
cat <<EOF > /home/vault/app-policy.hcl
path "secret*" {
  capabilities = ["read"]
}
EOF


vault policy write app /home/vault/app-policy.hcl
```

Now, you have a policy defining a privilege to read the secret under the `secret` path, such as `secret/postgres`. Next, you want to associate the policy with allowed entities, such as a service account in Kubernetes. This can be done by executing the following commands:

```
vault auth enable kubernetes
vault write auth/kubernetes/config \
    token_reviewer_jwt="$(cat /var/run/secrets/kubernetes.io/serviceaccount/token)" \
    kubernetes_host=https://${KUBERNETES_PORT_443_TCP_ADDR}:443 \
    kubernetes_ca_cert=@/var/run/secrets/kubernetes.io/serviceaccount/ca.crt
vault write auth/kubernetes/role/myapp \
    bound_service_account_names=app \
    bound_service_account_namespaces=demo \
    policies=app \
    ttl=24h
```

Vault can leverage naive authentication from Kubernetes and then bind the secret access policy to the service account. Now, the service account app in the namespace demo can access the `postgres` secret. Now, let's deploy a demo application in the `vault-app.yaml` file, as follows:

```
apiVersion: apps/v1
kind: Deployment
metadata:
```

```
    name: app
    labels:
      app: vault-agent-demo
spec:
  selector:
    matchLabels:
      app: vault-agent-demo
  replicas: 1
  template:
    metadata:
      annotations:
      labels:
        app: vault-agent-demo
    spec:
      serviceAccountName: app
      containers:
      - name: app
        image: jweissig/app:0.0.1
---
apiVersion: v1
kind: ServiceAccount
metadata:
  name: app
  labels:
    app: vault-agent-demo
```

Note that in the preceding .yaml file, there is no annotation added yet, so the secret is not injected, nor is the sidecar container added when the application is created. The code can be seen in the following snippet:

```
$ kubectl get pods
NAME                                READY     STATUS
RESTARTS     AGE
app-668b8bcdb9-js9mm                1/1       Running     0
3m23s
```

Next, we will show how secret injection works.

Provisioning and rotating secrets

The reason we don't show secret injection when the application is deployed is that we want to show you the detailed difference before and after injection to the demo application pod. Now, let's patch the deployment with the following Vault annotations:

```
$ cat patch-template-annotation.yaml
spec:
  template:
    metadata:
      annotations:
        vault.hashicorp.com/agent-inject: "true"
        vault.hashicorp.com/agent-inject-status: "update"
        vault.hashicorp.com/agent-inject-secret-postgres:
"secret/postgres"
        vault.hashicorp.com/agent-inject-template-postgres: |
          {{- with secret "secret/postgres" -}}
          postgresql://{{ .Data.data.username }}:{{ .Data.data.
password }}@postgres:5432/wizard
          {{- end }}
        vault.hashicorp.com/role: "myapp"
```

The preceding annotation dictates which secret will be injected, and in what format and using which role. Once we update the demo application deployment, we will find the secret has been injected, as follows:

```
$ kubectl get pods
NAME                                READY    STATUS
RESTARTS      AGE
app-68d47bb844-2hlrb                2/2      Running     0
13s
$ kubectl -n demo exec -it app-68d47bb844-2hlrb -c app -- cat /
vault/secrets/postgres
postgresql://alice:pass@postgres:5432/wizard
```

And let's look at the specification of the pod (not the patched deployment)—you will find the following (marked in bold) were added, compared to the specification of the patched deployment:

```
containers:
- image: jweissig/app:0.0.1
  ...
  volumeMounts:
  - mountPath: /vault/secrets
    name: vault-secrets
- args:
  - echo ${VAULT_CONFIG?} | base64 -d > /tmp/config.json &&
vault agent -config=/tmp/config.json
  command:
  - /bin/sh
  - -ec
  image: vault:1.3.2
  name: vault-agent
  volumeMounts:
  - mountPath: /vault/secrets
    name: vault-secrets
initContainers:
- args:
  - echo ${VAULT_CONFIG?} | base64 -d > /tmp/config.json &&
vault agent -config=/tmp/config.json
  command:
  - /bin/sh
  - -ec
  image: vault:1.3.2
  name: vault-agent-init
  volumeMounts:
  - mountPath: /vault/secrets
    name: vault-secrets
volumes:
- emptyDir:
    medium: Memory
  name: vault-secrets
```

A few things worth mentioning from the preceding changes listed: one `init` container named `vault-agent-init` and one sidecar container named `vault-agent` have been injected, as well as an `emptyDir` type volume named `vault-secrets`. That's why you saw two containers are running in the demo application pod after the patch. Also, the `vault-secrets` volume is mounted in the `init` container, the `sidecar` container, and the `app` container with the `/vault/secrets/` directory. The secret is stored in the `vault-secrets` volume. The pod specification modification is done by the `vault-agent-injector` pod through a predefined mutating webhook configuration (installed via `helm`), as follows:

```
apiVersion: admissionregistration.k8s.io/v1beta1
kind: MutatingWebhookConfiguration
metadata:
  ...
  name: vault-agent-injector-cfg
webhooks:
- admissionReviewVersions:
  - v1beta1
  clientConfig:
    caBundle: <CA_BUNDLE>
    service:
      name: vault-agent-injector-svc
      namespace: demo
      path: /mutate
  failurePolicy: Ignore
  name: vault.hashicorp.com
  namespaceSelector: {}
  rules:
  - apiGroups:
    - ""
    apiVersions:
    - v1
    operations:
    - CREATE
    - UPDATE
    resources:
    - pods
    scope: '*'
```

The mutating webhook configuration registered with `kube-apiserver` basically tells `kube-apiserver` to redirect any pods, create or update the request to the `vault-agent-injector-svc` service in the `demo` namespace. Behind the service is the `vault-agent-injector` pod. Then, the `vault-agent-injector` pod will look up the relevant annotations and inject the `init` container and the `sidecar` container, as well as the volume that stores the secret, to the specification of the pod on request. Why do we need one `init` container and one `sidecar` container? The `init` container is to prepopulate our secret, and the `sidecar` container is to keep that secret data in sync throughout our application's life cycle.

Now, let's update the secret by running the following code and see what happens:

```
vault kv put secret/postgres username=alice password=changeme
```

Now, the password has been updated to `changeme` from `pass` in the `vault` pod. And, on the `demo` application side, we can see from the following code block that it is updated as well, after waiting a few seconds:

```
$ kubectl -n demo exec -it app-68d47bb844-2hlrb -c app -- cat /vault/secrets/postgres
postgresql://alice:changeme@postgres:5432/wizard
```

Vault is a powerful secrets management solution and a lot of its features cannot be covered in a single section. I would encourage you to read the documentation and try it out to understand Vault better. Next, let's talk about runtime threat detection in Kubernetes with Falco.

Detecting anomalies with Falco

Falco is a CNCF open source project that detects anomalous behavior or runtime threats in cloud-native environments, such as a Kubernetes cluster. It is a rule-based runtime detection engine with about 100 out-of-the-box detection rules. In this section, we will first take an overview of Falco, and then we will show you how to write Falco rules so that you can build your own Falco rules to protect your Kubernetes cluster.

An overview of Falco

Falco is widely used to detect anomalous behavior in cloud-native environments, especially in the Kubernetes cluster. So, what is anomaly detection? Basically, it uses behavioral signals to detect security abnormalities, such as leaked credentials or unusual activity, and the behavioral signals can be derived from your knowledge of the entities in terms of what the normal behavior is.

Challenges faced

To identify what normal behaviors are in the Kubernetes cluster is not easy. From a running application's perspective, we may group them into three categories, as follows:

- **Kubernetes components**: `kube-apiserver`, `kube-proxy`, `kubelet`, the **Container Runtime Interface (CRI)** plugin, the **Container Networking Interface (CNI)** plugin, and so on

- **Self-hosted applications**: Java, Node.js, Golang, Python, and so on

- **Vendor services**: Cassandra, Redis, MySQL, NGINX, Tomcat, and so on

Or, from a system's perspective, we have the following types of activities:

- File activities such as open, read, and write

- Process activities such as `execve` and `clone` system calls

- Network activities such as accept, connect, and send

Or, from a Kubernetes object's perspective: `pod`, `secret`, `deployment`, `namespace`, `serviceaccount`, `configmap`, and so on

In order to cover all these activities or behaviors happening in the Kubernetes cluster, we will need rich sources of information. Next, let's talk about the event sources that Falco relies on to do anomalous detection, and how the sources cover the preceding activities and behaviors.

Event sources for anomaly detection

Falco relies on two event sources to do anomalous detection. One is system calls and the other is the Kubernetes audit events. For system call events, Falco uses a kernel module to tap into the stream of system calls on a machine, and then passes those system calls to a user space (`ebpf` is recently supported as well). Within the user space, Falco also enriches the raw system call events with more context such as the process name, container ID, container name, image name, and so on. For Kubernetes audit events, users need to enable the Kubernetes audit policy and register the Kubernetes audit webhook backend with the Falco service endpoint. Then, the Falco engine checks any of the system call events or Kubernetes audit events matching any Falco rules loaded in the engine.

It's also important to talk about the rationale for using system calls and Kubernetes audit events as event sources to do anomalous detection. System calls are a programmatic way for applications to interact with the operating system in order to access resources such as files, devices, the network, and so on. Considering containers are a bunch of processes with their own dedicated namespaces and that they share the same operating system on the node, a system call is the one unified event source that can be used to monitor activities from containers. It doesn't matter what programming language the application is written in; ultimately, all the functions will be translated into system calls to interact with the operating system. Take a look at the following diagram:

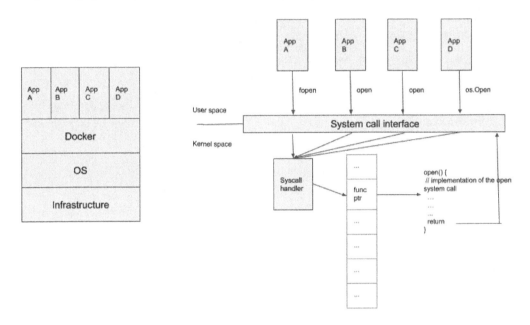

Figure 11.3 – Containers and system calls

In the preceding diagram, there are four containers running different applications. These applications may be written in different programming languages, and all of them call a function to open a file with a different function name (for example, fopen, open, and os.Open). However, from the operating system's perspective, all these applications call the same system call, open, but maybe with different parameters. Falco is able to retrieve events from system calls so that it doesn't matter what kind of applications they are or what kind of programming language is in use.

On the other hand, with the help of Kubernetes audit events, Falco has full visibility into a Kubernetes object's life cycle. This is also important for anomalous detection. For example, it may be abnormal that there is a pod with a busybox image launched as a privileged pod in a production environment.

Overall, the two event sources—system calls and Kubernetes audit events—are sufficient to cover all the meaningful activities happening in the Kubernetes cluster. Now, with an understanding of Falco event sources, let's wrap up our overview on Falco with a high-level architecture diagram.

High-level architecture

Falco is mainly composed of a few components, as follows:

- **Falco rules**: Rules that are defined to detect whether an event is an anomaly.

- **Falco engine**: Evaluate an incoming event with Falco rules and throw an output if an event matches any of the rules.

- **Kernel module/Sysdig libraries**: Tag system call events and enrich them before sending to the Falco engine for evaluation.

- **Web server**: Listen on Kubernetes audit events and pass on to the Falco engine for evaluation.

The following diagram shows Falco's internal architecture:

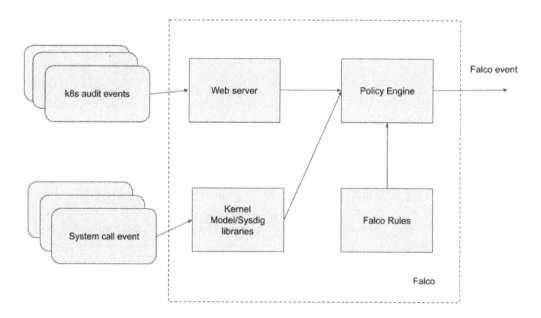

Figure 11.4 – Falco's internal architecture

Now, we have wrapped up our overview of Falco. Next, let's try to create some Falco rules and detect any anomalous behavior.

Creating Falco rules to detect anomalies

Before we dive into Falco rules, make sure you have Falco installed by running the following command:

```
helm install --name falco stable/falco
```

The Falco DaemonSet should be running in your Kubernetes cluster, as illustrated in the following code block:

```
$ kubectl get pods
NAME            READY   STATUS    RESTARTS   AGE
falco-9h8tg     1/1     Running   10         62m
falco-cnt47     1/1     Running   5          3m45s
falco-mz6jg     1/1     Running   0          6s
falco-t4cpw     1/1     Running   0          10s
```

To enable the Kubernetes audit and register Falco as the webhook backend, please follow the instructions in the Falco repository (https://github.com/falcosecurity/evolution/tree/master/examples/k8s_audit_config).

There are three types of elements in the Falco rules, as follows:

- **Rule**: A condition under which an alert will be triggered. A rule has the following attributes: rule name, description, condition, priority, source, tags, and output. When an event matches any rule's condition, an alert is generated based on the output definition of the rule.

- **Macro**: A rule condition snippet that can be reused by other rules or macros.

- **List**: A collection of items that can be used by macros and rules.

To facilitate Falco users in building their own rules, Falco provides a handful of default lists and macros.

Creating the system call rule

Falco system call rules evaluate system call events—more precisely, the enriched system calls. System call event fields are provided by the kernel module and are identical to the Sysdig (an open source tool built by the Sysdig company) filter fields. The policy engine uses Sysdig's filter to extract information such as the process name, container image, and file path from system call events and evaluate them with Falco rules.

The following are the most common Sysdig filter fields that can be used to build Falco rules:

- **proc.name**: Process name
- **fd.name**: File name that is written to or read from
- **container.id**: Container ID
- **container.image.repository**: Container image name without tag
- **fd.sip and fd.sport**: Server **Internet Protocol** (**IP**) address and server port
- **fd.cip and fd.cport**: Client IP and client port
- **evt.type**: System call event (open, connect, accept, execve, and so on)

Let's try to build a simple Falco rule. Assume that you have a nginx pod that serves static files from the /usr/share/nginx/html/ directory only. So, you can create a Falco rule to detect any anomalous file read activities as follows:

```
- rule: Anomalous read in nginx pod
    desc: Detect any anomalous file read activities in Nginx
pod.
    condition: (open_read and container and container.image.
repository="kaizheh/insecure-nginx" and fd.directory != "/usr/
share/nginx/html")
    output: Anomalous file read activity in Nginx pod
(user=%user.name process=%proc.name file=%fd.name container_
id=%container.id image=%container.image.repository)
    priority: WARNING
```

The preceding rule used two default macros: open_read and container. The open_read macro checks if the system call event is open in read mode only, while the container macro checks if the system call event happened inside a container. Then, the rule applies to containers running the kaizheh/insecure-nginx image only, and the fd.directory filter retrieves the file directory information from the system call event. In this rule, it checks if there is any file read outside of the /usr/share/nginx/html/ directory. So, what if there is misconfiguration of nginx that leads to file path traversal (reading files under arbitrary directories)? An example of this is shown in the following code block:

```
# curl insecure-nginx.insecure-nginx.svc.cluster.local/files../
etc/passwd
root:x:0:0:root:/root:/bin/bash
```

```
daemon:x:1:1:daemon:/usr/sbin:/usr/sbin/nologin
bin:x:2:2:bin:/bin:/usr/sbin/nologin
sys:x:3:3:sys:/dev:/usr/sbin/nologin
sync:x:4:65534:sync:/bin:/bin/sync
games:x:5:60:games:/usr/games:/usr/sbin/nologin
man:x:6:12:man:/var/cache/man:/usr/sbin/nologin
lp:x:7:7:lp:/var/spool/lpd:/usr/sbin/nologin
mail:x:8:8:mail:/var/mail:/usr/sbin/nologin
news:x:9:9:news:/var/spool/news:/usr/sbin/nologin
uucp:x:10:10:uucp:/var/spool/uucp:/usr/sbin/nologin
proxy:x:13:13:proxy:/bin:/usr/sbin/nologin
www-data:x:33:33:www-data:/var/www:/usr/sbin/nologin
backup:x:34:34:backup:/var/backups:/usr/sbin/nologin
list:x:38:38:Mailing List Manager:/var/list:/usr/sbin/nologin
irc:x:39:39:ircd:/var/run/ircd:/usr/sbin/nologin
gnats:x:41:41:Gnats Bug-Reporting System (admin):/var/lib/
gnats:/usr/sbin/nologin
nobody:x:65534:65534:nobody:/nonexistent:/usr/sbin/nologin
_apt:x:100:65534::/nonexistent:/bin/false
```

At the same time, Falco detects file access beyond the designated directory, with the following output:

```
08:22:19.484698397: Warning Anomalous file read activity
in Nginx pod (user=<NA> process=nginx file=/etc/passwd
container_id=439e2e739868 image=kaizheh/insecure-nginx) k8s.
ns=insecure-nginx k8s.pod=insecure-nginx-7c99fdf44b-gffp4
container=439e2e739868 k8s.ns=insecure-nginx k8s.pod=insecure-
nginx-7c99fdf44b-gffp4 container=439e2e739868
```

Next, let's look at how to use K8s audit rules.

Creating K8s audit rules

K8s audit rules evaluate Kubernetes audit events. We've already shown what a Kubernetes audit event record looks like, earlier in this chapter. Similar to Sysdig filters, there are two ways to retrieve the information out of a Kubernetes audit event. One is to use the **JavaScript Object Notation (JSON)** pointer; the other is to use Falco built-in filters. The following are a few commonly used Falco built-in filters to retrieve the information of Kubernetes audit events:

- `ka.verb`: The verb field of the Kubernetes audit event. `jevt.value[/verb]` is its corresponding JSON pointer.

- `ka.target.resource`: The resource field of the Kubernetes audit event. `jevt.value[/objectRef/resource]` is its corresponding JSON pointer.

- `ka.user.name`: The username field of the Kubernetes audit event. `jevt.value[/user/username]` is its corresponding JSON pointer.

- `ka.uri`: The `requestURI` field of the Kubernetes audit event. `jet.value[/requestURI]` is its corresponding JSON pointer.

Let's try to build a simple K8s audit rule. Assume that you don't want to deploy images in the `kube-system` namespaces except a few trusted images for services such as `kube-apiserver`, `etcd-manager`, and more. So, you can create a Falco rule, as follows:

```
- list: trusted_images
  items: [calico/node, kopeio/etcd-manager, k8s.gcr.io/kube-
apiserver, k8s.gcr.io/kube-controller-manager, k8s.gcr.io/kube-
proxy, k8s.gcr.io/kube-scheduler]


- rule: Untrusted Image Deployed in kube-system Namespace
  desc: >
    Detect an untrusted image deployed in kube-system namespace
  condition: >
    kevt and pod
    and kcreate
    and ka.target.namespace=kube-system
    and not ka.req.pod.containers.image.repository in (trusted_
images)
  output: Untrusted image deployed in kube-system namespace
(user=%ka.user.name image=%ka.req.pod.containers.image.
repository resource=%ka.target.name)
```

```
priority: WARNING
source: k8s_audit
tags: [k8s]
```

First, we define a list of trusted images that will be allowed to be deployed in the `kube-system` namespace. In the rule, we use two default macros: `pod` and `kcreate`. The `pod` macro checks if the target resource is a pod, while `kcreate` checks if the verb is `create`. We also check if the target namespace is `kube-system` and that the deploying image is not in the `trusted_images` list. The `k8s_audit` value from the `source` field of the rule indicates this rule evaluates the Kubernetes audit events. Then, if we try to deploy a `busybox` image pod in the `kube-system` namespace, we will see the following alert from Falco:

```
21:47:15.063915008: Warning Untrusted image deployed in kube-
system namespace (user=admin image=busybox resource=pod-1)
```

Note that in order for this rule to work, the audit level for a pod's creation needs to be at least at the `Request` level, with which the audit events include the pod's specification information, such as the image.

In this section, we introduced Falco and showed you how to create Falco rules from both event sources: system calls and Kubernetes audit events. Both rules are used to detect anomalous activities based on the known benign activities of the workload or cluster. Next, let's talk about how to do forensics in the Kubernetes cluster.

Conducting forensics with Sysdig Inspect and CRIU

Forensics in cybersecurity means collecting, processing, and analyzing information in support of vulnerability mitigation and/or fraud, counterintelligence, or law enforcement investigations. The more data you can preserve and the faster the analysis you can conduct on the collected data, the quicker you will trace down an attack and respond to the incident better. In this section, we will show you how to use the CRIU and Sysdig open source tools to collect data, and then introduce Sysdig Inspect, an open source tool for analyzing data collected by Sysdig.

Using CRIU to collect data

CRIU is the abbreviation of **Checkpoint and Restore In Userspace**. It is a tool that can freeze a running container and capture the container's state on disk. Later on, the container's and application's data saved on the disk can be restored to the state it was at the time of the freeze. It is useful for container snapshots, migration, and remote debugging. From a security standpoint, it is especially useful to capture malicious activities in action in the container (so that you may kill the container right after the checkpoint) and then restore the state in a sandboxed environment for further analysis.

CRIU works as a Docker plugin and is still in experimental mode, and there is a known issue that CRIU is not working properly in the most recent few versions (`https://github.com/moby/moby/issues/37344`). For demo purposes, I have used an older Docker version (Docker CE 17.03) and will show how to use CRIU to checkpoint a running container and restore the state back as a new container.

To enable CRIU, you will need to enable the `experimental` mode in the Docker daemon, as follows:

```
echo "{\"experimental\":true}" >> /etc/docker/daemon.json
```

And then, after restarting the Docker daemon, you should be able to execute the `docker checkpoint` command successfully, like this:

```
# docker checkpoint
Usage:      docker checkpoint COMMAND
Manage checkpoints
Options:
      --help    Print usage
Commands:
    create    Create a checkpoint from a running container
    ls        List checkpoints for a container
    rm        Remove a checkpoint
```

Then, follow the instructions to install CRIU (`https://criu.org/Installation`). Next, let's see a simple example to show how powerful CRIU is. I have a simple `busybox` container running to increase the counter by `1` every second, as illustrated in the following code snippet:

```
# docker run -d --name looper --security-opt seccomp:unconfined
busybox /bin/sh -c 'i=0; while true; do echo $i; i=$(expr $i +
1); sleep 1; done'
91d68fafec8fcf11e7699539dec0b037220b1fcc856fb7050c58ab90ae8cbd13
```

After sleeping for a few seconds, I then see the output of the counter increasing, as follows:

```
# sleep 5
# docker logs looper
0
1
2
3
4
5
```

Next, I would like to checkpoint the container and store the state to the local filesystem, like this:

```
# docker checkpoint create --checkpoint-dir=/tmp looper
checkpoint
checkpoint
```

Now, the checkpoint state has been saved under the /tmp directory. Note that the container looper will be killed after the checkpoint unless you specify a --leave-running flag when creating the checkpoint.

Then, create a mirror container without running it, like this:

```
# docker create --name looper-clone --security-opt
seccomp:unconfined busybox /bin/sh -c 'i=0; while true; do echo
$i; i=$(expr $i + 1); sleep 1; done'
49b9ade200e7da6bbb07057da02570347ad6fefbfc1499652ed286b874b59f2b
```

Now, we can start the new looper-clone container with the stored state. Let's wait another few seconds and see what happens. The result can be seen in the following code snippet:

```
# docker start --checkpoint-dir=/tmp --checkpoint=checkpoint
looper-clone
# sleep 5
# docker logs looper-clone
6
7
8
9
10
```

The new `looper-clone` container starts counting at 6, which means the state (the counter was 5) was successfully restored and used.

CRIU is very useful for container forensics, especially when there are some suspicious activities happening in a container. You can checkpoint the container (assuming you have multiple replicas running within the cluster), let CRIU kill the suspicious container, and then restore the suspicious state of the container in a sandboxed environment for further analysis. Next, let's talk about another way to capture data for forensics.

Using Sysdig and Sysdig Inspect

Sysdig is an open source tool for Linux system exploration and troubleshooting with support for containers. Sysdig can also be used to create trace files for system activity through instrumenting into the Linux kernel and capturing system calls and other operating system events. The capture capability makes it an awesome forensics tool for a containerized environment. To support capture system calls in the Kubernetes cluster, Sysdig offers a `kubectl` plugin, `kubectl-capture`, which enables you to capture system calls of the target pods as simply as with some other `kubectl` commands. After the capture is finished, Sysdig Inspect, a powerful open source tool, can be used to do troubleshooting and security investigation.

Let's continue to use `insecure-nginx` as an example, since we've got a Falco alert, as illustrated in the following code snippet:

```
08:22:19.484698397: Warning Anomalous file read activity
in Nginx pod (user=<NA> process=nginx file=/etc/passwd
container_id=439e2e739868 image=kaizheh/insecure-nginx) k8s.
ns=insecure-nginx k8s.pod=insecure-nginx-7c99fdf44b-gffp4
container=439e2e739868 k8s.ns=insecure-nginx k8s.pod=insecure-
nginx-7c99fdf44b-gffp4 container=439e2e739868
```

By the time the alert was triggered, it is still possible the `nginx` pod was undergoing an attack. There are a few things you can do to respond. Starting a capture and then analyzing more context out of the Falco alert is one of them.

To trigger a capture, download `kubectl-capture` from `https://github.com/sysdiglabs/kubectl-capture` and place it with the other `kubectl` plugins, like this:

```
$ kubectl plugin list
The following compatible plugins are available:
```

```
/Users/kaizhehuang/.krew/bin/kubectl-advise_psp
```

```
/Users/kaizhehuang/.krew/bin/kubectl-capture
```

```
/Users/kaizhehuang/.krew/bin/kubectl-ctx
```

```
/Users/kaizhehuang/.krew/bin/kubectl-krew
```

```
/Users/kaizhehuang/.krew/bin/kubectl-ns
```

```
/Users/kaizhehuang/.krew/bin/kubectl-sniff
```

Then, start a capture on the nginx pod, like this:

```
$ kubectl capture insecure-nginx-7c99fdf44b-4fl5s -ns insecure-
nginx
Sysdig is starting to capture system calls:

Node: ip-172-20-42-49.ec2.internal
Pod: insecure-nginx-7c99fdf44b-4fl5s
Duration: 120 seconds
Parameters for Sysdig: -S -M 120 -pk -z -w /capture-insecure-
nginx-7c99fdf44b-4fl5s-1587337260.scap.gz

The capture has been downloaded to your hard disk at:
/Users/kaizhehuang/demo/chapter11/sysdig/capture-insecure-
nginx-7c99fdf44b-4fl5s-1587337260.scap.gz
```

Under the hood, kubectl-capture starts a new pod to do the capture on the host where the suspected victim pod is running, with a 120-second capture duration, so that we can see everything that is happening right now and in the next 120 seconds in that host. Once the capture is done, the zipped capture file will be created in the current working directory. You can bring in Sysdig Inspect as a Docker container to start a security investigation, like this:

```
$ docker run -d -v /Users/kaizhehuang/demo/chapter11/sysdig:/
captures -p3000:3000 sysdig/sysdig-inspect:latest
17533f98a947668814ac6189908ff003475b10f340d8f3239cd3627fa9747769
```

Now, log in to `http://localhost:3000`, and you should see the login **user interface (UI)**. Remember to unzip the `scap` file so that you should be able to see the overview page of the capture file, as follows:

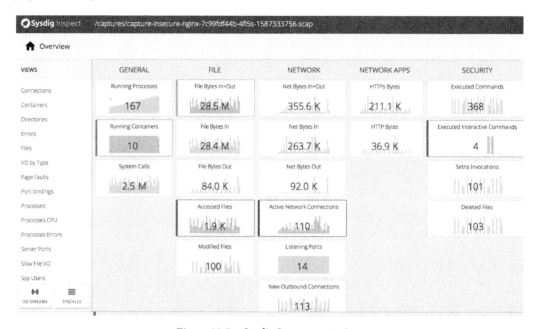

Figure 11.5 – Sysdig Inspect overview

Sysdig Inspect provides a full-blown insight into the activities happening inside the containers from the following angles:

- Executed commands
- File access
- Network connections
- System calls

Let's do a little more digging than just the Falco alert. From the alert, we may suspect this is a file path traversal issue as it is the `nginx` process accessing the `/etc/passwd` file, and we know that this pod serves static files only so that the `nginx` process should never access any files outside of the `/usr/share/nginx/html/` directory. Now, let's take a look at the following screenshot to see what the network requests sent to `nginx` pod were:

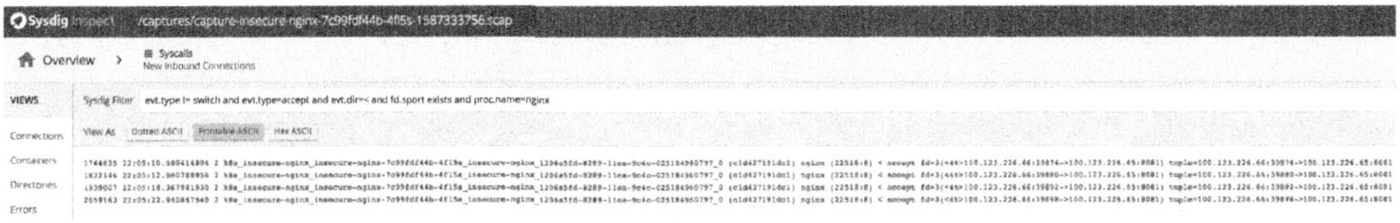

Figure 11.6 – Sysdig Inspect investigating network connections to nginx

After looking into the connections, we see that the requests came from a single IP, 100.123.226.66, which looks like a pod IP. Could it be from the same cluster? Click the **Containers** view on the left panel and specify fd.cip=100.123.226.66 in the filter. Then, you will find out it is from the anchore-cli container, as shown in the following screenshot:

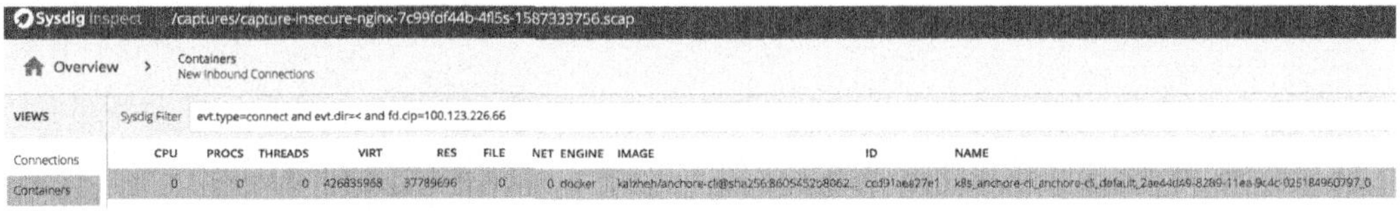

Figure 11.7 – Sysdig Inspect investigating a container sending a request to nginx

The anchore-cli pod actually happens to run on the same node as the nginx pod, as shown in the following code block:

```
$ kubectl get pods -o wide
NAME           READY    STATUS     RESTARTS    AGE    IP
NODE                                NOMINATED NODE    READINESS GATES
anchore-cli    1/1      Running    1           77m    100.123.226.66
ip-172-20-42-49.ec2.internal        <none>            <none>
$ kubectl get pods -n insecure-nginx -o wide
NAME                               READY    STATUS      RESTARTS
AGE    IP                 NODE                        NOMINATED
NODE     READINESS GATES
insecure-nginx-7c99fdf44b-4fl5s    1/1      Running     0
78m    100.123.226.65    ip-172-20-42-49.ec2.internal    <none>
<none>
```

Now we know that there might be some file path traversal attack launched from the `anchore-cli` pod, let's look at what this is (just double-click on the entry in the preceding **Sysdig Inspect** page), as follows:

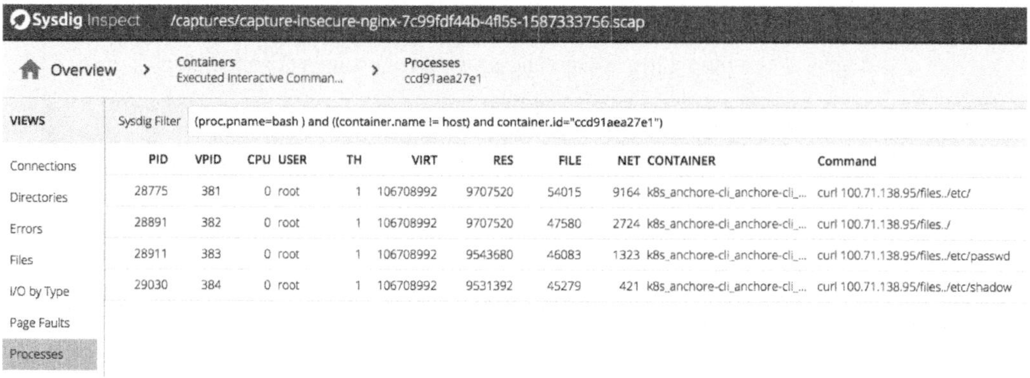

Figure 11.8 – Sysdig Inspect investigating path traversal attack commands

We found that there is list of file path traversal commands executed in the `anchore-cli` pod, detailed as follows:

- `curl 100.71.138.95/files../etc/`
- `curl 100.71.138.95/files../`
- `curl 100.71.138.95/files../etc/passwd`
- `curl 100.71.138.95/files../etc/shadow`

We're now able to get a step closer to the attacker, and the next step is to try to investigate more into how the attacker landed in the `anchore-cli` pod.

Both CRIU and Sysdig are powerful tools to conduct forensics in a containerized environment. Hopefully, the CRIU issue can be fixed soon. And note that CRIU also requires the Docker daemon to be run in `experimental` mode, while Sysdig and Sysdig Inspect work more at the Kubernetes level. Sysdig Inspect provides a nice UI to help navigate through different activities that happened in the pods and containers.

Summary

In this long chapter, we covered Kubernetes auditing, high availability for a Kubernetes cluster, managing secrets with Vault, detecting anomalous activities with Falco, and conducting forensics with CRIU and Sysdig. Though you may find it will take quite some time to get familiar with all the practices and tools, defense in depth is a huge topic and it is worth digging deeper into security so that you may build up a stronger fence for your Kubernetes cluster.

Most of the tools we talked about are easy to install and deploy. I would encourage you to try them out: add your own Kubernetes audit rules, use Vault to manage secrets in Kubernetes clusters, build your own Falco rules to detect anomalous behavior because you know your cluster better than anyone else, and use Sysdig to collect all the forensics data. Once you get familiar with all of these tools, you should feel confident that your Kubernetes cluster is a bit more under control.

In the next chapter, we're going to talk about some known attacks, such as the crypto mining hack against Kubernetes clusters, and see how we can use the techniques we learned in this book to mitigate these attacks.

Questions

1. Why should we not set the audit level to `Request` or `RequestResponse` for secret objects?
2. What flag is used to set up multiple master nodes in `kops`?
3. What does the sidecar container do when a secret is updated in Vault?
4. What are the event sources that Falco uses?
5. Which filter does Falco use to retrieve the process name from the system call event?
6. What can CRIU do to a running container?
7. What can you do with Sysdig Inspect?

Further references

- Kubernetes auditing: `https://kubernetes.io/docs/tasks/debug-application-cluster/audit/`

- High availability with kubeadm: `https://kubernetes.io/docs/setup/production-environment/tools/kubeadm/high-availability/`

- Vault: `https://www.vaultproject.io/docs/internals/architecture`

- Falco: `https://falco.org/docs/`

- Sysdig filtering: `https://github.com/draios/sysdig/wiki/Sysdig-User-Guide#user-content-filtering`

- CRIU: `https://criu.org/Docker`

- Sysdig kubectl-capture: `https://sysdig.com/blog/tracing-in-kubernetes-kubectl-capture-plugin/`

- Sysdig Inspect: `https://github.com/draios/sysdig-inspect`

- Sysdig: `https://github.com/draios/sysdig`

Section 3: Learning from Mistakes and Pitfalls

In this section, you will learn about some attack scenarios involving Kubernetes clusters, from known attacks and CVEs to mitigation and prevention strategies.

The following chapters are included in this section:

- *Chapter 12, Analyzing and Detecting Crypto-Mining Attacks*
- *Chapter 13, Learning from Kubernetes CVEs*

12
Analyzing and Detecting Crypto-Mining Attacks

Crypto-mining attacks are becoming more notable as blockchain and cryptocurrency are becoming more and more popular. Cryptocurrency is earned as the transaction fee of decentralized transactions on a blockchain for utilizing compute resources. The process of earning cryptocurrency for validating transactions using compute resources is called crypto-mining and is conducted by a software called a crypto-miner. Security researchers have found hacking incidents related to various crypto-miner binaries running within victims' infrastructures. The default openness of Kubernetes clusters and the availability of the extensive compute power required for mining makes Kubernetes clusters a perfect target for crypto-mining attacks. The complexity of Kubernetes clusters also makes crypto-mining activities hard to detect.

Since we've already been introduced to different Kubernetes built-in security mechanisms and open source tools to secure Kubernetes clusters, we'll now look at how to use them in a concrete scenario. In this chapter, we will first analyze a couple of known crypto-mining attacks, then we will discuss the detection mechanisms for crypto-mining attacks by using open source tools. Last but not least, we will recap the topics we discussed in previous chapters and see how they should be applied to defend our environment against attacks in general.

The following topics will be covered in this chapter:

- Analyzing crypto-mining attacks
- Detecting mining attacks
- Defending against attacks

Analyzing crypto-mining attacks

In this section, we will first provide a brief introduction to crypto-mining attacks, and then we will analyze some publicly disclosed crypto-mining attacks. We hope that you are aware of the crypto-mining attack patterns as well as the flaws that make the attack possible.

An introduction to crypto-mining attacks

Blockchain forms the basis for cryptocurrency. In short, blockchain is a chain of digital assets represented as blocks. These blocks have information about the transaction and who was involved in the transaction as a digital signature. Each cryptocurrency is associated with a blockchain. The process of verifying transactional records is called mining. Mining adds history to the blockchain to ensure that blocks cannot be modified in the future. Mining is designed to be resource-intensive to ensure the decentralized property of a blockchain. By successfully mining blocks, miners earn the transaction fee that is associated with the transaction. So, if you have a laptop or PC, you can use it to mine cryptocurrency, too; but most likely, you will need some dedicated GPUs or specialized hardware, such as **Field-Programmable Gate Arrays (FPGA)** and **Application-Specific Integrated Circuit (ASIC)** in order to do a good job of mining. The availability of resources in Kubernetes clusters makes them an ideal target for attackers to earn cryptocurrency.

A crypto-mining attack is just like free riding on Wi-Fi. Just as your network bandwidth will be shared by the free rider, some (or most) of your CPU or computing resources will be occupied by the mining processes without your consent. The impact is also similar. If the Wi-Fi free rider is downloading movies via BitTorrent using your Wi-Fi network, you may have a poor experience while watching Netflix. When there is a mining process running, other applications running in the same node will be severely impacted as the mining process may occupy the CPU most of the time.

Crypto-mining attacks have become one of the most appealing attacks to hackers as it is an almost guaranteed way of gaining some benefits out of a successful intrusion. Thieves come only to steal or destroy. If disruption is not the goal of the intrusion, a crypto-mining attack is probably one of the main choices for hackers.

At least two ways for hackers to launch a crypto-mining attack on a target victim have been reported. One is through application vulnerabilities, such as cross-site scripting, SQL injection, remote code execution, and more, so that the hacker gains access to the system, then downloads and executes the miner binary. The other way is through a malicious container image. When a container is created from the image that contains the mining binary, the mining process starts.

Although there are different types of crypto-mining binaries available on the internet, in general, the mining process is computation heavy and occupies a lot of CPU cycles. The mining process sometimes joins a mining pool in order to carry out mining in a collaborative way.

Next, let's look at a couple of crypto-mining attacks that have occurred in the real world. We will discuss the flaws that made the attacks possible and we will look at the attack patterns.

The crypto-mining attack on Tesla's Kubernetes cluster

A crypto-mining attack on Tesla's Kubernetes cluster occurred in 2018 and was reported by RedLock. Although the attack took place quite a while ago, there are at least two things we can learn from it—the flaw that made the attack possible and the attack patterns.

The flaw

The hacker infiltrated the Kubernetes dashboard, which was not protected by a password. From the dashboard, the hacker gained some important secrets to access the Amazon S3 buckets.

The attack patterns

The hackers did a pretty good job of hiding their footprint so that they could avoid being detected. The following are a few patterns worth mentioning:

- The mining process did not occupy too many CPU cycles, so the CPU usage of the pod was not too high.

- Unlike most crypto-mining cases, the mining process did not join any well-known mining pools. Instead, it had its own mining server, which sat behind Cloudflare, a **Content Delivery Network (CDN)** service.

- The communication between the mining process and the mining server was encrypted.

With the preceding maneuver, the hacker purposely tried to hide the crypto-mining pattern so that they could evade detection.

Graboid – a crypto-worm attack

This crypto-worm attack was discovered by the Palo Alto Network Unit42 research team in late 2019. Although the attack was not directed against Kubernetes clusters, this was aimed at Docker daemons, which is one of the foundation pillars in a Kubernetes cluster. In one of the attack steps, the toolkit downloaded images containing a crypto-mining binary from Docker Hub and launched. This step can also be applied to Kubernetes clusters too.

The flaw

The Docker engine was exposed to the internet while it was configured without authentication and authorization. The attacker could easily take full control of the Docker engine.

The attack patterns

Once the hacker took control over the Docker engine, they started downloading a malicious image and launched a container. The following are a few patterns worth mentioning regarding the malicious container:

- The malicious container contacted the command and control server to download some malicious scripts.

- The malicious container contained a Docker client binary, which was used to control other insecure Docker engines.

- The malicious container initiated commands via the Docker client to other insecure Docker engines to download and launch another image, which contained the crypto-mining binary.

According to Shodan, a search engine for internet-connected devices, more than 2,000 Docker engines were exposed to the internet. The preceding steps were repeated so that the crypto-mining worm spread.

Lessons learned

To recap what we have discussed about the two known crypto-mining attacks, misconfiguration is one of the major issues that make hacking easy. Crypto-mining has some typical patterns—for example, the mining process will communicate with mining pools and the mining process usually occupies a lot of CPU cycles. However, hackers may purposely disguise their mining behavior to evade detection. Once hackers get into the pod, they can start the contacting command and control server to download and execute the mining binary; on the other hand, they can also start reconnaissance. It would be easy for them to make a lateral move if the security domain in your Kubernetes cluster is not properly configured. Next, let's use the open source tools we introduced in previous chapters to detect typical crypto-mining activities in Kubernetes clusters.

Detecting crypto-mining attacks

In this section, we are going to talk about detecting crypto-mining activities in the Kubernetes cluster with some of the open source tools we introduced in earlier chapters. We detect crypto-mining activities based on the known patterns of crypto-mining: high CPU usage, communicating to mining pools, the executed command line of miner, and the binary signature. Note that each individual measure has its own limitations. Combining them improves the efficiency of detection for sure. However, there are still some advanced crypto-mining attacks, such as the one that attacked Tesla. It's necessary for you to work with your security team to apply a comprehensive detection strategy for your Kubernetes cluster to cover all kinds of intrusion.

In order to demonstrate each tool to detect crypto-mining, we simulate a victim `nginx` pod:

```
$ kubectl get pods -n insecure-nginx
NAME                              READY   STATUS    RESTARTS
AGE
insecure-nginx-8455b6d49c-z6wb9   1/1     Running   0
163m
```

Inside the `nginx` pod, there is a miner binary located in the `/tmp` directory:

```
root@insecure-nginx-8455b6d49c-z6wb9:/# ls /tmp
minerd2  perg
```

`minerd2` is the mining binary. We can assume that `minerd2` is either seeded in the image or downloaded from a command and control server. First, let's see how monitoring the CPU usage can help detect crypto-mining activities.

> **Note**
>
> It is not recommended that you run crypto-mining binaries in your production servers. This is for educational purposes only.

Monitoring CPU utilization

As we discussed in *Chapter 10, Real-Time Monitoring and Resource Management of a Kubernetes Cluster*, resource management and resource monitoring are crucial to maintaining a service's availability. Crypto-mining usually occupies tons of CPU cycles, which leads to the CPU usage of a container or a pod reaching a significantly higher level. Let's take a look at an example by comparing the CPU usage before and after crypto-mining happens within an `nginx` pod:

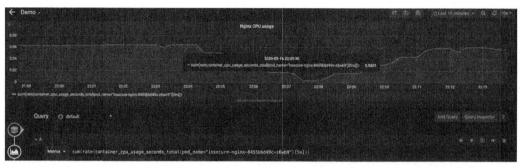

Figure 12.1 – The CPU usage of an nginx pod before mining happens in Grafana metrics

The preceding screenshot shows the CPU usage of the `insecure-nginx` pod monitored by Prometheus and Grafana. In general, the maximum CPU usage rate is less than `0.1`. When the crypto-mining binary is executed, you will find that the CPU usage skyrockets:

Figure 12.2 – The CPU usage of an nginx pod after mining happens

The CPU usage rate hikes from an average rate of 0.07 to around 2.4. No matter what happens behind the scenes, such a huge CPU usage hike should get your attention immediately. It's also quite obvious that even with this CPU surge, it doesn't mean there is a crypto-mining binary running inside the pod. The CPU surge can be caused by some other reasons, too.

On the flip side, if the hacker purposely restricts the crypto-mining attack progress, as was the case with the attack on Tesla, there may only be a little hike in the CPU that is hard to notice. Next, let's look at how Falco can help detect crypto-mining activities.

Detecting network traffic to a mining pool

One typical crypto-mining process behavior is where the mining process works collaboratively with other mining processes within the same mining pool for the purpose of mining efficiently. The mining processes communicate with the mining pool server during mining.

In Falco's default rules, there is one rule to detect outbound connections to known mining pools. Let's take a closer look at this rule. First, there are predefines lists for mining ports and the mining domain (https://github.com/falcosecurity/falco/blob/master/rules/falco_rules.yaml#L2590):

```
- list: miner_ports
  items: [
        25, 3333, 3334, 3335, 3336, 3357, 4444,
        5555, 5556, 5588, 5730, 6099, 6666, 7777,
```

```
        7778, 8000, 8001, 8008, 8080, 8118, 8333,
        8888, 8899, 9332, 9999, 14433, 14444,
        45560, 45700
    ]


- list: miner_domains
  items: [
      "Asia1.ethpool.org","ca.minexmr.com", "monero.crypto-
pool.fr",

      ...

      "xmr-jp1.nanopool.org","xmr-us-east1.nanopool.org",
      "xmr-us-west1.nanopool.org","xmr.crypto-pool.fr",
      "xmr.pool.minergate.com"
    ]
```

Then, there is a predefined macro for network connections to the preceding miner ports and miner domains:

```
- macro: minerpool_other
  condition: (fd.sport in (miner_ports) and fd.sip.name in
(miner_domains))
```

Besides the `minerpool_other` macro, there are two other macros for HTTP and HTTPS connections, respectively—`minerpool_http` and `minerpool_https`—and all of them combine to get the main detection logic:

```
- macro: net_miner_pool
  condition: (evt.type in (sendto, sendmsg) and evt.dir=<
and (fd.net != "127.0.0.0/8" and not fd.snet in (rfc_1918_
addresses)) and ((minerpool_http) or (minerpool_https) or
(minerpool_other)))
```

The `net_miner_pool` macro is then used by the `Detect outbound connections to common miner pool ports` rule to detect outbound connections to miner domains:

```
# The rule is disabled by default.
# Note: Falco will send DNS requests to resolve miner pool
domains which may trigger alerts in your environment.
- rule: Detect outbound connections to common miner pool ports
  desc: Miners typically connect to miner pools on common
ports.
```

```
   condition: net_miner_pool and not trusted_images_query_miner_
domain_dns
   enabled: true
   output: Outbound connection to IP/Port flagged by cryptoioc.
ch (command=%proc.cmdline port=%fd.rport ip=%fd.rip
container=%container.info image=%container.image.repository)
   priority: CRITICAL
   tags: [network, mitre_execution]
```

If there is a crypto-mining process running and communicating to the miner domains defined in the list, the alert will be triggered, as follows:

```
19:46:37.939287649: Critical Outbound connection to
IP/Port flagged by cryptoioc.ch (command=minerd2 -a
cryptonight -o stratum+tcp://monero.crypto-pool.fr:3333 -u
49TfoHGd6apXxNQTSHrMBq891vH6JiHmZHbz5Vx36nLRbz6WgcJunTtgcxno
G6snKFeGhAJB5LjyAEnvhBgCs5MtEgML3LU -p x port=37110
ip=100.97.244.198 container=k8s.ns=insecure-nginx k8s.
pod=insecure-nginx-8455b6d49c-z6wb9 container=07dce07d5100
image=kaizheh/victim) k8s.ns=insecure-nginx k8s.pod=insecure-
nginx-8455b6d49c-z6wb9 container=07dce07d5100 k8s.
ns=insecure-nginx k8s.pod=insecure-nginx-8455b6d49c-z6wb9
container=07dce07d5100
```

The Detect outbound connections to common miner pool ports rule is straightforward. If there is an alert generated by this rule, you should address it as high-priority. The limitation of the rule is also obvious; you will have to keep the mining domain and mining ports updated. If there is a new mining domain available or a new mining server port is used and they are not added to the Falco list, then the rule will miss detecting the crypto-mining activities. Note that the rule is disabled by default. As Falco needs to send DNS requests to resolve the miner pool domains, these DNS requests will be alerted by some cloud providers. A side note is that an open source tool such as Hubble from Cilium can help monitor network traffic.

Another approach is to use the whitelist approach. If you know the target port or IP blocks in the outbound connections of your microservices, you can create Falco rules to alert any outbound connection's destination IPs or ports that are not on the whitelist. The following is an example:

```
- list: trusted_server_addresses
   items: [...]
- list: trusted_server_ports
```

```
   items: [...]
- rule: Detect anomalous outbound connections
   desc: Detect anomalous outbound connections
   condition: (evt.type in (sendto, sendmsg) and container and
evt.dir=< and (fd.net != "127.0.0.0/8" and not fd.snet in
(trusted_server_addresses) or not fd.sport in (trusted_server_
ports)))
   output: Outbound connection to anomalous IP/
Port(command=%proc.cmdline port=%fd.rport ip=%fd.rip
container=%container.info image=%container.image.repository)
   priority: CRITICAL
```

The preceding rule alerts any outbound connection to IP addresses or ports outside of
trusted_server_ports or trusted_server_addresses. Given that the attack
happened in Tesla, Falco will alert that there is an anomalous connection, even though
the IP address looks normal. Next, let's look at another Falco rule to detect potential
crypto-mining activities based on patterns in the command line.

Detecting launched crypto-mining processes

Stratum mining protocol is the most common protocol for the mining process
to communicate with mining servers. Some mining binaries allow users to specify
protocols to communicate with the mining pool server when executed.

In Falco's default rules, there is one to detect the crypto binaries' execution based on
keywords in the command line:

```
- rule: Detect crypto miners using the Stratum protocol
   desc: Miners typically specify the mining pool to connect to
with a URI that begins with 'stratum+tcp'
   condition: spawned_process and proc.cmdline contains
"stratum+tcp"
   output: Possible miner running (command=%proc.cmdline
container=%container.info image=%container.image.repository)
   priority: CRITICAL
   tags: [process, mitre_execution]
```

The `Detect crypto miners using the Stratum protocol` rule will raise an alert if Falco detects any processes launched with `stratum+tcp` and is specified in the process's command line. The output looks as follows:

```
19:46:37.779784798: Critical Possible miner running
(command=minerd2 -a cryptonight -o stratum+tcp://monero.crypto-
pool.fr:3333 -u 49TfoHGd6apXxNQTSHrMBq891vH6JiHmZHbz5Vx36
nLRbz6WgcJunTtgcxnoG6snKFeGhAJB5LjyAEnvhBgCs5MtEgML3LU -p
x container=k8s.ns=insecure-nginx k8s.pod=insecure-nginx-
8455b6d49c-z6wb9 container=07dce07d5100 image=kaizheh/victim)
k8s.ns=insecure-nginx k8s.pod=insecure-nginx-8455b6d49c-z6wb9
container=07dce07d5100 k8s.ns=insecure-nginx k8s.pod=insecure-
nginx-8455b6d49c-z6wb9 container=07dce07d5100
```

The `minerd2 -a cryptonight -o stratum+tcp://monero.crypto-pool. fr:3333 -u 49TfoHGd6apXxNQTSHrMBq891vH6JiHmZHbz5Vx36nLRbz6Wgc JunTtgcxnoG6snKFeGhAJB5LjyAEnvhBgCs5MtEgML3LU -p x` command line that was executed contains the `stratum+tcp` keyword. That's why the alert was triggered.

Like other name-based detection rules, the limitation of the rule is obvious. If the crypto binary execution does not contain `stratum+tcp`, the rule will not be triggered.

The preceding rule uses the blacklist approach. Another way is to use a whitelist approach if you know the processes that are going to run in the microservices. You can define a Falco rule to raise an alert when any process that is not on the trusted list is launched. The following is an example of this:

```
- list: trusted_nginx_processes
  items: ["nginx"]
- rule: Detect Anomalous Process Launched in Nginx Container
  desc: Anomalous process launched inside container.
  condition: spawned_process and container and not proc.name in
(trusted_nginx_processes) and image.repository.name="nginx"
  output: Anomalous process running in Nginx container
(command=%proc.cmdline container=%container.info
image=%container.image.repository)
  priority: CRITICAL
  tags: [process]
```

The preceding rule will alert any anomalous process launched in an `nginx` container, which includes the crypto-mining processes. Last but not least, let's look at how image scanning tools can help detect the existence of crypto-mining binaries through integrating with malware feed services.

Checking the binary signature

Crypto-mining binaries can sometimes be recognized as malware. Like traditional anti-virus software, we can also check the hash value of running binaries against the malware feeds. With the help of an image scanning tool, such as Anchore, we can get the file's hash values:

```
root@anchore-cli:/# anchore-cli --json image content kaizheh/
victim:nginx files | jq '.content | .[] | select(.filename=="/
tmp/minerd2")'
{
  "filename": "/tmp/minerd2",
  "gid": 0,
  "linkdest": null,
  "mode": "00755",
  "sha256": "e86db6abf96f5851ee476eeb8c847cd73aebd0bd903827a362
c07389d71bc728",
  "size": 183048,
  "type": "file",
  "uid": 0
}
```

The hash value of the `/tmp/minerd2` file is `e86db6abf96f5851ee476eeb8c847` `cd73aebd0bd903827a362c07389d71bc728`. Then, we can check the hash value against VirusTotal, which provides malware feed service:

```
$ curl -H "Content-Type: application/json" "https://www.
virustotal.com/vtapi/v2/file/report?apikey=$VIRUS_FEEDS_API_
KEY&resource=e86db6abf96f5851ee476eeb8c847cd73aebd0bd903827a
362c07389d71bc728" | jq .
```

$VIRUS_FEEDS_API_KEY is your API key to access the VirusTotal API service, which then provides the following report:

```
{
    "scans": {
        "Fortinet": {
            "detected": true,
            "version": "6.2.142.0",
            "result": "Riskware/CoinMiner",
            "update": "20200413"
        },
        . . .
        "Antiy-AVL": {
            "detected": true,
            "version": "3.0.0.1",
            "result": "RiskWare[RiskTool]/Linux.BitCoinMiner.a",
            "update": "20200413"
        },
    },
    . . .
    "resource":
"e86db6abf96f5851ee476eeb8c847cd73aebd0bd903827a362c07389d71bc
728",
    "scan_date": "2020-04-13 18:22:56",
    "total": 60,
    "positives": 25,
    "sha256":
"e86db6abf96f5851ee476eeb8c847cd73aebd0bd903827a362c07389d71bc
728",
}
```

The VirusTotal report shows that /tmp/minerd2 has been reported as malware by 25 different feed sources, such as Fortinet and Antiy AVL. By integrating an image scanning tool and malware feeds service in your CI/CD pipeline, you can help detect malware at an early stage in the development life cycle. However, the downside of this single approach is that you will miss the crypto-mining attack if the mining binary is downloaded from the command and control server into a running pod. Another limitation is that if the feed server doesn't have any information about the crypto binary, you will definitely miss it.

We have talked about four different approaches to detect crypto-mining attacks. Each of these approaches has its own advantages and limitations; it would be ideal to apply some of these approaches together to improve their detection capability and detection efficacy.

Next, let's recap what we've discussed in this book, and comprehensively use this knowledge to prevent attacks in general.

Defending against attacks

In the previous section, we talk about a few ways of detecting crypto-mining activities. In this section, we will talk about defending against attacks in general by securing Kubernetes clusters. So, this involves more than just defending against a particular attack, but defending against all kinds of attacks. The four major defense areas are Kubernetes cluster provisioning, build, deployment, and runtime. First, let's talk about securing Kubernetes cluster provisioning.

Securing Kubernetes cluster provisioning

There are multiple ways to provision Kubernetes clusters such as kops and kubeadm. No matter which tool you use to provision a cluster, each Kubernetes component needs to be configured securely. Use kube-bench to benchmark your Kubernetes cluster and improve the security configurations. Make sure that RBAC is enabled, the --anonymous-auth flag is disabled, network connections are encrypted, and so on. The following are the key areas we covered in *Chapter 6, Securing Cluster Components*, and *Chapter 7, Authentication, Authorization, and Admission Control*:

- Properly configuring authentication and authorization for the Kubernetes control plane, kubelet, and so on

- Securing communication between Kubernetes components—for example, communication between kube-apiserver, kubelet, kube-apiserver, and etcd

- Enabling data encryption at rest for etcd

- Ensuring you do not launch unnecessary components, such as the dashboard

- Making sure all the necessary admission controllers are enabled while the deprecated ones are disabled

With the Kubernetes clusters securely provisioned, there are fewer chances for hackers to hack into your Kubernetes cluster easily, as was the case with Tesla's clusters (where the dashboard did not require authentication). Next, let's talk about securing the build.

Securing the build

Securing Kubernetes clusters also includes securing microservices. Securing microservices has to start at the beginning of the CI/CD pipeline. The following are some key countermeasures, as discussed in *Chapter 8*, *Securing Kubernetes Pods*, and *Chapter 9*, *Image Scanning in DevOps Pipelines* to secure microservices at the build stage:

- Address vulnerabilities discovered by image scanning tools properly for your microservices so that the possibility of a successful intrusion through exploiting application vulnerabilities is slim.

- Benchmark Dockerfiles to improve security configuration for images. Make sure no sensitive data is stored in the image, that all the dependent packages are updated, and so on.

- Scan executable files in the image to make sure no malware is seeded inside the image.

- Configure Kubernetes security contexts properly for workloads. Follow the principle of least privileges, limit access to system resources, such as using host-level namespaces, host paths, and so on, and remove unnecessary Linux capabilities, only granting the ones that are required.

- Do not enable an auto-mount service account. If no service account is required for the workload, don't create a service account for it.

- Follow the principle of least privileges, try to understand the tasks your workloads are carrying out, and only grant the required privileges to the service account.

- Follow the principle of least privileges, try to estimate the resource usage for workloads, and apply proper resource requests and limits to workloads.

Of course, securing the build can also be expanded to secure the entire CI/CD pipeline, such as source code management and CI/CD components. However, that is beyond the scope of this book. We will only suggest the options we think are most relevant to securing your Kubernetes clusters. Next, let's talk about securing deployment.

Securing deployment

We've already talked about different kinds of admission controllers in Kubernetes clusters in *Chapter 7, Authentication, Authorization, and Admission Control*, and *Chapter 8, Securing Kubernetes Pods*, and the need to use them properly with an example of an image-scanning admission controller (*Chapter 9, Image Scanning in DevOps Pipelines*). Using admission controllers and other built-in mechanisms serves as a great security gatekeeper for your workloads. The following are some key counter-measures:

- Apply network policies for namespaces and workloads. This could either be to restrict access to workloads (inbound network policies) or to implement the principle of least privileges (outbound network policies). When given a workload, if you know the destination IP block for outbound connection, you should create a network policy for that workload to restrict its outbound connection. The outbound network policy should block any traffic with a destination beyond the whitelisted IP block, such as downloading a crypto-mining binary from command and control server.

- Use **Open Policy Agent** (**OPA**) to ensure only images from trusted image registries are allowed to run in the cluster. With this policy, OPA should block any images from untrusted sources from running. For example, malicious images that contain crypto-mining binaries may reside in Docker Hub, so you should never consider Docker Hub as a trusted image registry.

- Use image-scanning admission controllers to ensure only images compliant with the scanning policy are allowed to run in the cluster. We already talked about this in *Chapter 9, Image Scanning in DevOps Pipelines*. New vulnerabilities may be discovered and the vulnerabilities' databases will be updated when you deploy workloads. It is necessary to scan before deploying.

- Use OPA or pod security policies to ensure workloads with limited Linux capabilities and restricted access to the host-level namespaces, host paths, and so on.

- It would be ideal to have AppArmor enabled on worker nodes and for each image that is deployed to have an AppArmor profile applied to it. Confining AppArmor profiles is done when workloads deploy, although the actual protection happens during runtime. A good use case is to build an AppArmor profile to whitelist the allowed processes when you know the processes that are running inside the container so that other processes, such as crypto-mining processes, will be blocked by AppArmor.

Do leverage the power of admission controllers and build a gatekeeper for your workload's deployment. Next, let's talk about securing workloads in runtime.

Securing runtime

Most likely, your Kubernetes clusters are the front battlefield to fight against hackers. Although we discussed different tactics to secure the build and deployment, all of these tactics ultimately aim to reduce the attack surface in the Kubernetes clusters. You cannot simply close your eyes and assume everything is going to be fine in your Kubernetes cluster. That's why we talk about resource monitoring in *Chapter 10*, *Real-Time Monitoring and Resource Management of a Kubernetes Cluster*, and auditing, secret management, detection, and forensics in *Chapter 11*, *Defense in Depth*. To recap what was covered in those two chapters, the following are the key counter-measures to secure runtime:

- Deploy decent monitor tools, such as Prometheus and Grafana, to monitor resource usage in your Kubernetes cluster. This is critical to ensure the availability of services and also, attacks such as crypto mining may trigger surges in CPU usage.

- Enable Kubernetes' audit policy to log Kubernetes events and activities.

- Ensure high availability across your infrastructure, Kubernetes components, and workloads.

- Use decent secret management tools, such as Vault, to manage and provision secrets for microservices.

- Deploy decent detection tools, such as Falco, to detect suspicious activities in Kubernetes clusters.

- It would be ideal to have forensics tools to collect and analyze suspicious events.

You may notice that securing communication among microservices is not mentioned. Service meshes are a hot topic that could help secure communication among microservices and beyond. However, service meshes are not covered in this book for two reasons:

- A service mesh introduces performance overhead to workloads and Kubernetes clusters, so they are not yet a perfect solution to secure communication among services.

- From an application security standpoint, it is easy to enforce service listening on port 443 with a CA-signed certificate so that the communication is encrypted. If microservices also perform authentication and authorization, then only trusted microservices can access authorized resources. A service mesh is not an irreplaceable solution to secure communication among services.

To defend against attacks to Kubernetes clusters, we need to secure the provisioning, build, deployment, and runtime of our Kubernetes clusters from end to end. They should all be considered as equally important as the strength of your defense is determined by your weakest link.

Summary

In this chapter, we went through a couple of the crypto-mining attacks that occurred over the last two years that brought a lot of attention to the need for securing containerized environments. Then, we showed you how to detect crypto-mining attacks with different open source tools. Last but not the least, we talked about how to defend your Kubernetes clusters against attacks in general by recapping what we discussed in previous chapters.

We hope you understand the core concepts of securing a Kubernetes cluster, which means securing the cluster provisioning, build, deployment, and runtime stages. You should also feel comfortable with starting to use Anchore, Prometheus, Grafana, and Falco.

As we know, Kubernetes is still evolving and it's not perfect. In the next chapter, we're going to talk about some known Kubernetes **Common Vulnerabilities and Exposures (CVEs)** and some mitigations that can protect your cluster against unknown variations. The purpose of the following chapter is to prepare you to be able to respond to handling any Kubernetes CVEs discovered in the future.

Questions

- What was the flaw that made a crypto-mining attack possible in Tesla's Kubernetes cluster?
- If you were the DevOps of Tesla, what would you do to prevent the crypto-mining attack?
- When you see CPU usage surge in a container, can you conclude that there has been a crypto-mining attack?
- Can you think of a crypto-mining process that can bypass the `Detect crypto miners using the Stratum protocol` Falco rule?
- What are the four areas you need to secure in order to secure your Kubernetes cluster?

Further reading

Refer to the following links for more information on the topics covered in this chapter:

- The Tesla crypto-mining attack: `https://redlock.io/blog/cryptojacking-tesla`
- The crypto-worm attack: `https://unit42.paloaltonetworks.com/graboid-first-ever-cryptojacking-worm-found-in-images-on-docker-hub/`

- Prometheus: `https://prometheus.io/docs/introduction/overview/`

- Falco: `https://falco.org/docs/`

- The VirusTotal API: `https://developers.virustotal.com/v3.0/reference`

- The crypto-mining attack analysis: `https://kromtech.com/blog/security-center/cryptojacking-invades-cloud-how-modern-containerization-trend-is-exploited-by-attackers`

- Hubble: `https://github.com/cilium/hubble`

13
Learning from Kubernetes CVEs

Common Vulnerabilities and Exposures (CVEs) are identifications for publicly known security vulnerabilities and exposures that are found in popular applications. The CVE ID is made up of the CVE string followed by the year and the ID number for the vulnerability. The CVE database is publicly available and is maintained by the MITRE Corporation. The CVE entries include a brief description of each issue, which is helpful to understand the root cause and severity of the issue. These entries do not include technical details about the issue. CVEs are useful for IT professionals to coordinate and prioritize updates. Each CVE has a severity associated with it. MITRE uses a **Common Vulnerability Scoring System (CVSS)** to assign a severity rating to a CVE. It is recommended to patch high-severity CVEs immediately. Let's look at an example of a CVE entry on cve.mitre.org.

As you can see in the following screenshot, a CVE entry includes the ID, a brief description, references, the name of the **CVE Numbering Authority (CNA)**, and the date on which the entry was created:

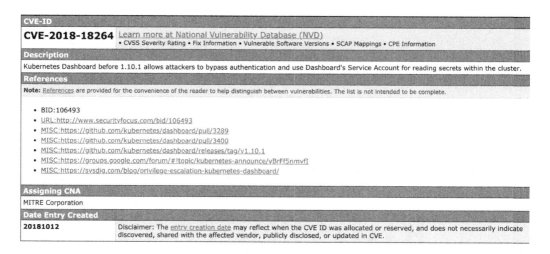

Figure 13.1 – MITRE entry for CVE-2018-18264

For security researchers and attackers, the most interesting part of a CVE entry is the **References** section. References for CVEs are links to blogs published by researchers covering the technical details of the issue, as well as links to issue descriptions and pull requests. Security researchers study the references to understand the vulnerability and develop mitigations for similar issues or for known issues that don't have a fix yet. Attackers, on the other hand, study the references to find unpatched variations of the issue.

In this chapter, we'll discuss four publicly known security vulnerabilities of Kubernetes. First, we will look at a path-traversal issue—CVE-2019-11246. This issue allowed attackers to modify the content on the client side, which could potentially lead to exfiltration or code execution on the cluster administrator's machine. Next, we will discuss CVE-2019-1002100, which allows users to cause **Denial-of-Service (DoS)** attacks on the API server. Then, we will discuss CVE-2019-11253, which allows unauthenticated users to cause DoS attacks on `kube-apiserver`. Lastly, we will discuss CVE-2019-11247, which allows users with namespace privileges to modify cluster-wide resources. We will discuss mitigation strategies for each CVE. Upgrading to the latest version of Kubernetes and `kubectl`, which patches vulnerabilities, should be your first priority. The latest stable version of Kubernetes can be found at `https://github.com/kubernetes/kubernetes/releases`. The mitigation strategies that we will discuss will help strengthen your cluster against attacks of a similar nature. Finally, we will introduce `kube-hunter`, which can be used to scan Kubernetes clusters for known security vulnerabilities.

We will cover the following topics in this chapter:

- The path traversal issue in kubectl cp—CVE-2019-11246
- The DoS issue in JSON parsing—CVE-2019-1002100
- The DoS issue in YAML parsing—CVE-2019-11253
- The privilege-escalation issue in role parsing—CVE-2019-11247
- Scanning known vulnerabilities using kube-hunter

The path traversal issue in kubectl cp – CVE-2019-11246

Developers often copy files to or from containers in a Pod for debugging. `kubectl cp` allows developers to copy files from or to a container in a Pod (by default, this is done in the first container within the Pod).

To copy files to a Pod, you can use the following:

```
kubectl cp /tmp/test <pod>:/tmp/bar
```

To copy files from a Pod, you can use the following:

```
kubectl cp <some-pod>:/tmp/foo /tmp/bar
```

When files are copied from a pod, Kubernetes first creates a TAR archive of the files inside the container. It then copies the TAR archive to the client and then finally unpacks the TAR archive for the client. In 2018, researchers found a way to use `kubectl cp` to overwrite files on the client's host. If an attacker has access to a pod, this vulnerability could be used to replace the TAR archive with special files that use relative paths by overwriting the original TAR binary with a malicious one. When the malformed TAR file was copied to the host, it could overwrite the files on the host when it was extracted. This could lead to data compromise and code execution on the host.

Let's look at an example where the attacker modifies the TAR archive to have two files: `regular.txt` and `foo/../../../../bin/ps`. In this archive, `regular.txt` is the file that the user is expecting and `ps` is a malicious binary. If this archive is copied to `/home/user/admin`, the malicious binary overwrites the well-known `ps` binary in the `bin` folder. The first patch for this issue was incomplete and attackers found a way to exploit the same issue using symlinks. Researchers found a way to bypass the fix for symlinks, which was finally addressed in versions 1.12.9, 1.13.6, and 1.14.2, and was assigned CVE-2019-11246.

Mitigation strategy

You can use the following strategies to harden your cluster against this issue and issues similar to CVE-2019-11246 that haven't yet been found:

- **Always use the updated version of kubectl**: You can find the latest version of the kubectl binary by using the following command:

```
$ curl https://storage.googleapis.com/kubernetes-release/
release/stable.txt
v1.18.3
```

- **Use admission controllers to limit the use of kubectl cp**: As we discussed in *Chapter 7, Authentication, Authorization, and Admission Control*, Open Policy Agent can be used as an admission controller. Let's look at a policy that denies calls to kubectl cp:

```
deny[reason] {
    input.request.kind.kind == "PodExecOptions"
    input.request.resource.resource == "pods"
    input.request.subResource == "exec"
    input.request.object.command[0] == "tar"
    reason = sprintf("kubectl cp was detected on %v/%v by
user: %v", [
        input.request.namespace,
        input.request.object.container,
        input.request.userInfo.username])
}
```

This policy denies the execution of a TAR binary in the pod, thereby disabling kubectl cp for all users. You can update this policy to allow kubectl cp for specific users or groups.

- **Apply appropriate access controls to the client**: If you are an administrator of a production cluster, there are many secrets on your work machine that the attackers might want access to. Ideally, the build machine should not be your work laptop. Having dedicated hardware that admins can ssh into to access the Kubernetes cluster is good practice. You should also ensure that any sensitive data on the build machine has appropriate access controls.

- **Set the security context for all pods**: As discussed in *Chapter 8, Securing Kubernetes Pods*, ensure that pods have `readOnlyRootFilesystem`, which will prevent the files from being tampered with (for example, overwrite `/bin/tar` `binary`) by attackers in the filesystem:

```
spec:
    securityContext:
        readOnlyRootFilesystem: true
```

- **Use Falco rules to detect file modification**: We discussed Falco in *Chapter 11, Defense in Depth*. Falco rules (which can be found at `https://github.com/falcosecurity/falco/blob/master/rules/falco_rules.yaml`) can be set up to do the following:

Detect modification of a binary in a pod: Use `Write below monitored dir` in the default Falco rules to detect changes to the TAR binary:

```
- rule: Write below monitored dir
  desc: an attempt to write to any file below a set of
binary directories
  condition: >
    evt.dir = < and open_write and monitored_dir
    and not package_mgmt_procs
    and not coreos_write_ssh_dir
    and not exe_running_docker_save
    and not python_running_get_pip
    and not python_running_ms_oms
    and not google_accounts_daemon_writing_ssh
    and not cloud_init_writing_ssh
    and not user_known_write_monitored_dir_conditions
  output: >
    File below a monitored directory opened for writing
(user=%user.name
    command=%proc.cmdline file=%fd.name parent=%proc.
pname pcmdline=%proc.pcmdline gparent=%proc.aname[2]
container_id=%container.id image=%container.image.
repository)
  priority: ERROR
  tags: [filesystem, mitre_persistence]
```

Detect the use of a vulnerable kubectl instance: kubectl versions 1.12.9, 1.13.6, and 1.14.2 have a fix for this issue. The use of any versions earlier than this will trigger the following rule:

```
- macro: safe_kubectl_version
  condition: (jevt.value[/userAgent] startswith "kubectl/
v1.15" or
           jevt.value[/userAgent] startswith "kubectl/
v1.14.3" or
           jevt.value[/userAgent] startswith "kubectl/
v1.14.2" or
           jevt.value[/userAgent] startswith "kubectl/
v1.13.7" or
           jevt.value[/userAgent] startswith "kubectl/
v1.13.6" or
           jevt.value[/userAgent] startswith "kubectl/
v1.12.9")


# CVE-2019-1002101
# Run kubectl version --client and if it does not say
client version 1.12.9,
1.13.6, or 1.14.2 or newer,  you are running a vulnerable
version.
- rule: K8s Vulnerable Kubectl Copy
  desc: Detect any attempt vulnerable kubectl copy in pod
  condition: kevt_started and pod_subresource and kcreate
and
           ka.target.subresource = "exec" and ka.uri.
param[command] = "tar" and
           not safe_kubectl_version
  output: Vulnerable kubectl copy detected (user=%ka.
user.name pod=%ka.target.name ns=%ka.target.namespace
action=%ka.target.subresource command=%ka.uri.
param[command] userAgent=%jevt.value[/userAgent])
  priority: WARNING
  source: k8s_audit
  tags: [k8s]
```

CVE-2019-11246 is a great example of why you need to keep track of security advisories and read through the technical details to add mitigation strategies to your cluster to ensure that if any variations of an issue are discovered, your cluster is safe. Next, we will look at CVE-2019-1002100, which can be used to cause DoS issues on `kube-apiserver`.

DoS issues in JSON parsing – CVE-2019-1002100

Patching is a commonly used technique used to update API objects at runtime. Developers use `kubectl patch` to update API objects at runtime. A simple example of this can be adding a container to a pod:

```
spec:
  template:
    spec:
      containers:
      - name: db
        image: redis
```

The preceding patch file allows a pod to be updated to have a new Redis container. `kubectl patch` allows patches to be in JSON format. The issue was in the JSON parsing code of `kube-apiserver`, which allowed an attacker to send a malformed `json-patch` instance to cause a DoS attack in the API server. In *Chapter 10, Real-Time Monitoring and Resource Management of a Kubernetes Cluster*, we discussed the importance of the availability of services within Kubernetes clusters. The root cause of this issue was unchecked error conditions and unbounded memory allocation to `kube-apiserver` for the `patch` requests.

Mitigation strategy

You can use the following strategies to harden your cluster against this issue and issues similar to CVE-2019-100210 that haven't yet been found:

- **Use resource monitoring tools in Kubernetes clusters**: As discussed in *Chapter 10, Real-Time Monitoring and Resource Management of a Kubernetes Cluster*, resource-monitoring tools such as Prometheus and Grafana can help identify issues of higher memory consumption in the master node. High values in the graphs for Prometheus metrics could look as follows:

```
container_memory_max_usage_bytes{pod_ name="kube-
apiserver-xxx" }
sum(rate(container_cpu_usage_seconds_total{pod_
name="kube-apiserver-xxx"}[5m]))
```

```
sum(rate(container_network_receive_bytes_total{pod_
name="kube-apiserver-xxx"}[5m]))
```

These resources graph maximum memory, CPU, and network usage by `kube-apiserver` over 5-minute intervals. Any abnormality in these usage patterns is a sign of an attack on `kube-apiserver`.

- **Set up high-availability Kubernetes masters**: We learned about high-availability clusters in *Chapter 11, Defense in Depth*. High-availability clusters have multiple instances of Kubernetes components. If the load on one component is high, other instances can be used until the load is reduced or the first instance is restarted.

Using `kops`, you can use `--master-zones={zone1, zone2}` to have multiple masters:

```
kops create cluster k8s-clusters.k8s-demo-zone.com \
   --cloud aws \
   --node-count 3 \
   --zones $ZONES \
   --node-size $NODE_SIZE \
   --master-size $MASTER_SIZE \
   --master-zones $ZONES \
   --networking calico \
   --kubernetes-version 1.14.3 \
   --yes \
kube-apiserver-ip-172-20-43-65.ec2.internal
1/1      Running   4         4h16m
kube-apiserver-ip-172-20-67-151.ec2.internal
1/1      Running   4         4h15m
```

As you can see, there are multiple `kube-apiserver` pods running in this cluster.

- **Limit users' privileges using RBAC**: Privileges to users should also follow the principle of least privilege, which was discussed in *Chapter 4, Applying the Principle of Least Privilege in Kubernetes*. If a user does not require access to `PATCH` privileges for any resource, the role should be updated so that they don't have access.

- **Test your patches in the staging environment**: Staging environments should be set up as a replica of the production environment. Developers are not perfect, so it's possible for a developer to create a malformed patch. If patches or updates to the cluster are tested in the staging environment, bugs in the patch can be found without disrupting the production services.

DoS is often considered a low-severity issue, but if it happens to the core component of your cluster, you should take it seriously. DoS attacks on `kube-apiserver` can disrupt the availability of the whole cluster. Next, we look at another DoS attack against an API server. This attack can be performed by unauthenticated users, making it more severe than CVE-2019-1002100.

A DoS issue in YAML parsing – CVE-2019-11253

XML bombs, or billion laughs attacks, are popular with any XML parsing code. Similar to parsing issues in XML, this was a parsing issue in YAML files that were sent to `kube-apiserver`. If a YAML file sent to the server has recursive references, it triggers the `kube-apiserver` to consume CPU resources, which causes availability issues on the API server. In most cases, requests parsed by `kube-apiserver` are restricted to authenticated users, so unauthenticated users should not be able to trigger this issue. There was an exception to this rule in the Kubernetes versions preceding 1.14 that allowed unauthenticated users to check whether they could perform an action using `kubectl auth can-i`.

This issue is similar to CVE-2019-1002100, but is more severe as unauthenticated users can also trigger this issue.

Mitigation strategy

You can use the following strategies to harden your cluster against this issue and issues similar to CVE-2019-11253 that haven't yet been found:

- **Use resource-monitoring tools in Kubernetes clusters**: Similar to CVE-2019-1002100, resource-monitoring tools, such as Prometheus and Grafana, which we discussed in *Chapter 10, Real-Time Monitoring and Resource Management of a Kubernetes Cluster,* can help identify issues of higher memory consumption in the master node.

- **Enable RBAC**: The vulnerability is caused by the improper handling of recursive entities in the YAML file by `kube-apiserver` and the ability of unauthenticated users to interact with the `kube-apiserver`. We discussed RBAC in *Chapter 7, Authentication, Authorization, and Admission Control.* RBAC is enabled by default in the current version of Kubernetes. You can also enable it by passing `--authorization-mode=RBAC` to the `kube-apiserver`. In this case, unauthenticated users should not be allowed to interact with `kube-apiserver`. For authenticated users, the principle of least privilege should be followed.

- **Disable auth can-i for unauthenticated users (for v1.14.x):** Unauthenticated users should not be allowed to interact with `kube-apiserver`. In Kubernetes v1.14.x, you can disable `auth can-i` for unauthenticated servers using the RBAC file at `https://github.com/kubernetes/kubernetes/files/3735508/rbac.yaml.txt`:

```
kubectl auth reconcile -f rbac.yaml --remove-extra-
subjects --remove-extra-permissions
```

```
kubectl annotate --overwrite clusterrolebinding/
system:basic-user rbac.authorization.kubernetes.io/
autoupdate=false
```

  The second command disables auto-updates for `clusterrolebinding`, which will ensure that the changes are not overwritten on restart.

- **kube-apiserver should not be exposed to the internet:** Allowing access to the API servers from trusted entities using a firewall or VPCs is good practice.

- **Disable anonymous-auth:** We discussed `anonymous-auth` as an option that should be disabled if possible in *Chapter 6, Securing Cluster Components*. Anonymous authentication is enabled by default in Kubernetes 1.16+ for legacy policy rules. If you are not using any legacy rules, it is recommended to disable `anonymous-auth` by default passing `--anonymous-auth=false` to the API server.

As we discussed earlier, a DoS attack on `kube-apiserver` can cause a disruption of services throughout the cluster. In addition to using the latest version of Kubernetes, which includes a patch for this issue, it is important to follow these mitigation strategies to avoid similar issues in your cluster. Next, we will discuss an issue in the authorization module that triggers privilege escalation for authenticated users.

The Privilege escalation issue in role parsing – CVE-2019-11247

We discussed RBAC in detail in *Chapter 7, Authentication, Authorization, and Admission Control*. Roles and RoleBindings allow users to get the privileges to perform certain actions. These privileges are namespaced. If a user needs a cluster-wide privilege, ClusterRoles and ClusterRolebindings are used. This issue allowed users to make cluster-wide modifications even if their privileges were namespaced. Configurations for admission controllers, such as Open Policy Access, could be modified by users with a namespaced role.

Mitigation strategy

You can use the following strategies to harden your cluster against this issue and issues similar to CVE-2019-11247 that haven't yet been found:

- **Avoid wildcards in Roles and RoleBindings**: Roles and ClusterRoles should be specific to the resource names, verbs, and API groups. Adding * to roles can allow users to have access to resources that they should not have access to. This adheres to the principle of least privilege, which we discussed in *Chapter 4, Applying the Principle of Least Privilege in Kubernetes.*

- **Enable Kubernetes auditing**: We discussed auditing and audit policies for Kubernetes in *Chapter 11, Defense in Depth.* Kubernetes auditing can help identify any unintended actions in a Kubernetes cluster. In most cases, a vulnerability such as this will be used to modify and delete any additional controls within the cluster. You can use the following policy to identify instances of these kinds of exploits:

```
apiVersion: audit.k8s.io/v1 # This is required.
kind: Policy
rules:
- level: RequestResponse
  verbs: ["patch", "update", "delete"]
  resources:
  - group: ""
    resources: ["pods"]
    namespaces: ["kube-system", "monitoring"]
```

This policy logs any instances of the deletion or modification of pods in kube-system or the monitoring namespace.

This issue is certainly an interesting one since it highlights that the security features provided by Kubernetes can also be harmful if they are misconfigured. Next, we will talk about kube-hunter, which is an open source tool to find any known security issues in your cluster.

Scanning for known vulnerabilities using kube-hunter

Security advisories and announcements (`https://kubernetes.io/docs/reference/issues-security/security/`) published by Kubernetes are the best way to keep track of new security vulnerabilities found in Kubernetes. The announcements and advisory emails can get a bit overwhelming and it's always possible to miss an important vulnerability. To avoid these situations, a tool that periodically checks the cluster for any known CVEs comes to the rescue. `kube-hunter` is an open source tool that is developed and maintained by Aqua that helps identify known security issues in your Kubernetes cluster.

The steps to set up `kube-hunter` are as follows:

1. Clone the repository:

   ```
   $git clone https://github.com/aquasecurity/kube-hunter
   ```

2. Run the `kube-hunter` pod in your cluster:

   ```
   $ ./kubectl create -f job.yaml
   ```

3. View the logs to find any issues with your cluster:

   ```
   $ ./kubectl get pods
   ```

NAME AGE	READY	STATUS	RESTARTS
kube-hunter-7hsfc 12s	0/1	ContainerCreating	0

The following output shows a list of known vulnerabilities in Kubernetes v1.13.0:

```
Vulnerabilities
For further information about a vulnerability, search its ID in:
https://github.com/aquasecurity/kube-hunter/tree/master/docs/_kb
+--------+------------------+--------------------+----------------------+--------------------+----------------------+
| ID     | LOCATION         | CATEGORY           | VULNERABILITY        | DESCRIPTION        | EVIDENCE             |
+--------+------------------+--------------------+----------------------+--------------------+----------------------+
| KHV005 | 10.96.0.1:443    | Unauthenticated    | Unauthenticated      | The API Server port| b'{"kind":"APIVersio |
|        |                  | Access             | access to API        | is accessible.     | ns","versions":["v1" |
|        |                  |                    |                      | Depending on       | ...                  |
|        |                  |                    |                      | your RBAC settings |                      |
|        |                  |                    |                      | this could expose  |                      |
|        |                  |                    |                      | access to or control|                     |
|        |                  |                    |                      | of your cluster.   |                      |
+--------+------------------+--------------------+----------------------+--------------------+----------------------+
| KHV026 | 10.96.0.1:443    | Privilege Escalation| Arbitrary Access To | Api Server not     | v1.13.0              |
|        |                  |                    | Cluster Scoped       | patched for        |                      |
|        |                  |                    | Resources            | CVE-2019-11247.    |                      |
|        |                  |                    |                      | API server         |                      |
|        |                  |                    |                      | allows access to   |                      |
|        |                  |                    |                      | custom resources via|                     |
|        |                  |                    |                      | wrong scope        |                      |
+--------+------------------+--------------------+----------------------+--------------------+----------------------+
| KHV005 | 10.96.0.1:443    | Information         | Access to API using  | The API Server port| b'{"kind":"APIVersio |
|        |                  | Disclosure         | service account      | is accessible.     | ns","versions":["v1" |
|        |                  |                    | token                | Depending on       | ...                  |
|        |                  |                    |                      | your RBAC settings |                      |
|        |                  |                    |                      | this could expose  |                      |
|        |                  |                    |                      | access to or control|                     |
|        |                  |                    |                      | of your cluster.   |                      |
+--------+------------------+--------------------+----------------------+--------------------+----------------------+
| KHV002 | 10.96.0.1:443    | Information         | K8s Version          | The kubernetes     | v1.13.0              |
|        |                  | Disclosure         | Disclosure           | version could be   |                      |
|        |                  |                    |                      | obtained from the  |                      |
|        |                  |                    |                      | /version endpoint  |                      |
+--------+------------------+--------------------+----------------------+--------------------+----------------------+
| KHV025 | 10.96.0.1:443    | Denial of Service  | Possible Reset Flood | Node not patched for| v1.13.0             |
|        |                  |                    | Attack               | CVE-2019-9514. an  |                      |
|        |                  |                    |                      | attacker could cause|                     |
|        |                  |                    |                      | a                  |                      |
|        |                  |                    |                      | Denial of          |                      |
```

Figure 13.2 – Results of kube-hunter

This screenshot highlights some of the issues discovered by `kube-hunter` for a Kubernetes v1.13.0 cluster. The issues found by `kube-hunter` should be treated as critical and should be addressed immediately.

Summary

In this chapter, we discussed the importance of CVEs. These publicly known identifiers are important for cluster administrators, security researchers, and attackers. We discussed the important aspects of CVE entries, which are maintained by MITRE. We then looked at four well-known CVEs and discussed the issue and the mitigation strategy for each CVE. As a cluster administrator, upgrading the `kubectl` client and Kubernetes version should always be your first priority. However, adding mitigation strategies to detect and prevent exploits caused by similar issues that have not been reported publicly is equally important. Finally, we discussed an open source tool, `kube-hunter`, which can be used to periodically identify issues in your Kubernetes cluster. This removes the overhead of cluster administrators keeping a close eye on security advisories and announcements by Kubernetes.

Now, you should be able to understand the importance of publicly disclosed vulnerabilities and how these advisories help strengthen the overall security posture of your Kubernetes cluster. Reading through these advisories will help you identify any problems in your cluster and help harden your cluster going forward.

Questions

1. What are the most important parts of a CVE entry for cluster administrators, security researchers, and attackers?

2. Why are client-side security issues such as CVE-2019-11246 important for a Kubernetes cluster?

3. Why are DoS issues in the kube-apiserver treated as high-severity issues?

4. Compare authenticated versus unauthenticated DoS issues in the API server.

5. Discuss the importance of `kube-hunter`.

Further references

- The CVE list: `https://cve.mitre.org/cve/search_cve_list.html`

- Detecting CVE-2019-11246 with Falco: `https://sysdig.com/blog/how-to-detect-kubernetes-vulnerability-cve-2019-11246-using-falco/`

- Preventing CVE-2019-11246 with OPA: `https://blog.styra.com/blog/investigate-and-correct-cves-with-the-k8s-api`

- The GitHub issue for CVE-2019-1002100: `https://github.com/kubernetes/kubernetes/issues/74534`

- The GitHub issue for CVE-2019-11253: `https://github.com/kubernetes/kubernetes/issues/83253`

- The GitHub issue for CVE-2019-11247: `https://github.com/kubernetes/kubernetes/issues/80983`

- kube-hunter: `https://github.com/aquasecurity/kube-hunter`

- The GitHub issue for CVE 2020-8555: `https://github.com/kubernetes/kubernetes/issues/91542`

- The GitHub issue for CVE 2020-8555: `https://github.com/kubernetes/kubernetes/issues/91507`

Assessments

Chapter 1

1. Scaling, operational cost, and longer release cycle.

2. Master components run on the master node. These components are responsible for the management of the worker nodes. The master components include `kube-apiserver`, `etcd`, `kube-scheduler`, `kube-controller-manager`, `cloud-controller-manager`, and `dns-server`.

3. Kubernetes Deployments help scale pods up/down based on labels and selectors. Deployments encapsulate replica sets and pods. The YAML spec for a Deployment consists of number of instances of pods and `template`, which is identical to a Pod specification.

4. OpenShift, K3S, and Minikube.

5. Kubernetes environments are highly configurable and are composed of a myriad of components. Configurability and complexity with insecure defaults is a big cause of concern. Additionally, the compromise of master components in cluster is the easiest way to cause a breach.

Chapter 2

1. Pod.

2. Network namespace and IPC namespace.

3. A placeholder to hold a network namespace for other containers.

4. ClusterIP, NodePort, LoadBalancer, and ExternalName.

5. Ingress supports layer 7 routing and doesn't require extra load balancers from the cloud provider, while LoadBalancer services require one load balancer per service.

Chapter 3

1. Threat modeling is an iterative process that starts at the design phase.

2. End user, internal attacker, and privileged attacker.

3. Unencrypted data stored in `etcd`.

4. The complexity of the Kubernetes environment increases the difficulty of using threat modeling applications in Kubernetes environments.

5. Kubernetes introduces additional assets and interactions with applications. This increases the complexity of applications in Kubernetes, increasing the attack surface.

Chapter 4

1. A `Role` object contains rules consisting of verbs and resources that indicate the operational privileges for resources in a namespace.

2. A `RoleBinding` object links the `Role` object in a namespace to a group of subjects (for example, `User` and `ServiceAccount`). It is used to grant privileges defined in the Role objects to the subjects.

3. `RoleBinding` indicates that the privileges the subjects have are effective in the `RoleBinding` object's namespace. `ClusterRoleBinding` indicates that the privileges the subjects have are effective in the entire cluster.

4. `hostPID`, `hostNetwork`, and `hostIPC`.

5. Create a network policy for the Pod with an egress rule.

Chapter 5

1. Master components, worker components, and Kubernetes objects.

2. Pod, service/Ingress, `api-server`, nodes, and namespace.

3. RBAC and network policy.

4. Processes in the Pod can access host the PID namespace, viewing all the processes running in the worker node.

```
kind: NetworkPolicy
metadata:
  name: allow-good
```

```
spec:
  podSelector:
    matchLabels:
      app: web
  policyTypes:
  - Ingress
  ingress:
  - from:
    - namespaceSelector:
        matchLabels:
          from: <allowed_label>
```

Chapter 6

1. Token-based authentication enables static tokens to be used to identify the origin of requests in the cluster. Static tokens cannot be updated without restarting the API server and so should not be used.

2. The `NodeRestriction` admission controller ensures that a kubelet can only modify the node and Pod objects for the node that it is running on.

3. Pass `--encryption-provider-config` to the API server to ensure data is encrypted at rest in `etcd`.

4. Security vulnerabilities in `dnsmasq`, performance issues in SkyDNS, and a single container instead of three for `kube-dns` to provide the same functionality.

5. You can use `kube-bench` on an EKS cluster as follows:

```
$ git clone : https://github.com/aquasecurity/kube-bench
$ kubectl apply -f job-eks.yaml
```

Chapter 7

1. Static tokens and basic authentication should not be used in production clusters. These modules use static credentials, which require a restart of the API server to be updated.

2. Cluster administrators can use the user impersonation privileges to test the permissions granted to a new user. Using `kubectl`, cluster administrators can use the `--as` `--as-group` flags to run requests as a different user.

3. Node and RBAC are enabled by default in Kubernetes. These should be used. If the cluster uses a remote API for authorization, Webhook mode should be used instead.

4. The `EventRateLimit` admission controller specifies the maximum limit for requests that can be serviced by the API server. On the other hand, LimitRanger ensures that Kubernetes objects adhere to the resource limits specified by the `LimitRange` object.

5. The `rego` policy to deny the creation of an Ingress with the `test.example` endpoint is as follows:

```
package kubernetes.admission
import data.kubernetes.namespaces
operations = {"CREATE", "UPDATE"}
deny[msg] {
    input.request.kind.kind == "Ingress"
    operations[input.request.operation]
    host := input.request.object.spec.rules[_].host
    host == "test.example"
    msg := sprintf("invalid ingress host %q", [host])
}
```

Chapter 8

1. Defines a command to ask Docker Engine to check the health status of the container periodically.

2. The `COPY` instruction can only copy files from build machine to the filesystem of the image, while the `ADD` instruction can not only copy files from localhost but also retrieve files from remote URLs to the filesystem of the image. Using `ADD` may introduce the risk of adding malicious files from the internet to the image.

3. `CAP_NET_BIND_SERVICE`.

4. With the `runAsNonRoot` setting set to `true`, kubelet will block the container from starting if run as root user.

5. Create a role with privilege, use the `PodSecurityPolicy` object, and create a `rolebinding` object to assign the role to the service account that is used by the workload.

Chapter 9

1. Docker history <image name>.

2. 7-8.9.

3. anchore-cli image add <image name>.

4. anchore-cli image vuln <image name> all.

5. anchore-cli evaluate check <image digets> --tag <image full tag>.

6. It helps identify images with latest publicly known vulnerabilities.

Chapter 10

1. Resource requests specify what a Kubernetes object is guaranteed to get, whereas limits specify the maximum resources a Kubernetes object can use.

2. The resource quota that limits memory to 500 mi is as follows:

```
apiVersion: v1
kind: ResourceQuota
metadata:
    name: pods-medium
spec:
    hard:
        memory: 500Mi
```

3. LimitRanger is an admission controller that enforces LimitRanges. LimitRange defines constraints on a Kubernetes resources. A limit range can be applied to a Pod, container, or persistantvolumeclaim. Namespace resource quotas are similar to LimitRange, but are enforced for the entire namespace.

4. Service account tokens.

5. Prometheus and Grafana.

Chapter 11

1. The secret data will be recorded in the Kubernetes audit log.

2. `--master-zones`.

3. Sync the updated secret to the Pod's mounted volume.

4. System calls and Kubernetes audit events.

5. `proc.name`.

6. Checkpoint a running container, which can be restored later in a sandboxed environment.

7. Troubleshooting and security investigation.

Chapter 12

1. Dashboard is used without authentication enabled.

2. Do not run Dashboard, or enable authentication for Dashboard.

3. No. It could be a crypto mining attack, but it could also be caused by some other things, such as application errors.

4. The crypto mining binary uses the HTTP or HTTPS protocol to connect to the mining pool server instead of stratum.

5. Kubernetes cluster provisioning, build, deployment, and runtime.

Chapter 13

1. Cluster administrators keep track of CVE IDs to ensure that the Kubernetes cluster is not vulnerable to a publicly known issue. Security researchers study the references section to understand the technical details of the issue to develop mitigations for a CVE. Lastly, attackers study the references section to find unpatched variations or use similar techniques to discover issues in other parts of the code.

2. Client-side issues often lead to data exfiltration or code execution on the client side. Build machines or machines of cluster administrators often contain sensitive data, and an attack on such machines can have a significant economic impact on the organization.

3. DoS issues on `api-server` can lead to disruption of the availability of the entire cluster.

4. Unauthenticated DoS issues are more severe than authenticated DoS issues. Ideally, unauthenticated users should not be able to communicate with `api-server`. If an unauthenticated user is able to send requests and cause a DoS issue for `api-server`, it is worse than an authenticated user. Authenticated DoS requests are also very severe since a misconfiguration in the cluster can allow an unauthenticated user to escalate privileges and become an authenticated user.

5. Security advisories and announcements by Kubernetes are a great way to learn about any new publicly known vulnerabilities. These announcements and advisories are fairly noisy, and administrators can easily miss an important issue. Running `kube-hunter` regularly helps cluster admins identify any publicly known issues that administrators might have missed.

Other Books You May Enjoy

If you enjoyed this book, you may be interested in these other books by Packt:

Hands-On Kubernetes on Windows

Piotr Tylenda

ISBN: 978-1-83882-156-2

- Understand containerization as a packaging format for applications
- Create a development environment for Kubernetes on Windows
- Grasp the key architectural concepts in Kubernetes
- Discover the current limitations of Kubernetes on the Windows platform
- Provision and interact with a Kubernetes cluster from a Windows machine
- Create hybrid Windows Kubernetes clusters in on-premises and cloud environments

Kubernetes - A Complete DevOps Cookbook

Murat Karslioglu

ISBN: 978-1-83882-804-2

- Deploy cloud-native applications on Kubernetes
- Automate testing in the DevOps workflow
- Discover and troubleshoot common storage issues
- Dynamically scale containerized services to manage fluctuating traffic needs
- Understand how to monitor your containerized DevOps environment
- Build DevSecOps into CI/CD pipelines

Leave a review - let other readers know what you think

Please share your thoughts on this book with others by leaving a review on the site that you bought it from. If you purchased the book from Amazon, please leave us an honest review on this book's Amazon page. This is vital so that other potential readers can see and use your unbiased opinion to make purchasing decisions, we can understand what our customers think about our products, and our authors can see your feedback on the title that they have worked with Packt to create. It will only take a few minutes of your time, but is valuable to other potential customers, our authors, and Packt. Thank you!

Index

L

M

N

Printed in Great Britain
by Amazon